DATE DUE

JE 9 '04			

DEMCO 38-296

HYPERCULTURE

HYPERCULTURE

The Human Cost
of Speed

STEPHEN BERTMAN

PRAEGER

Westport, Connecticut
London

Library of Congress Cataloging-in-Publication Data

Bertman, Stephen.
    Hyperculture : the human cost of speed / Stephen Bertman.
      p. cm.
    Includes bibliographical references (p.) and index.
    ISBN 0–275–96205–9 (alk. paper)
    1. United States—Civilization—1970– 2. Technological
innovations—Social aspects—United States. 3. Speed—Social
aspects. I. Title.
    E169.12.B397 1998
    973.92—dc21   97–32951

British Library Cataloguing in Publication Data is available.

Library of Congress Catalog Card Number: 97–32951
ISBN: 0–275–96205–9

First published in 1998

Praeger Publishers, 88 Post Road West, Westport, CT 06881
An imprint of Greenwood Publishing Group, Inc.

Printed in the United States of America

The paper used in this book complies with the
Permanent Paper Standard issued by the National
Information Standards Organization (Z39.48–1984).

10 9 8 7 6 5 4 3 2 1

Copyright Acknowledgments

The author and publisher gratefully acknowledge permission for use of the following material:

Excerpts from "The Hamlet of A. MacLeish." COLLECTED POEMS 1917–1982 by Archibald MacLeish. Copyright © 1985 by The Estate of Archibald MacLeish. Reprinted by permission of Houghton Mifflin Co. All rights reserved.

"Upon this age that never speaks its mind" by Edna St. Vincent Millay. From COLLECTED POEMS, HarperCollins. Copyright 1939, 1967 by Edna St. Vincent Millay and Norma Millay Ellis. All rights reserved. Reprinted by permission of Elizabeth Barnett, literary executor.

Excerpts from the script of the motion picture *Network* (MGM/UA 1976) by Paddy Chayefsky.

No man in a hurry
is quite civilized.

—Will Durant

Contents

Contents

Acknowledgments

I AM INDEBTED to Anthony Harrigan for his friendship and encouragement, so generously given. Both inspired me to think the thoughts and write the words out of which this book has grown.

I also owe thanks to a number of people who were willing to share their time with me through conversation or correspondence. For stimulating my thinking by challenging my views—or by encouraging those views with their inspiration, information, and insight—I wish to thank Craig Brod, Reid Buckley, William P. Cheshire, Thomas R. Cole, Edward Cornish, J. T. Fraser, Francis Fukuyama, Grace Goodell, Robert Grudin, John A. Howard, C. David Jenkins, Russell Kirk, Robert W. Kubey, Richard D. Lamm, Michael Larsen, Robert V. Levine, Norman Liberman, S. Robert Lichter, Tom Lutz, Daniel Malvin, Jerry Mander, Bill McKibben, Paul T. Menzel, John Nelson, Philip T. Nicholson, Paul Pearsall, George Roche III, John P. Robinson, Herbert I. Schiller, Andrew Bard Schmookler, Richard Sclove, John P. Sisk, Gregory Stock, James B. Stockdale, Jeremy Tarcher, Robert Theobald, Dave Wagner, Shelley Waldenberg, James C. Wetherbe, and James Q. Wilson.

Ideas and even sentences, however, cannot become a book without publication. I am therefore grateful to my literary agent, Edward Knappman, for his dedication and energy, and to my publishers for their faith in this project. Special thanks are also due my secretary, Margie Prytulak, for giving my typescript electronic form.

To my wife, Elaine, I owe gratitude impossible to measure for sharing her life with mine. Out of our long talks over decaffeinated coffee, and our common concerns, came the substance of this book.

Introduction

The Time Machine

THE TIME MACHINE, written by H. G. Wells a century ago, told the tale of a daring adventurer who traveled through the fourth dimension to the other side of time. Journeying at breathtaking speed, he landed in the year 802,701 on an earth he barely recognized, a future world of both savage desolation and tender promise in which creatures of darkness battled creatures of light in a struggle that would determine our planet's destiny.

By the standards of 1895, Wells's machine was state-of-the-art—"a glittering metallic framework" fashioned of ivory and brass and transparent crystal, a device fitted with a saddle and two white levers: one for moving forward into the future, the other for moving back into the past.[1]

Accustomed as we now are to space exploration, Wells's design may seem technically naive. But simplistic as it was, it nevertheless embodied a visionary concept: that human beings by their inventive genius might someday be able to break the restraining bonds of time and travel to other eras, future or past.

Though the fulfillment of such a dream may be far off, a time machine of sorts already exists—in fact, one more powerful than Wells's imagination could ever have conceived. The machine can accommodate not merely one passenger but an entire society. And it is energized not by a mysterious crystal but by the spirit of technology itself.

Unlike Wells's time-traveler, we shall not arrive on an alien landscape. For it will not be the world, as much as ourselves, that will be altered. For we are being transformed, even at this very moment, by our extraordinary velocity and by the emergence of a newly insistent force—the power of now.

This book is about our transformation: how and why it is taking place, and what its long-term consequences may be.

Chapter 1 describes the speed-up of our everyday activities and the impact this acceleration is having on the quality of our lives. Chapter 2 investigates the reasons for this speed-up. Chapters 3 through 8 explore in detail the profound changes it is causing and illustrate how a new sense of time is redefining the very meaning of the individual and the family, of democratic society and international relations, and of the natural environment around us. Finally, chapter 9 calls upon us to rethink radically some of our contemporary assumptions in order to insure a humane future for ourselves and our children.

In writing this book my aim has been to identify and describe what I believe to be the primary force responsible for shaping contemporary consciousness, to propose a central unifying principle that connects the separate phenomena of current society. In addition, my intention is to propose ways of dealing with this force so we may better live our lives. Any theory that advances one explanation for so many features of reality is bound to go too far. And any author who theorizes so broadly is certain to be faulted. But in confronting life today and trying to understand it, to dare less would be a greater flaw.

HYPERCULTURE

Chapter 1

Warp Speed

OVER TWENTY-FIVE years ago, Alvin Toffler clinically described the symptoms of a new disease he had discovered, a disease he called "future shock."[1] According to Toffler, future shock was a psychobiological condition induced by subjecting individuals to "too much change in too short a time."[2] Toffler argued that technological and social changes were taking place faster than people could adjust to them. As a consequence, large numbers of individuals were beginning to exhibit symptoms of confusion. Though most evident in the United States, signs of future shock were becoming visible in other nations as well. "Future shock," he wrote, "is the dizzying disorientation brought on by the premature arrival of the future. . . . Unless man quickly learns to control the rate of change in his personal affairs as well as in society at large, we are doomed to a massive adaptational breakdown."[3]

Since the publication of *Future Shock* in 1970, the pace of social change has increased even more. Largely responsible for this increase has been the rapid development and deployment of earlier technologies and the swift introduction and growth of new ones. Supported by an electronic network of instantaneous communications, our culture has been transformed into a "synchronous society," a nationally and globally integrated culture in which the prime and unchallenged directive is to keep up with change.

In order to adapt to change, the synchronous society has abandoned traditional values. Whatever values remain have become warped in the process of accommodating themselves to the faster pace of life. Because of this adaptation and accommodation, future shock itself has undergone a transformation, changing from an acute state to a chronic condition permeating and affecting every aspect of our daily lives. Its effects, moreover, are no longer only psychological; they have become ethical and moral as well.

WARP SPEED

Driven by the momentum of technologies operating at the speed of light, our social speedometer has continued to climb. Like the crew of the Starship Enterprise, "boldly go[ing] where no man has gone before,"[4] we are now nearing a velocity called "warp speed." But, unlike a "Star Trek" adventure, the speed we travel at is one that can, if we are not wise or strong enough, warp the fundamental nature of our lives.

It can do this because this highest of all speeds changes our relationship to time.

First, warp speed disengages us from the past. The speed of our ascent leaves the past far behind us, like a receding landscape viewed from the rear of a roaring rocket, a landscape so progressively miniaturized by increasing velocity that its features lose all recognizable form. Traditions become incomprehensible; history, irrelevant; memories, a blur.

Second, warp speed plunges us toward the future. The features of the future rush toward us like the fireballs of a meteor storm, blinding us to what lies farther ahead hidden in the cosmic night. Brilliant inventions, glittering products, glistening data, and luminous celebrities—each swarm brighter than the last—sweep past us in successive waves, dazzling our eyes.

Nullifying a vision of the past and negating a true view of the future, warp speed isolates us in the present. Marooned there, floating in temporal zero-gravity, we turn to the present as our exclusive basis for fulfillment and gratification, as our sole source of security in a cosmos where all other sources of security have been stripped from us by our onrushing speed. Hurtling through time, we cling to the moment.

THE POWER OF NOW

When we travel at warp speed, we fall under the sway of a new force, the power of now. The power of now is the intense energy of an unconditional present, a present uncompromised by any other dimension of time. Under its all-consuming power, the priorities we live by undergo transformation in a final act of adaptation to electronic speed. Our lives cease to be what they once were, not so much because life itself has changed, but because *the way we see it* has.

The power of now replaces the long-term with the short-term, duration with immediacy, permanence with transience, memory with sensation, insight with impulse.

Unlike the monastery or the desert where mystics once attained transcendant perspective by withdrawing from the world, the realm of now is an environment of pervasive sensory stimulation and swift flux, a continually altered cosmos that offers us no fixed horizon. As a consequence, our lives come to be characterized more by their random trajectory than by any reasoned destination.

All of this is not our fault. Instead, we are like disoriented astronauts who have suddenly awakened, encapsulated in deep space. But until we get our bearings, we shall forever remain lost in space and time.

THE EXPLOSION OF TECHNOLOGY

The power of electronic technology to accelerate our lives took us by surprise. The computer, for example, received only minimal attention in *Future Shock*—understandably so because it had not yet assumed a major role in American society. The first word processor did not appear until 1970; the first silicon chip, not until 1971; the first personal computer, not until 1975. Yet, according to estimates, one out of every two workers in America today uses a computer terminal,[5] a percentage that doubled in just ten years.[6]

Equally striking is the computer's rapid domestication.[7] As late as 1984, only eight out of 100 American households had a computer. In just two years, however, the figure doubled. And, by 1994, a computer could be found in more than one out of every three American homes. By 1995, 25 percent of American homes with computers had two.[8]

At the same time, modem sales climbed, doubling to over two million units between 1983 and 1988, and rising to three million by 1995.[9] While modems could only transmit 300 bits of data per second in 1983 (somewhat slower than normal reading speed), 28.8 thousand bits were being transmitted in 1994. During the same period, computer speed itself was doubling every eighteen months. Today, for example, top-of-the-line PCs are almost 200 times faster than IBM's original model.[10]

Meanwhile, cellular phone sales radically grew, jumping from 300,000 in 1986 to 6,750,000 in just a decade.[11] By 1993, cordless phones were in one out of every two American homes. Fax machine sales also took off, skyrocketing from under 100,000 in 1983 to well over three million in 1997.[12] In addition, at least 30 million Americans now carry electronic pagers, fifteen times the number that carried them in 1985.[13]

None of these electronic technologies, however, can match television's rate of growth as a medium of instant communication.[14] Back in 1950, fewer than one out of ten American homes had a television set. By 1955, however,

TV sets could be found in almost seven out of ten homes, an increase of 30 million households in just five years. By 1970, 96 percent of America's families were watching TV; by 1993, 98 percent. Sales records show that in just one year, 1992, a total of 22.5 million sets were bought. In fact, more American families have television sets than have indoor plumbing.[15]

The increase in TV stations is also notable. In 1970, there were 677 in the United States. By 1993, there were 1,541. The same period saw the number of cable subscribers grow from 4 million to 57 million.[16]

Yet, more important than the popularity of any one of these technologies is their combination, which radically reinforces and intensifies the accelerative effect that each separate technology would have had alone. It is their electronic linkage that keeps pictures, sounds, and data continually coursing on a nonstop, high-speed track, saturating our environment with instancy. And the more our society depends upon electronic information flow and entertainment, the more our everyday lives need to keep up with its speed-of-light pace, since our economic and emotional existence is wired into its circuitry.[17]

Although the upward curve on the electronics sales chart may some day level off, nearly universal ownership will signify that an integrated system of instantaneous social communication has come into being, a system national and even global in scope. Indeed, concerted efforts are already proceeding to fuse these separate technologies into interactive multimedia systems that will function in every American home.

Many hail the promise such systems hold out, the promise of satisfying our needs and fulfilling our wishes as never before. With the help of a television screen and computer, shopping and banking will be done at home. With the aid of E-mail, faxing and teleconferencing, workers will commute to offices electronically rather than fight rush-hour traffic. Through personalized access to kaleidoscopic databanks, young and old will educate themselves without ever needing to "go to school." And home entertainment will burgeon in infinite variety. Indeed, these descriptions are but extensions of electronic capabilities already in current use in tens of thousands of American homes.

"This will change the world," said John Sculley, former CEO of Apple Computer.[18] "It's starting already. It's not science fiction." John Malone, CEO of the nation's largest cable company, foresees it "taking down any barrier between fulfillment and imagination."[19]

But others, like psychologist Kenneth J. Gergen, have predicted the emergence of a new kind of personality, a "saturated self," a self awash in a multitude of societally generated stimuli.[20] Unlike normal stress, this harried state of consciousness would not be the product of particular situations. Instead, it would be the result of the overall environment in which we come to live, an electronic environment in which information overload, overstimulation, and overchoice are the order of the day. The media we use, rather than allowing us to relax as a result of their efficiency, will instead keep revving us up with their infectious speed. As one pioneer on the electronic frontier has already complained: "Technology is increasing the heartbeat. We are inundated with information. The mind can't handle it all. The pace is so fast now, I sometimes feel like a gunfighter dodging bullets."[21]

Such stress doesn't just come from having to know everything we should know. It also comes from the gnawing anxiety that we'll never know enough. Richard Saul Wurman calls this condition "information anxiety," a state "produced by the ever-widening gap between what we understand and what we think we should understand."[22] On the domestic front, information anxiety is what many of us experience in the evening when we want to watch something on television and feverishly scan the cable guide before the program begins to be sure there isn't something better to watch instead. Of course, such a problem never existed until cable networks sprang up in the late 1970s. But "cable-guide panic" is only the tip of the anxiety iceberg in a society that continually offers us more and more choices.[23] Though media moguls herald the coming of 500 (or 5,000) channels some day, for many viewers fifty is already quite enough.

The most significant challenge that may face us, however, may not be based on the number of things that confront us as much as the speed at which they travel, a speed that requires our instantaneous response. For the rate of electronic flow is not governed by the natural limits of the human nervous system as much as it is by the almost boundless speed of the nonhuman systems that serve us. And when a technology's speed exceeds limits inherent in nature, conflict can ensue.

BREAKING THE SOUND BARRIER

The potential dangers of such a situation are evident in the experiences of aviators in World War II. Early in the war, as the English and Germans battled for supremacy in the skies over Europe, both sides raced to build faster and faster fighters and bombers for tactical advantage. Allied and Axis planes, however, soon struck an invisible and deadly wall. As test pilots neared the speed of sound (approximately 760 miles per hour) they encountered a mysterious force—a force that shook their fuselages violently and overpowered their controls, a force capable of disintegrating a plane in mid-air.

What *was* this powerful force?

As an airplane flies through the atmosphere, it creates waves of compressed air. Like invisible ripples, these waves rush outward from the plane at the speed of sound. As long as the plane itself flies at subsonic speed, the waves it generates run ahead of it. As it nears the speed of sound, however, the plane begins to catch up to its own pressure waves. Should the plane attempt to penetrate these waves,

> [s]hock waves crawl across the wings. The airplane's controls no longer work normally, and the turbulent airflow exerts tremendous forces on the airframe itself. Airplanes approaching the speed of sound tended to pitch down all at once. Pilots who tried to pull up the nose put too much stress on the tail, already feeling the powerful wake from the wings. The tremendous forces wrenched the tails right off some airplanes.[24]

After a number of fatal crashes, aeronautical engineers finally discovered how to "break the sound barrier." They reduced the thickness of the wings and swept them back so they would knife through the air; they also streamlined the plane's nose so it would pierce the invisible wall. Such structural changes ultimately enabled man to fly faster than sound.

But military hardware was not the only kind of technology that was speeding up in the mid-twentieth century. The pace of peacetime technology was picking up also; and, along with it, the speed of everyday life. This acceleration has continued down to our own day, heightened by electronic technologies that operate not at the speed of sound but at the much higher speed of light, 186,000 miles per second. Like it or not, today we all live in fast times.

Very often this speed is exhilarating. It brings us what we need and want faster than ever before—from hot entrees to hot entertainment. But that same speed can also add stress to our lives.

SPEED AND STRESS

The principles of physics that underlie the sound barrier can help us understand the origin of this stress. As the velocity of everyday life increases—as we fly faster and faster through the "atmosphere" of daily experience—our craft encounters a turbulence it was never designed to withstand, indeed a turbulence it *cannot* withstand. As our "air speed" increases, invisible pressures build up, pressures strong enough to shatter the structural integrity of our personalities, of our human relationships, and of society itself. Ultimately, we may lose control, or the craft itself may disintegrate. Or we may desperately hold on for dear life, knowing we have neither parachute nor ejection seat to save us.

Measured against the backdrop of human history, these destructive pressures appear to be a new phenomenon. Physical stress, to be sure, had long been a part of the human struggle to survive. But emotional stress was less common. Yet today it is grudgingly accepted as a basic fact of life.

For example, in a national survey conducted in 1986 by the Louis Harris organization, one out of three Americans said they lived with stress nearly every day.[25] And six out of ten said they experienced "great stress" once or twice a week. In addition, in 1994, two out of ten people questioned reported feeling such great stress almost every day, according to the findings of the Prevention Index survey.[26]

The presence of stress in our lives is also revealed by the printed word.[27] In the last five years, almost 400 articles on stress and time management have appeared in popular national magazines. In addition, there are some 900 books currently in print on these topics. All these publications do more than just show how popular a subject stress is. They also demonstrate how little control we seem to have over it.

To be sure, there is "good" stress and "bad" stress. Stress is probably an essential component of any difficult but valuable endeavor, especially when the results matter to us. When *McCall's* magazine, for example, polled working women in 1990, two out of three said on-the-job stress actually made their lives more stimulating.[28] Similarly, the tension actors and musicians feel before going on stage can lead to finer performances than they give in rehearsal. But unquestionably, stress also has a downside.[29]

We manifest that downside in a number of ways. Externally, we exhibit it in our behavior toward others, when we are irritable and short-tempered. Internally, we express it through a variety of physical and emotional symptoms: nervousness and anxiety, headaches, muscular tension, stomach and intestinal problems, quickened heartbeat and elevated blood pressure, loss of sleep and insomnia, and depression. In fact, according to one estimate, stress is partly responsible for two out of every three visits to a primary-care physician.[30] The American Institute of Stress goes further, identifying stress as a contributing factor in 75 to 90 percent of all illnesses, in part because of the negative effect it has on the body's immune system.[31] Indeed, as one scientific study has shown, just *thinking* your life is stressful can be enough to make you sick![32]

There is no question that stress is waiting for us when we arrive at work. After surveying 40,000 employees in 1985, the National Center for Health Statistics found that more than half had experienced a significant level of stress in the two weeks prior to the survey.[33] In 1991–92, Peggy Lawless was project director for an investigation of worker stress sponsored by the Northwestern National Life Insurance Company.[34] "Stress," concluded Lawless, "is running like a fire through the American workplace. . . . The idea that high stress is a motivator is simply not true. Instead, stress may have become the number one debilitator of the American workplace."[35] Supporting her view is the fact that workers' compensation claims based on stress have risen dramatically, straining many state budgets.[36] Indeed, stress-related losses from accidents, illnesses, and absenteeism may be costing American industry between 150 and 200 billion dollars annually.[37]

The rage that job stress can sometimes provoke has also taken its toll. From 1989 to 1993, incidents of workplace violence tripled,[38] making murder in the workplace America's fastest-growing form of homicide.[39]

Many factors contribute to on-the-job stress: long hours and mandatory overtime, frustrating rules and regulations, conflicts with bosses and co-workers, fear of being laid off or fired, isolation, and even boredom. But one of the most commonly identified causes is the inability to control the pace of work. When employees are not free to determine their own speed, the result is stress.[40]

We can readily understand why a company would speed its workers up: speed leads to higher productivity and higher productivity leads to bigger profits.

But the demand for greater speed is also a byproduct of technology. Factory machinery and assembly lines long ago forced workers to step up their speed if they wanted to keep their jobs. What factory workers had to do then—and still have to do today—is match the speed of nonhuman, mechanical devices.

Today, however, electronic equipment has picked up the pace even more, creating what one critic has called "electronic sweat-shops,"[41] workplaces in which the speed of human activity is governed not by turning gears or moving belts but by invisible signals traveling at the speed of light. Increasingly, electronic information systems using fax machines, computers, and video monitors are inserting the word "fast" into every job description.[42] The problem, according to psychologist Craig Brod, is that "we have taken the standards of the machine and applied them to humans, not the standards of humans and applied them to machines."[43]

The major negative effect of this speed-up is what Brod calls "techno-stress"—stress induced by technology.[44] The malady is an infectious one, affecting not only how we act and feel, but even how we think. For, instead of being in conflict with a machine, the worker actually becomes *like* the machine. As one frequent fax machine user reports, it "makes me want to work faster and makes me believe I should be keeping up. . . . The more I have used . . . this equipment, the faster I want it to go."[45] Says another user: "It leads to bouncing the ball back and forth much faster. You feel like you've got to move faster. When mail comes through on the fax, you shouldn't have to feel you have to turn it around faster, but you do."[46] E-mail can similarly instill in us a real sense of urgency, even about matters that are not urgent at all.[47]

Workplace speed can be addictive. But it is an addiction that burns us out even as it speeds us up. When we come home at the end of the day,[48] it may not be just work we bring with us, but also our high-speed frustrations and electronic expectations.[49] In short, we may come to expect the imperfect human beings in our lives to operate as efficiently as our equipment, quickly losing patience with those we might otherwise love because they do not answer as swiftly, or respond as rapidly, or obey as readily as the machines we know.

Culturally, we have been conditioned to believe our technology frees us of labor. The more technology, the easier our lives. Or so the story goes. But some researchers aren't so sure.

From statistical evidence, Harvard economist Juliet Schor has shown that Americans are actually working longer hours today than they did fifty years ago.[50] We may own and consume twice as much as we did a half century ago, but we end up working longer just to own and consume it. As one consumer puts it: "All these 'labor-saving devices'. . . don't save anybody any labor. They just make more stuff. Everybody's got more stuff. I got stuff. You got stuff. He's got stuff. All this stuff. And there's more stuff than people can deal with now."[51] Schor's calculations reveal that from 1970 to 1990 Americans put in nine more hours on the job each year than the year before—a whole extra month of work in just two decades.

Our standard of living includes many things—like home air-conditioning, TV sets, and a second car—that would have once been considered luxuries but are now thought of as absolute necessities.[52] Being able to afford all those things (and all the other new products and services we come to want) means working more.[53] Thus, says Schor, Americans find themselves trapped in a vicious cycle of work-and-spend, spend-and-work.[54] As a consequence, leisure—the very thing that would allow us to enjoy life more—becomes more and more elusive.

Sociologist John Robinson[55] of the University of Maryland points out that many Americans, especially those over 51, have actually gained more free time, as much as five extra hours a week since 1965. But even Robinson admits that for those between 36 and 50 years of age life is more harried than ever before, especially if, in addition to holding down jobs, they are married and have children. The paradox is, even those Americans who *have* more free time than before actually feel they have less![56]

Robinson's "Americans' Use of Time Project" reveals a progressive increase in hurriedness over the years.[57] In 1965, 25 percent of those surveyed said their lives were rushed all the time. By 1975, the figure had risen to 28 percent. By 1985, it had climbed to 32 percent. And, more recently in 1992, Penn State researchers Geoffrey Godbey and Alan Graefe put the figure at 38 percent, almost a 50 percent increase from 1965.[58] Strikingly, those who live in small towns feel as rushed as those who live in big cities. Just as strikingly, both groups feel their lives are hurried not only at work but also at play. Even leisure, it seems, isn't leisurely any more!

All of this is understandable. With so many Americans working longer hours or holding down two jobs (including mothers who return home from work to a "second shift"), time off is bound to suffer.[59] The fact is, despite all our technological inventiveness, there are still only twenty-four hours in a day. More time on the job inevitably means less time at home, or anywhere else for that matter.

As a result, all the things we would have otherwise done—before work, after work, and on weekends—now have to be fitted into fewer hours. Errands get bunched together, while other "less necessary" activities (browsing in a shop, brewing a cup of tea, chatting with a friend, watching a sunset) are simply eliminated because there's "no time." Still others are doubled up.[60] Thus we eat while talking on the phone, shave or put on make-up while driving, and read while "watching" TV. Other tasks get delegated and become less personal in turn: day-care centers and sitters take the place of parents; carry-out food and microwave meals replace home cooking. Even the family dog is being replaced by the family cat, a lower-maintenance pet that doesn't demand time-consuming walks.[61]

The time crunch, moreover, makes us speed up whatever we do, as though the creeping minute hands on all the world's clocks had suddenly become whirling second hands. Even so-called recreation accelerates as we crowd in work-outs and hectic vacations into the little time we have left.[62] No wonder almost half the workers in America say they'd gladly trade a day's pay for an extra day off.[63]

Like it or not, we've all been drafted into an army, a peacetime army that fights its battles on the battlefield of everyday life. It's "time wars" we wage, to use Jeremy Rifkin's term, wars between the slower pace our minds and bodies crave and the faster tempo our technology demands.[64] And, in such wars, all of us are combat veterans.

Listen now to some voices from the trenches. As in many a modern army, troops are male and female and come from all walks of life. Perhaps in their war stories you'll hear an echo of your own.

> I have a calendar and I'm totally lost without it. If I didn't keep appointments, children's activities, school sports, days the kids have dental appointments, the days I'm going to work, etc., etc., written on my calendar, I'd be lost. I'd go crazy. When I'm without my calendar I'm like a lost person.[65]
>
> If I'm reading, I think I should be writing. If I'm writing, I wonder if I should have gone to that meeting instead. If I go to the meeting, I think maybe I should have spent the evening on the phone.[66]
>
> If I get more productive I'm going to scream.[67]
>
> Sometimes it seems I can't run fast enough.[68]
>
> My life is on fast forward.[69]
>
> Time . . . is the most precious commodity I've got and I don't have enough of it. It used to be money. Now it's time.[70]

There are times I move so fast I get frightened. At times my life is moving so fast all I can do is steer it, not change the pace. But as it picks up speed, it's harder to steer.[71]

Time??? It's no longer an issue. There is none.[72]

These personal comments are confirmed by the findings of a scientific survey funded in 1991 by Hilton Hotels. When adult Americans were polled, one out of three said: "I feel that I'm constantly under stress—trying to accomplish more than I can handle," "I worry that I don't spend enough time with my family and friends," and "At the end of the day, I often feel that I haven't accomplished what I set out to do." More than one out of five complained, "I just don't have time for fun anymore," and confessed, "Sometimes I feel that my spouse doesn't know who I am anymore."[73]

Even though these are the views of a minority of Americans, the anguish in their voices deserves to be heard, especially since every day more and more such cries are being raised.

The Adventures of Charlie and Lucy

Strikingly, the feelings they express and the issues they address were anticipated many years ago.

A decade before the sound barrier was broken, an English comedian named Charlie Chaplin was already exploring how high-speed technology can cause stress. Filmed in the midst of the Great Depression, *Modern Times* was written and directed by Chaplin as a tribute to the indomitable resiliency of Everyman and Everywoman as they search for happiness in a harsh society governed by brute capitalism and the unfeeling force of machines.[74]

As the film opens, the president of the Electro Steel Corporation issues his first order of the day: "Section 5. Speed 'er up. 4.1." A symbol of heartless authoritarianism, the president has the only audible lines of dialogue in the whole film, lines barked out over a loudspeaker to his chief engineer. We see his face on a futuristic wall-sized television screen, part of a two-way video system that lets him monitor his workers even when they take a toilet break.

Chaplin, our hero in overalls, frantically wields two wrenches—one in each hand—as he races to tighten nuts speeding by on a moving conveyor belt. "Section 5. More speed. 4.7." Now Chaplin is flailing his elbows as he works the twin wrenches, desperately trying to keep up. "Section 5. Give it the limit," the loudspeaker barks, and the belt accelerates still more.

But it has all become too fast for a mere human, however nimble and conscientious he may be. In the throes of a nervous breakdown, our poor nut-tightener is drawn by the conveyor belt into an open shaft and down into the gear-filled innards of the great machine. Finally, he dizzily emerges, and proceeds to tighten all the nuts in sight, till his eager eyes fall on the nut-like buttons of a matron's dress. Arrested for almost wrenching a wench, he is hauled off to a mental hospital, only the first in a series of misadventures and imprisonments.

In the end, Charlie discovers true love in the person of a lovely street urchin. When she wants to give up her struggle to find happiness, he urges her to keep on trying, to "never say die." Gesturing to her to put a smile on her lips, with the strains of Chaplin's own song, "Smile," rising in the background, he takes her hand. Silhouetted against the dawn, the two walk down the road of life, hand in hand.

Years later, the medium of television would take up the same theme. One of the most popular, most watched, and most talked about programs in television's "Golden Age" was the comedy series "I Love Lucy," starring Lucille Ball and Desi Arnaz.[75] The 1952–53 season premiered with an episode entitled "Job Switching."[76]

To prove to their husbands that they are not "just housewives" but can hold down a "real job," Lucy and her friend Ethel start work in the wrapping department at Kramer's Kandy Kitchen. Their job: to wrap newly-dipped chocolates for boxing. As the supervisor yells "Let 'er roll!," the candy conveyor belt begins to move—slowly at first, enough to give Lucy and Ethel confidence in their new-found roles.

But then the pace picks up. In a frantic effort to keep pace with the belt (if a chocolate gets by them, they'll be fired), Lucy and Ethel eat passing candies, scoop them off the belt, stuff them in their uniforms—anything to survive. Returning, the supervisor surveys the empty belt with satisfaction, only to shout "Speed it up a little!" to the belt operator. All ends happily, though, when Lucy and Ethel, fired from the factory, go home and receive gifts of appreciation from their frustrated homemaker-husbands—two five-pound boxes of chocolate!

Like Chaplin's *Modern Times*, "Job Switching" pitted human beings against machines, and human beings came in last. As Lucy at one point declares, "I think we're fighting a losing game."

What had made the difference was not the machine's power but its speed, a speed that tested the outer limits of human reflex and endurance. What makes us laugh at the comedians is the universal truth we sense behind their antics, a truth we are all too familiar with in our everyday lives.

THE ACCELERATION OF SOCIETY

Some technological changes are probably hard to appreciate because they do not occur all at once but gradually, infiltrating our everyday lives little by little even as they transform them.

Listen now to author Jerry Mander as he "brings us up to speed" by describing the technological changes he has witnessed in his own lifetime:

I was born in 1936. At that time there were no jet planes and commercial plane traffic was effectively non-existent. There were no computers, no space satellites, no microwave ovens, no electric typewriters, no Xerox machines, no tape recorders. There were no stereo music systems nor compact disks. There was no television in 1936. No space travel, no atomic bomb, no hydrogen bomb, no "guided missiles," as they were first called, no "smart" bombs. There were no fluorescent lights, no washing machines nor dryers, no Cuisinarts, no VCRs. There was no air conditioning. Nor were there freeways, shopping centers, or malls. There were no suburbs as we know them. There was no Express Mail, no fax, no telephone touch dialing, no birth-control pill. There were no credit cards, no synthetic fibers. There were no antibiotics, no artificial organs, no pesticides or herbicides. . . . During my lifetime all of this changed.[77]

The inventions Mander lists are quite specific, but something far more subtle, and much more pervasive, was going on. The very pace of life was picking up, accelerated by new technologies that more and more began to characterize American culture.

Many of these were not mechanical technologies with slow-moving parts but electronic ones that operated instantaneously. In the time it takes for a human eye to blink, an electronic signal could travel half-way to the moon.

But we were not sending signals to the moon—at least not yet. We were sending them to each other, with greater and greater frequency. In the '50s and '60s, America's phone was ringing, its radio was blaring, its TV was on—all at the same time. And factories were cranking out more and more electronic appliances and gadgets for us to buy.

If life on the job was speeding up, life at home wasn't getting any slower. What we soon had to adapt to wasn't just a shift at Chaplin's Electro Steel Corporation or Kramer's Kandy Kitchen. It was our whole waking existence in a new open-24-hours world.

Not only were things getting faster. By the '70s and '80s, even the definition of "fast" was getting faster: "instant" this and "express" that— with us caught in the middle. By the '90s, if one thing saved us time, three things were already there to take its place.

If that wasn't bad enough, everything seemed to be connected to everything else in one great big fast-moving system that wouldn't let us go, that wouldn't let us lead our lives at a pace *we* chose—a pace less stressful and more humane.

In struggling to adapt to the nonhuman tempo of their society, many Americans were thankful just to be keeping up. But in the process of keeping up, they had begun to lose something very precious: a sense of what life should be for.

From now on, neither a simple Chaplinesque smile nor a five-pound box of chocolates would be enough to insure a happy ending. For the velocity we were traveling at was robbing us of the perspective we would need to find our way.

The power of now had begun to transform our lives.

Chapter 2

The Three Sources of Now's Power

THE POWER OF NOW, like a mighty river, draws its strength from a number of tributaries. In this chapter we shall explore these tributaries one by one.

TECHNOLOGY

The most visible of these tributaries is technology. But like any tributary, its currents can be traced upstream to even more distant—and more hidden—sources. Two ancient Greek stories reveal the direction and depth of those waters.

The Wings of Icarus

According to a legend, the Mediterranean island of Crete was once ruled by a mighty king named Minos.[1] Imprisoned in his palace was a half-human, half-animal monster called the Minotaur. The prison, called the Labyrinth, was a subterranean maze of intricate design. So intertwined were its passageways that no one who entered it could ever find his way out. The architect of the maze was Daedalus.

But Daedalus gave away the secret of the Labyrinth to let a brave hero slay the terrible monster. Discovering Daedalus's treachery, King Minos ordered Daedalus and his son Icarus placed under house arrest and executed. While imprisoned, Daedalus directed his creative imagination toward finding a means of escape. The palace, however, was patrolled by guards, including the stairways that led to the top floor where Daedalus and his son Icarus were held captive.

Observing birds that flew by his window, Daedalus suddenly conceived a daring plan. Snapping off twigs from branches that overhung his chamber, removing feathers from his pillows, and taking wax from his workshop, Daedalus fashioned artificial wings. Fitting the devices to his son's arms and his own, he instructed Icarus in their use. He especially warned him not to fly too low else the salt spray of the sea would weigh down the feathers and make the wings too heavy to lift, nor to fly too high else the heat of the sun's rays would melt the wax and cause the wings to collapse.

Climbing onto the parapet outside the window, the two flapped their arms, tentatively at first, then boldly stepped into the air and flew! Soaring like birds, Daedalus and Icarus marveled at their power, delighting in their new-found freedom.

But young Icarus, intoxicated by the exhilaration of flight, forgot his father's words of warning. Higher and higher he flew into the sky, nearer and nearer the sun. Slowly, the wax grew soft from the growing heat until the wings fell apart, sending Icarus plummeting into the sea to his death. Grieving, Daedalus flew on to a place of refuge, a sanctuary won at the cost of his son's very life.

The legend of Daedalus celebrates human resourcefulness, but it is also a tragic story, for resourcefulness, however brilliant, may lead to painful consequences we never anticipate. In the bright glare of the present the dark contours of the future may lie unseen.

What led Icarus to ignore his father's warnings was the thrill of flight, the exhilaration of a powerful experience never before known to man. Ascending to the heavens, the realm of the gods, was a transcendant experience because it left behind the human limitations Icarus had always known. Daedalus, his father, more intimately understood the limitations of the device he had invented, that the transcendant power it offered man was conditional upon man's own self-control. Yet even wise Daedalus had failed to appreciate the impulsiveness of youth. More adept with things than with people, more at home with reason than emotion, Daedalus had not fully understood the implications of freedom and its exercise by human beings. He had not foreseen that, once invented, a device acquires a life of its own, its power now available to whomever would use it in whatever way they might wish—for good or ill. Once generated, the invention—like a grown child—may cease to respond to its creator's will.

Like Icarus, we have witnessed how mechanical devices can alter our lives. The automotive engine and the winged airplane, once they were invented, set into motion a multiplicity of forces and subordinate inventions whose trajectories were impossible to control. Both automobile and airplane have caused fatalities in peacetime and, adapted to military purposes as tanks and bombers, have multiplied them deliberately in war.

"If God had meant man to fly, He would have given him wings," said critics of the first experimental planes. They pointed to Nature to prove human beings were overstepping their bounds in trying to fly. But such critics overlooked a crucial component in the makeup of the human animal: while birds are already equipped with bodily parts that enable them to fly, human beings are endowed with an even greater, albeit less visible, attribute—the power to reason and invent—an attribute as much a part of human nature as arms and legs. Through the application of this power the human animal is able to redefine itself with the creative acquisition of powers it never before possessed.

Each technology we acquire endows us with an artificial power that expands the capabilities we would otherwise possess through nature alone. But even as it grants us this power, it obscures the invisible limitations that may prove to be our undoing, for it entrusts us with instrumentalities whose wise use demands a level of self-control we may not—or may not ever—possess. It is our internal limitations, rather than some external, impersonal foe named technology, that are our truest and most natural enemies.

To save himself and his son from a deadly environment, Daedalus invented a device only to discover it had become the instrument of his beloved son's death. In a similar way, we have endeavored to make our lives easier and faster by technical means only to discover that these very artifices now threaten the health and wholeness of the society in which we live. Trapped within a technological labyrinth of our own invention, we search for the means to our liberation.

Our task would be less difficult if the challenge we faced was only physical. But the labyrinth we have designed—as we will later see—distorts our very perception of reality, bending in its corridors our sense of space and time.

Technology's Children

Like our children, inventions spring from within us. To reject technology totally is to disown before birth the very offspring of our minds. Our responsibility as parents, however, does not end, but instead begins, when our children are born. It is our duty to protect and nurture them, but also to instruct them firmly in what is right and wrong. In a similar way, society has an obligation to set prudent limits to the technology it generates.

Childrearing is of course unpredictable, as is marriage itself. Despite this unpredictability, individuals contemplating marriage would be foolhardy not to analyze realistically their long-term compatibility with their prospective partners in life. To fail to assess their relationship as carefully as possible, to assume naively that everything will "work out," is to court disaster. So, too, with technology. We cannot and should not accept its blandishments of comfort and ease on blind faith.

Yet, ironically, so technicized has our age become that the mere asking of such questions marginalizes the asker and often invites ridicule. The asker is usually dismissed as a "Luddite" or "neo-Luddite," terms that recall a series of dramatic events that took place in early nineteenth-century England.[2]

The traditional handicrafts of spinning, weaving, and cloth shearing were then being threatened by the introduction of factory machinery. Operated by a small number of unskilled workers, such machines could mass produce textiles at very low cost. To protect their livelihoods and keep food on their families' tables, skilled workers banded together to attack the mills and break the machines. With popular support, they waged guerilla warfare on mill owners from 1811 to 1816 until repressive legislation, military arrests, deportations, and hangings crushed their revolt. In Parliament their cause had been championed by none other than Lord Byron, who had proclaimed: "However we may rejoice in any improvement in the arts which may be beneficial to mankind, we must not allow mankind to be sacrificed to improvements in Mechanism."[3]

The ringleader of this lost cause had been a mythical general named Lud. As one version has it, the name arose from an incident in the 1770s when a young apprentice knitter named Ned Lud (or Ludd, or Ludlam) got angry and smashed his knitting frame when his father told him to get back to work.

Today, the name "Luddite" is applied to activists who would like to see the clock of technological progress turned backward. "They complain that words should not be processed, want phones answered by warm-blooded receptionists and insist that no matter how small a computer becomes, there's nothing 'personal' about it."[4] On a more public front, they oppose the dangers they see in such seemingly benevolent technologies as television and genetic engineering.[5]

To be sure, idealistic neo-Luddite arguments about the human spirit and the quality of life might have been barely intelligible to the original Luddites; their concerns had more to do with having bread than defining the future of man. Likewise, their enemies, the mill owners, were not defending abstract progress as much as private property and crass profit. But after taking account of these distinctions, the fundamental question still remains: do human beings have the right to reject a specific technology, or have they lost that right, even when the applications of that technology negatively affect their everyday lives? Do we have the authority to sit in judgment on the public uses to which inventions are put, or have we lost that power, or meekly ceded it, to the machines themselves and the owners who profit from them?

This is not to claim that technological advancement is inherently evil. Our lives have been made immeasurably safer, healthier, and richer by an infinite number of inventions. But our lives have also been damaged and diminished by their impact.

Surveying modern mechanization in the aftermath of World War II, critic Sigfried Giedion concluded: "Means have outgrown man."[6] If Giedion's judgment is correct, we can only regain control over our lives by evaluating the full human consequences of our technology. Yet, raising such objections in a technological society can be construed as evidence of treason or, at least, of mental instability.

Those who decry technology's direction and warn of the effects of its unrestrained momentum are often berated as "Jeremiahs."[7]

The original Jeremiah lived in the kingdom of Judah during a tragic period in its history, the late seventh to the early sixth centuries B.C. Jeremiah denounced his society's moral corruption—its greed and selfishness—and urged his people to mend their ways or suffer the consequence of military destruction. Believing themselves invulnerable, the Judeans rejected Jeremiah's impassioned plea. In 586 B.C., the Babylonian king Nebuchadnezzar captured Jerusalem, burned its Temple, and marched its people into captivity.

Those who dismiss modern social critics as latter-day Jeremiahs ignore the reality of Jeremiah's love for his people and his abiding faith in their promise. But, most of all, they fail to acknowledge the painful accuracy of his prediction.

For everything we buy or do there is a price. And so we must always ask: What is the price we will be asked to pay? And what price will be asked of our children? In exploring the temporal implications of electronic technology and the moral implications of an accelerated culture, we must always keep these questions in mind.

Plato's Cave

Our second instructive tale from Greece is not a myth like the story of Daedalus and Icarus, but a philosopher's story. Like the legend of the Labyrinth, however, it deals with imprisonment and escape and the consequences of technology.

It was the ancient Greeks who created what we call philosophy, the rational search for truth. Philosophy sought with the power of the mind to replace the dark unknown with understanding. Though philosophers lived in many parts of Greece, no city became as renowned for philosophy as Athens, a city whose very name echoed the name of Athena, goddess of wisdom.

A man named Socrates once lived in Athens, a man who committed his life to the search for truth and who gave mortal witness to the importance

of that search. Tried as a subversive because his interrogations had infuri-
ated the pompous, he was offered his life in exchange for his silence. If he
would only stop asking questions, they would leave him alone; but if he
persisted, he would be executed.

Socrates' answer is recorded in his defense speech.[8] It is simply this: "a
life that cannot be questioned isn't worth living." In short, if he couldn't be
free to ask questions, then it wasn't worth being alive. What Socrates meant,
and what he gave his life to prove, is that existence alone is insufficient; one
must also have the freedom to examine one's existence.

Thanks to his disciple, Plato, Socrates lived on as the central character in
a series of philosophical dialogues Plato wrote, the most famous of which
is *The Republic*. In the seventh chapter, or "book," of this work, Plato paints
a picture, a picture of an imaginary cave.

Facing the back wall of the cave are people who have spent their entire
lives in its darkness, bound in such a way that they can only look at the
wall, unable to turn their heads. As they have lived in the cave since
childhood, that wall is all they have ever seen. Behind them is a blazing fire
whose light is used by mysterious puppeteers to create shadow images on
the wall. The prisoners believe these shadows to be reality, for the shadows
are the only reality they have ever known.

Plato tells us the cave is a metaphor for our intellectual lives. All of us
live in a cave, all of us are trapped by its darkness, and we must somehow
break free of the bondage of misinformation to find our way out into the
sunlight of truth.

Ever since the *Republic*, the notion of escaping the darkness of ignorance
and seeking the light of knowledge has become the classic symbol of human
progress, of humankind's quest for fulfillment. Yet for us today, and
for the rest of this century and on into the twenty-first, the enemy will
not be darkness, but light. Too much light, light 186,000 miles-per-sec-
ond fast.

While the history of technology can be traced along many lines, one of
the most intriguing lines of development is that of phototechnology, the
technology of light. From the prehistoric invention of fire to laser beams
and fiber optics, light has continually occupied the minds of inventors.
Their inventions fall into two categories: the use of light to aid vision and,
more fascinating still, the use of light for purposes of communication.

The use of light for communication is one of the major directions that
technology has taken ever since the middle of the nineteenth century. From
still photography to motion pictures to television (with a progression from
black-and-white to color imagery in each), phototechnology has had a
profound effect upon mass communication and mass education. Unlike the
printed word, visual images have more impact because they are more
immediate: they simulate reality in a way that the printed word cannot.
Unlike alphabetic shapes, they are not abstract; unlike words, they require

no symbolic interpretation by the mind. Coupled with the widespread and uniform dissemination of such images, phototechnology affects the thinking of vast audiences and shapes their perception of reality.

Ironically, this was all anticipated by our friend, Plato, for the prisoners in the cave are not conditioned by darkness per se but by images projected through the use of light. Nor should the prisoners be termed a captive audience only. So conditioned are they by their lifelong education, they would challenge anyone who denied their shadowy truth. And if somebody went into that cave and tried to free them, free them and pull them from their seats and bring them into the sunlight, they might even kill such a person, Plato says, recalling the fate of his very own teacher, Socrates.

The Burden of Choice

Like the prisoners in Plato's cave, millions of Americans are simultaneously affected by the commercially inspired electronic manipulation of artificial images. They call it "entertainment" and can't wait to get more. Lest the shadows slip through their fingers, they set their VCRs.

As the number of commercially available television channels multiplies, the freedom of choice for viewers increases, but so does the burden of that choice. Increasingly, viewers are bombarded with multiple stimuli and are asked to make instantaneous choices of growing complexity—all in the name of personal fulfillment.

Meanwhile, in the workplace as well, the rapidity of mass communications has created a regenerating supply of information greater than can readily be absorbed, one that threatens executives with "datacide."[9] Deluged by information, people in business struggle to swim a dangerous channel churning with random data.[10] Though "decision stress" and "information overload" were identified over two decades ago, they continue to be symptomatic of our social condition.[11]

In the face of overstimulation, the distinction between what is more important and what is less important can easily be lost. But just as threatening are the mechanisms that have been developed, both personal and social, to protect the psyche from this overload. Forced to handle too much data, the individual may practice "psychological absenteeism": avoiding responsibility and decisions, chemically insulating his psyche from the reality, and seeking various forms of sensual gratification as substitutes for understanding. Just as the pupil of the eye contracts in response to excessive light, so the receptors of the mind contract in response to excessive information.

In addition to these mechanisms, there is also the tendency to oversimplify deliberately, to jettison data because there is simply too much on board. In mass communications, such simplification can soothe the harried brain. The use of the "happy talk" format for local TV news, the minimal treatment of world issues on such programs, the reduction of complex stories on television to headlines and captions, and the success of the picture-oriented newspaper *USA Today*, all illustrate this phenomenon.

The desire for simplification also led to the development of the computer. Having invented the means for the instantaneous collection of information, human beings discovered that such technology produces impulses too many and too rapid for the human neurological system to absorb. What was needed was that human beings become as efficient as the nonhuman devices they had designed. The solution was to develop an ancillary technology: to delegate the organization and analysis of data and the making of appropriate decisions to devices capable of operating more swiftly than the unaided human brain. Now vast quantities of information could be stored and interpreted.

Long regarded by many as a danger because of its alien and remote nature, the computer has become personal, user-friendly, and a part of our everyday lives. Though many once looked upon it as a monster, others now see it as a savior. In reality, of course, it is neither. Like technology itself, the computer is a tool that can serve purposes both good and bad. The computer cannot "solve all our problems," for we must first define what our problems truly are and which of them can be addressed meaningfully in quantitative terms.

In 1928, long before the computer age dawned, American poet Archibald MacLeish wrote the following lines:

> We have learned the answers, all the answers
> It is the question that we do not know.[12]

Yes, we do have the answers, lots of answers, more answers than we know what to do with. Our computers are crammed with answers. But what is the question, the question that will endow those random facts with significance, with purpose? Like orphaned keys found in an attic drawer, facts by themselves are useless, however bright and shiny they may seem. Better to have a lock without a key, a puzzle in steel to solve, than keys to nothing.

Yet, knowing how many people hunger for answers to make them feel secure, I hasten to provide a brief list:

1. Yes	6. False
2. Never	7. Everyone
3. No	8. True
4. Always	9. No one
5. Sometimes	10. 17

All of the above are guaranteed to be correct, even the last. There is not a single wrong answer here.

And yet all of these answers by themselves are useless, for the value of any answer is proportionate to the significance of the question that generated it. And when more than one answer is possible, responsibility reverts to the human spirit to choose the direction it wishes to take, the outcome it wants to see.

The chooser must take time to reflect, to meditate. But reflection and meditation are functions inconsistent with the computer's nature, its mandate from society, and society's own pace.[13] Though a computer may save us time, its very quickness can condition us to disdain slower, more peculiarly human, modes of operation.

Ours is a quantitative age in which even quality has been quantified. Instant answers are in demand, and the sooner the better. "We don't know where we're going but we're on our way," sings Carl Sandburg's song of Kalamazoo.[14] In such a world, contemplation is so much useless "downtime."

Wishes and Wisdom

Electronic technology radically contracts the interval between need and fulfillment. And therein lies its ability to amplify the power of now. Like Aladdin's genie, it can achieve for us incredible and almost instant results. All we need to do, it seems, is rub the lamp of technology and wish.

Technology, in fact, is the inevitable and natural outgrowth of human needs and desires. But, like human nature itself, it also possesses an intrinsic potential for good or evil.

From one angle, technology looks value-neutral. It seems we can no more blame it for our ills than we can blame Aladdin's lamp for the consequences of its master's wishes, as the tool is the unbiased instrument of its user's choice. Thus, depending on its application, fire can either warm a home or destroy it. As Adlai Stevenson said of nuclear fire: "Man has wrested from nature the power to make the world a desert or to make the desert bloom. There is no evil in the atom; only in men's souls."[15] If we dream, then, of a better world, it is to our own souls that we must first look to insure that wisdom governs our wishes.

Yet, though technology itself is uncolored by intent, its very existence colors the choices we make. First of all, technology makes possible a type and magnitude of action that otherwise would have been impossible. Thus, no matter how great the hatred of two Neanderthals toward each other, no matter how sharp the spear each hurled at the other's cave, neither could have caused the devastation of a nuclear missile. Our progressive technology has indeed expanded the circumference of our everyday blessings, but it has also enlarged the diameter of our destructive capacity. And it has speeded up our capacity for destruction as well.

Secondly, technology tends to multiply geometrically, and its cultural influence increases accordingly. The inventions of one age quickly spawn others, exponentially expanding the totality of technology's power, including its power over our thoughts and actions. For a pervasive technology has the ability to permeate the human spirit rapidly with its own intrinsic principles.

As Jacques Ellul wrote:

> When technique enters into every area of life, including the human, it ceases to be external to man and becomes his very substance. It is no longer face to face with man but is integrated with him, and it progressively absorbs him. . . .
>
> Technique never observes the distinction between moral and immoral use. It tends, on the contrary, to create a completely independent technical morality.[16]

Like a brakeless car rolling downhill, technology acquires a momentum all its own, one that accelerates even as the vehicle plunges downward. And we are the passengers who once steered the car. Now brakeless, we maintain only the illusion of control, trying to stay on the roadway even as we hurtle onward.

The third way technology influences our choices comes from the very fact that it exists, for the existence of a technology constitutes an invitation for its use. It is too facile to argue that criminals, not weapons, commit crimes. For the very existence of handguns and their easy accessibility make possible the commission of certain violent acts that otherwise never would have taken place. If we are weak then, technology can seduce us into forgetting our concerns by tempting us with power.

Lastly, the products of technology can, in certain critical ways, inhibit us from obtaining the perspective we need to use our power wisely. The technological society eagerly replaces the old with the new and the atechnical with the technical. As a result, what is old is called outdated and what is unquantifiable is regarded as useless. Yet, as wisdom is marked by age and traditional values are not easily quantified, both wisdom and tradition soon become incongruous with society's sensibilities. A technological culture thus inevitably severs its people from the past, depriving them of historical and spiritual perspective.

By displacing the natural environment with an artificial one, mankind has replaced nature's tempo with a faster one of his own devising. Like a rapidly ticking metronome, it dictates an insistent rhythm our movements must obey. Having invented a myriad of mechanical and electronic inventions to do more and more in less and less time, we now find ourselves inhabiting an environment that artificially quickens the pulse. A "technopulse" animates our souls, a rhythm antithetical to reflection. It is precisely in this way—through the acceleration of our lives—that contemporary technology most threatens the wisdom of our decisions, decisions that will ultimately prove critical for the building of a humane world.

As Edna St. Vincent Millay wrote:

> Upon this age, that never speaks its mind,
> This furtive age, this age endowed with power
> To wake the moon with footsteps, fit an oar
> Into the rowlocks of the wind, and find
> What swims before his prow, what swirls behind—
> Upon this gifted age, in its dark hour,
> Rains from the sky a meteoric shower
> Of facts . . . they lie unquestioned, uncombined.
> Wisdom enough to leech us of our ill
> Is daily spun; but there exists no loom
> To weave it into fabric; undefiled
> Proceeds pure Science, and has her say; but still
> Upon this world from the collective womb
> Is spewed all day the red triumphant child.[17]

HISTORY

Second among the sources of now's power is our history as a nation. Nowism—the preoccupation with the present—is not caused by technology alone. Technology's influence is reinforced by the land we Americans live in, a land whose history exemplifies and celebrates the new.

The New World

The "New" World discovered by Christopher Columbus was already an old world to the natives who lived here when Columbus landed. But the false notion of newness was to persist because it described how European explorers perceived America. To them at least, this world *was* new and, as conquest made theirs the dominant ideology, their definition prevailed.

Calling the land new also served to justify their seizure of it. Acknowledging native claims hallowed by tradition would have only complicated the question of ownership. On the other hand, converting the surviving natives into Europeans (by religion, language, and law) would erase any vestiges of a past. Indeed, the conversion of natives to Christianity would, by the salvation it granted them, cleanse their conquerors of all guilt. Thus, the colonization of America was as much a conquest of time as it was a conquest of space. Old was forcibly transformed into new.

The seeming newness of America was further affirmed—if any affirmation was needed—by the unurbanized, uncivilized, undeveloped land later

explorers and colonists found. And, when American patriots broke their
ties to a British past and united under a revolutionary constitution, the
newness of their country acquired a political dimension.

As Americans, the aura of newness in our environment has conditioned
and continues to condition our cultural attitude toward reality. This attitude
was reinforced by industrialization and the spirit of private enterprise. Our
economic system values the new over the old, first as a consequence of true
technological progress, and second as a means of earning profits—as sales
are generated not only by actual consumer need but also by the public's
belief that a new model or style is better than the old one it replaces.

If a nowist society, then, is a modern phenomenon, the mood of nowism
itself is rooted in our national experience. Our preference for now derives
from the strands of newness woven into the fabric of our history.

This national compatibility with the new is the corollary of our discom-
fort with the old. By and large, Americans disdain the study of history
because history isn't concerned with the new. Attuned instead to the
present, we prefer the "news" to history. Because its content is ephemeral,
the news suits our temporal taste. Besides, its very novelty provides the
sensory stimulation we crave. History, on the other hand, only becomes
attractive when it is packaged as entertainment.

Because our historical memory is short, our culture has traditionally
exhibited personality traits that belong to the young: enthusiasm and
impulsiveness. These, however, are traits that persist only as long as life is
untarnished by the memory of defeat or by the more dulling realization
that no victory is final.

It is the repeated abrasion of harsh experience that sculpts the realism of
the mature adult, and such traits likewise characterize nations with long
histories and cultural memories. Such nations look across wider vistas of
time's landscape and see the dark valleys as well as the sunlit heights.

Significantly, America's Founding Fathers were deeply immersed in
history, especially ancient history. But that was because they drew their
spiritual nourishment from the chronologically deep and fertile soil of
European culture. Ironically, however, the American Revolution itself
served to sever the roots through which such sustenance was drawn.

Of course, it can be argued that ignorance is bliss, but historical ignorance is a bliss short-lived. To those ignorant of the past, all new fruits seem
equally inviting because they have never been tasted. But novelty alone is
an insufficient indicator of the nourishment they can give. If we are ignorant of history, we can easily assume that the way we see reality is the way
it has always been seen or, as we know little else, that our way—the way
of today—is the best way to live. Novelty, you see, is curiously self-reinforcing: the shorter our cultural memory, the more uncritical our acceptance
of what we are shown. By denying our eyes the lens of history, we validate
the correctness of our myopia.

But that is not all. For, even as we affirm the new, we destroy the old. We condemn historic sites to demolition and old neighborhoods to "development." Eliminating the vestiges of an earlier time makes forgetting all the easier and the next wave of conquest more free of guilt. For in the nowist society, each new generation stands as a chronological conquistador, slaying and converting in order to build a shining new world upon the ruins of the past. And ultimately a generation arises that can only live as a stranger in its own land.

Exiles from Time

Most cultures arise and persist in the same geographical area. This area becomes the native land, the motherland or fatherland, honored in memory and song. At the same time it serves as a stabilizing force, undergirding the structure of tradition with the love of one's country. Thus, in patriotism, space and time are fused.

But what if space is changed? Will the sense of time change as well?

Five centuries ago, America was truly a "New World." Those who came to this continent as colonists brought their old world with them to help make them feel more secure. They brought with them the familiar objects of their everyday lives—from pipes to thimbles—as well as their religious beliefs and language, naming their new homes for the European cities they had left behind ("New" Amsterdam or "New" York). In so doing, the colonists sought to invent, though an ocean apart from their original homeland, the illusion of spatial continuity.

As long as America was merely a land and not a nation with its own intrinsic culture, the task of sustaining one's own culture was easier. But once a revolutionary new nation was born, founded upon an ideology that united disparate ethnic groups, the task became more difficult, for the United States of America made its own claims for allegiance as a new American society was born.

As later waves of immigration broke upon American shores, the newcomers found it necessary to choose between old country and new, between past and present. The fact that they had sought out America as a haven from hunger and oppression gave them an incentive to turn from the past. Yet, because they discovered themselves in a land alien in both culture and language, they tended to settle in ethnic neighborhoods that offered them the security of a familiar culture. Their children and grandchildren, however, increasingly found the ways and speech of the "old country" alien and committed themselves unabashedly to an American future, becoming—in the words of immigrant George M. Cohan—"real, live nephews of their Uncle Sam, born on the Fourth of July."[18] Behind the vigor of such patriotism, however, was a subtle spiritual transformation wrought by a movement in geographical space that stretched and sometimes tore the bonds of time.

During the eras of early colonization and later immigration, two groups suffered special traumas. Each group was degraded by the forcible violation of its own spatial and spiritual home. Native Americans, for whom this was not a "New" World at all, were robbed of their ancestral lands and freedom, then confined to artificial reservations whose narrow bounds were drawn by the very government that had despoiled them. Blacks, abducted from their African homeland and enslaved on white-owned plantations, were landlessly "emancipated," then persecuted for lacking the very things—property and education—they were historically denied. Such violent acts stripped each group of its own cultural history. Even the Civil War, in its destruction of antebellum splendor, functioned as a cultural leveler, along with the Reconstruction, by uprooting the old.

During the nineteenth and twentieth centuries, the expansion of the American frontier and the growth of America's cities produced a continuously changing, kaleidoscopic definition of what America was territorially, an evolution that did not slow until the inclusion of Alaska and Hawaii as states in 1959. The subsequent explosion of suburbs, the recent implosion of inner cities, and the pressure of new immigration continue to alter the landscape of urban America. In spatial terms, America has always been in flux, has always been "new."

Architecture reflects the spirit of a civilization. We seldom recognize, however, how much architecture can affect a civilization's spirit. The very newness of our buildings reinforces the power of now over our land. In every city of Europe, on the other hand, there are visible, physical reminders of the past. As residents of an Italian city stroll down a winding street, they may pass a Roman statue, a medieval church, and a Renaissance palace. These monuments in stone do not merely denote particular periods in history. They testify to the continuity of time itself and the durability of civilization. From their marble threads is interwoven a tapestry of time, worn but rich in texture. From such a monumental fabric can come a sense of one's place in time, a warmth that colder, newer American cities—ascendant in steel and glass above the demolished brick of yesterday—cannot provide.

It is for this reason that tourists from the New World are inexorably drawn back to the Old. At once befuddled by the clutter of monuments and encumbered by cameras to record them, they struggle to understand the language of a foreign land—the land of time, a time measured not in days or decades but in centuries and millennia. No wonder they seem so lost, or so insistent upon the "foreigners" conforming to their needs. Yet the texture draws them on, the illusive texture of time, woven by generations, the texture that speaks not only of today but of a million yesterdays, flowing one into the other, the fabric that could warm—and even nourish—them if only a way could be found.

The restless mobility of Americans and the anguished homelessness of Americans are merely points on the same national spectrum. As Americans, we will always be chronic emigrants in search of a home. Emma Lazarus put it best:

> Here at our sea-washed, sunset gates shall stand
> A mighty woman with a torch, whose flame
> Is the imprisoned lightning, and her name
> Mother of Exiles.[19]

Inhabitants of a land ever new, we will always be exiles from time.

The Need for Continuity

If matter is time made visible (autumn immanent in the browning leaf, spring signified by the greening bud), then a human generation is time made visible in flesh and blood. Each generation is the physical embodiment of a particular time.

But like a link in a chain, a generation has a function that transcends its own intrinsic substance. Connecting what has gone before with what is yet to come, each generation also constitutes a component that sustains the continuity of a larger whole, a whole defined by time.

Yet in addition to serving as a link to which adjacent parts are attached, a generation also functions as a conduit through which the past flows to the future. Like an electrical conductor, the linkage of generations permits the transmission of a current of ideas. One generation may differ from another in particular ways, but it is the common bond between and among its members that accounts for a distinct culture's existence. Though individual generations may die, the culture itself lives on.

This persistence, however, is by no means automatic or guaranteed. Like human beings, generations of less complex organisms maintain their physical and instinctual continuity by the mere act of organic propagation. But human beings possess an additional and special talent: the ability to perpetuate by mind and language a nonphysical continuity, that fragile continuity of ideas that we know as civilization.

It is of this fragile continuity that French aviator Antoine de Saint-Exupéry wrote, while serving in World War II.

> First things must come first, I agree. The war must be fought and won. . . . But when that will have been made secure, we will face the problem that is fundamental in our time: What is the meaning of man? To this question no answer is being offered, and I

have the feeling we are moving toward the darkest era our world has ever known.

It does not matter to me that I may be killed in this war. Of all that I have loved, what will remain? I am speaking not only of people but of customs, of irreplaceable modulations, of a certain spiritual light, of lunch under the olive trees on a farm in Provence, of Handel. The things that will survive I don't give a damn about!

What does matter is a certain ordering of things. Civilization is an intangible possession; it does not reside in things but in the invisible bonds that link them one to the other in this way and not in that way. Suppose we do achieve the mass distribution of perfectly machined musical instruments; where will the musician be?[20]

The perpetuation of our civilization is by no means the automatic consequence of our mere existence. Unlike the leaves of a tree that are mindlessly reduplicated every spring, the intangible values of a civilization depend upon voluntary and deliberate actions for their rebirth. Without the willing transmission of these values, the tree of civilization dies.

Down through history most cultures have maintained a bond with the past. By training and example, younger generations were schooled by older generations in the forms of behavior respected by the group. In certain cases, ancestors were worshipped (as in Confucian China) or were held in such high esteem (as in Republican Rome) that they continued—in an almost ghostly way—to influence morality long after they died. The very antiquity of these ancestors endowed their images with special sanctity and potency.

Yet even in such traditional societies, younger and older generations sometimes stood at odds, grappling for power and for the right to define the shape of the future. Such conflicts between generations arose because times changed. The world turned, and values conceived centuries earlier seemed inadequate to deal with problems and opportunities (economic or military) that had never before been anticipated. Thus, the very distance that once inspired reverence for tradition in an unchanging world now undermined the authority and validity of that tradition.

Today, the velocity of change in American society increases as never before. As a result, the distance between past and present grows ever wider, exacerbating the desperate need for continuity in our lives.

THE SENSES

In addition to technology and national history, there is a third source of now's power—the senses of the human body. While the first two sources lie outside us, the sensory origins of the power of now lie within.

The Mandate of the Senses

As animate creatures, human beings are obedient to the mandate of the senses—to the seductive reign of pleasure and the repulsive rule of pain. The domains of pleasure and pain exist fundamentally in the present, not in the distant future or past. Primarily, animals are answerable to their nerve endings, to the call that lies beneath the skin, and humanity is no different. That is not to say that animate beings owe allegiance solely to their senses. Animals may suffer pain to protect their territory and kin. Likewise, human beings may fight and die to defend family and home and (because of their capacity for belief) that most insubstantial thing, an idea. Nevertheless, notwithstanding examples of noble self-sacrifice, the pleasure principle remains—after the instinct for survival itself—the most generally potent force in determining animate behavior.

Because the past and the future cannot be directly experienced but can only be conceptualized, the present is the only dimension of time that offers direct sensory stimulation to the nerves. The voice of pleasure, therefore, speaks through the lips of the present. And, as the will of pleasure is so dominant in our lives, of all temporal powers the power of the present stands supreme.

Because the power of the present is rooted deep in human neurology and psychology, it can never be excised. It would be a mistake, for example, to assume that the power of now is rooted simply in culture alone, that by somehow altering the structure of our society (were that even possible) we could end now's influence once and for all.

Nor should we. For our openness to the present offers us access to the only dimension of life we can ever fully experience. And, without the sensual pleasures the present offers, our lives would be impoverished.

Combined, however, with the energy of technology and the effects of history, our inborn affinity for now acquires an overpowering strength capable of shutting out life's larger meaning. Our senses and the pleasures they give thus paradoxically desensitize us to a further reality.

The Landscape of Time

The palace of pleasure has many doors; for the senses are not one, but many. Each of the senses—touch, taste, smell, hearing, and sight—opens our internal consciousness to a facet of the world outside. Which of these senses was the first to arise primordially when life on this planet began? And which of these senses was the last to arise before man himself appeared?

Whatever the answer may be, of these five portals to external reality it is the sense of sight that has exerted the most influence on humanity's career. For each of the other four—touch, taste, smell, and hearing—is more narrowly focused, whereas the sense of sight offers to the brain a far wider, deeper, and more diverse range of information about the world.

In sensory terms, therefore, the biography of humankind is a visual story. The present and the future have a primacy that the past does not. It is a primacy based upon the sense of sight, for our understanding of time is conditioned by our perception of space. Our attitudes are thus colored not merely by the particular things we see, but by the very existence of sight.

Our eyes show us what stands in front of us, not what lies behind. As we walk through life, the world recedes behind us. Except for the fleeting backward glance that slows our forward momentum, the places we pass disappear. We see what exists now, not what existed then.

Only through memory can the past be recalled, memory that recreates where we have been and recounts the stages in our journey. But memory is less immediate than sight, less vivid than vision. Answering to subconscious stimuli or deliberate summons, memory is a secondary sense whose impulses require conversion into mental images or sounds.

Had we 360° vision—like mythical Janus with eyes front and back—not only would our perception of space be different, but so would our understanding of time. Though movement would carry us in one direction, the mind would perceive that movement as motion *away from* one horizon as much as *toward* another. We would feel ourselves relinquish the past even as we neared the future.

But such is not the case, for the human body is *forward*-oriented. Eyes and nose are front-mounted; feet and toes point ahead; knees and elbows are articulated to favor frontal movement. Of the body's sensory organs, only the ears are side-mounted—to permit the stereophonic tracking of sounds.

In evolutionary terms, the development of the human brain coupled with the frontal placement of the eyes made progress literally inevitable. From our earliest beginnings, our eyes aimed our energies ahead. Biologically, we were not meant to look back.

Our perception of space is, in fact, formed by the objects before us as we walk. What lies beneath our feet is hidden. Beyond the depth of the ploughshare's cut and the grave's marker lay a region of inscrutable mystery for the primitive mind. In the subterranean dimension resided the dark powers of death and the fertile secrets of earth.

What arched above, the sky—with its gliding clouds and sun, its moon, planets, and stars—was in ancient religion just as mysterious, though different. Seemingly within reach but yet beyond, visible yet immeasurable, the sky taunted man as the more tangible earth did not. Looking to celestial bodies, ancient astronomers sought direction for their earthly lives. Tracking stars and planets long before the earliest telescopes, they drew comfort from the discovery of order in the heavens, finding security in the fact that these phenomena were, if not explicable, then at least predictable.

To make the heavens more intelligible, they connected stellar dots into constellations, seeing in star clusters the familiar shapes of humans or animals. Yet there were no standards, no scale or frame of reference, to permit man to measure the heavens, to gauge them against his own human standard. How distant were the stars and planets? How big the sun and moon?

Compared to the dark world below and the distant world above, the world ahead was more intelligible, and from its appearance and organization human beings constructed a set of values: what was nearer was bigger and more important; what was farther was smaller and—except for predator or prey—of lesser concern. Prehistoric demands for survival accordingly defined spatial and temporal priorities. For those who had to live and die in the here and now, "far behind" and "far ahead" were not as important as the present.

Our eyes have thus played a dominant role in shaping our values. But, as we shall now see, it is the weaknesses of our senses as much as their strengths that have given the present the place it has in our lives. For our senses are limited and susceptible to manipulation.

Sensory Vulnerability

In a classroom or at a meeting, when a speaker begins to speak, a listener may begin to write, copying what he hears. The attentive listener is able to copy every word faithfully and accurately, as long as the speaker speaks slowly, pausing and pacing his utterances to the ability of the listener to comprehend and transcribe.

If the speaker begins to speak more quickly, the listener will adjust by accelerating the speed of his transcription. Should the pace of dictation increase still more, the listener will hasten to copy what he can, catching only phrases or occasional words as he tries to capture the speaker's message.

What such a listener experiences is the result of a disparity between two different rates of speed: the speed at which words can be spoken and the slower speed at which the same words can be written down. When the speed of speech exceeds the speed of writing, the writer can only adjust by writing fewer words. The speaker, however, can continue to increase the rate of his verbal output. He can even speak so rapidly that the listener becomes incapable of understanding the meaning of what is said, especially if the content is complex. In such a situation, the rate of speech will have exceeded the listener's rate of absorption and the level of his rational comprehension.

Such an experience can apply to visual as well as auditory perception. By increasing the speed of projection, for example, an enjoyable slide show can quickly be converted into a meaningless blur of colors and shapes.

These examples illustrate how our senses are limited in their ability to process and absorb information.

Natural human limits have, in fact, historically defined the tempo of the arts as well as of communication in general. As long as the production of sights and sounds was governed by human physiology (by the nimbleness of the dancer or the dexterity of the musician), an equation existed between the activity of the performer and the perception of that activity by the audience. Mechanical and electronic technology, however, have made it possible not only to record creative sights and sounds but to transmit them at a rate faster than they were originally produced by their human creators.

Imagine how much music we could appreciate if our neurological system were able to operate at a more rapid rate, absorbing in seconds the entire content of a compact disc. Or imagine how many films we could enjoy if "fast forward" were not simply a setting to advance a videotape but an accelerated mode of absorbing a visual message.

But such is not the case, for the tempo of the arts is a function not of how fast notes and images can be generated but of how fast they can be comprehended. To accelerate the speed of delivery beyond the natural power of reception is to distort experience itself: to fracture its integrity into disjointed parts or to compress its substance into an incomprehensible mass.

Imagine now a society modeled on this principle, a society in which the rate of data transmission presses the outer limits of natural absorption. In such a society the harried listener will struggle to transcribe the hurried message but will never be able to capture its wholeness. And even while he struggles, other messages will compete for his attention, messages simultaneously offered or delivered, each one only marginally comprehensible in its own right.

Like an air-traffic controller with failing equipment, struggling alone to land multiple flights in the night, the listener will suffer chronic tension. But the tension of the air-traffic controller is a tension familiar to others as well. For the celebrated age of communication in which we live tests by its nonhuman speed the very sanity of our lives.

As Jerry Mander has written:

> In our society, speed is celebrated as if it were a virtue in itself. And yet as far as most human beings are concerned, the acceleration of the information cycle has only inundated us with an unprecedented amount of data, most of which is unusable in any practical sense. The true result has been an increase in human anxiety, as we try to keep up with the growing stream of information. Our nervous systems experience the acceleration more than our intellects do. It's as if we were all caught at a socially approved video game, where the information on the screen comes faster and faster as we earnestly try to keep up.[21]

Increased beyond its optimal human level toward its almost unlimited technical one (a speed limited only by light's own speed), information transmission becomes increasingly counterproductive, for excessive speed and the cumulative effects of multiple systems operating simultaneously overwhelm, rather than aid, the individual.

The handwritten letter of colonial days that took weeks to reach its recipient represented a method of communication that invited reverie and reflection before reply. E-mailed, the same message today demands an instantaneous response. The telephone, which once allowed friends the leisure to share time in open-ended conversation, now electronically interrupts one call with the admonition that another is waiting.

To be sure, no one actually forces such changes upon us, for the features described—E-mail and call-waiting—are merely technological options. Yet what is the allure that leads us to choose interruption over tranquillity and tension over composure?

To begin with, it is an allure based upon the desire not to miss something: not to miss the call, not to miss the deal. Another way of stating this is to say that our society by its very speed invites us to use (or invent) certain devices to make sure we are not left out. And there would be no fault in this were it not for the possibility that in the act of "keeping up" we may in fact be falling behind—allowing our lives to be diminished qualitatively as the tempo of life steps up.

To answer a question quickly is not necessarily to answer it wisely. And to conduct two conversations simultaneously is to converse less well in each. Indeed, the trade-offs we make to attain high speed may at times come at the cost of our very humanity, however much our efficiency may seem to increase.

Because of the stimulation it receives and its own vulnerability, the human nervous system spontaneously grants to the power of now the authority it has over our lives. In addition, that same nervous system makes us susceptible to manipulation by individuals and groups who see us only as a means to a profitable end. Such people create an artificial now that serves their own selfish ends.

As Herbert I. Schiller observes:

> There is a vast amount of research going on, most of which never gets to see the light of day because it's proprietary research, . . . for very specific and very money-making objectives. The whole idea is sort of to "psych out," to discover, human behavioral characteristics. . . human vulnerabilities, human susceptibilities, and to turn these to account. . . . If you look at current media products, you find that they are deliberately being constructed, increasingly so, to short-circuit reflection and short-circuit rational thought and to emphasize and to go directly to visceral

approaches. . . . I don't think you can overstate what kind of an effort goes into this—a research effort, an "expenditure of resources" effort, and a development of the technology.

I do think underneath it all is a very strong search for money-making that operates not only as an individual activity but. . . system-wide. And this has become absolutely pervasive in this society.[22]

Thus, Schiller argues, a deliberate corporate strategy exists to manipulate consumers on a subrational level for the purposes of profit—to get the audience where they *feel*, not where they *think*, through what Vance Packard once called "hidden persuaders."[23] This manipulation has a long history, a history that is technological and peculiarly American.

Through motivational research techniques pioneered in the late 1940s and early 1950s, "people's subsurface desires, needs, and drives were probed in order to find their points of vulnerability. . . . Once these were isolated, the psychological hooks were fashioned and baited and placed deep in the merchandising sea for unwary prospective customers."[24] Guided by the principles of Freudian theory, a scientist named Ernest Dichter used sophisticated questionnaires and in-depth interviews to discover the prejudices, inhibitions, and emotions that secretly governed consumers' choices.[25] Once their true motivations were uncovered, Dichter devised psychologically appropriate marketing strategies for his clients. Thus, if they wanted to sell more perfume, he advised them to sell not a scent but sexual attraction; if they wanted to sell more power tools, he counseled them to sell not a machine but masculine sexual potency.

While Dichter was developing his "strategy of desire," another researcher named Louis Cheskin was exploring how the perception of color influences people's choices.[26] Packaging the same detergent in differently colored boxes, he asked a group of housewives to try out the detergent for a few weeks and report how well it washed delicate fabrics. Though the detergent was exactly the same, the women who poured it out of bright yellow boxes said it was too strong and ruined their clothes; those who poured it out of blue boxes said it left their clothes dirty; while those who had yellow and blue boxes called it "wonderful" and "fine." In a similar experiment using identical roll-on deodorants[27] in differently colored holders, one test group reported their deodorant had a strong smell,[28] another said theirs was irritating and worthless, and a third called theirs quick-drying and effective. Thus, a manufacturer could attract and build a loyal clientele for a product by shrewdly choosing the appropriate color for its package.

In 1957, market researcher James Vicary claimed to have dramatically boosted refreshment-stand sales at a movie theater by using subliminal stimulation.[29] Messages were flashed on the screen twelve times a minute for only 1/3000th of a second, enough time for the stimuli to reach the brain but too short a time for the audience to be consciously aware of their transmission. By projecting "Eat popcorn" and "Drink Coca-Cola" on the screen, Vicary claimed to have increased popcorn sales by 58 percent and cola sales by 18 percent. Later research findings have demonstrated that subliminal messages can indeed arouse hunger, thirst, and sexual appetite, but no evidence so far shows that such arousals can be converted into the purchase of a particular product or translated into a particular action.[30]

Vicary had used a projection device he called the "tachistoscope." By the 1960s, researchers were using other types of technology to improve marketing.[31] To predict the effectiveness of certain TV commercials, they measured the galvanic skin response of viewers. To gauge how much attention readers paid to magazine ads, they measured how much the pupils of their eyes widened or closed. Meanwhile, cameras hidden in stores and markets secretly tracked the movements and reactions of shoppers as they passed particular displays of merchandise.

By the 1970s, "neuromarketers"[32] were attaching electrodes to volunteers' scalps to observe how commercial stimuli affect brain wave patterns and frequencies.

In the 1980s, marketers turned to psychographics, or life-style studies.[33] By identifying activities, interests, and opinions that certain people had in common, marketing strategies could be developed to target promising groups. By pressing the right life-style button, a psychographic marketer could drive up sales. For example, if he found a lot of ecologically conscious health enthusiasts, he played up the healthfulness of his client's product and the biodegradability of its packaging. If most potential buyers were cost-conscious, he emphasized low prices.

By the 1990s, marketers discovered that gold could be mined from commercially available databases.[34] Using personal information culled from credit files, magazine subscription lists, membership rolls, and warranty cards (among other sources), direct-mail marketers were able to identify the names and addresses of likely customers by virtue of income, interests, or past buying practices. It was the computer that made possible the melding and sorting of such vast data. At the same time, electronic scanners at check-out counters were letting big business keep a running file on the everyday lives and choices of willing consumers, who were all too eager to exchange their privacy for the privilege of having a scannable VIP "frequent buyer" card that gave them a small discount. Later, sitting at home in front of their television sets, these same consumers would be showered by a pulsating electronic stream of carefully contrived commercial messages holding out to them the world of things that was theirs to buy, own, or experience.

In a materialistic society, individuals are fundamentally perceived (by others and even by themselves) as consumers—whether of goods, of services, or even of ideas. A consumerist society, in turn, is one in which the senses play an extraordinarily significant role, not only because the senses are the socially preferred avenue to gratification, but also because they are so readily available as an avenue of economic and political exploitation. The primacy of the senses in such a society facilitates the subversion of reason. This is because the senses respond to things spontaneously and rapidly, whereas, by comparison, reason is slow and deliberate.

A free-market economy, emboldened by psychological research and empowered by electronic technology, can easily enter the neurological portal to the self. Since "in the United States, unrestricted capitalistic behavior has been far more noticeable over time than in any other country,"[35] our land provides fertile ground for nowist greed to grow and thrive. Indeed, to the extent that this very greed reflects an appetite for pleasure, it too is rooted in now.

The Eyes of Teiresias

Even if our senses were not manipulated by others, they would still be hypnotized by the power of now. It is their very responsiveness to stimuli that makes them vulnerable.

To regard the blind as handicapped because they cannot see is natural. But the sighted are handicapped too—paradoxically by their very ability to see. To appreciate the paradox we must recognize that there are two different kinds of vision: the ability to see objects and the ability to see nonphysical realities.

The ancient Greeks, who were fascinated by what it meant to be human, long ago realized how the lives we possess are shaped by the kinds of people we are, by the invisible—but nonetheless real—entities of character and personality. They also understood how easy it is to blame what is wrong in our life on other people rather than ourselves.

In the plays of Sophocles, there is a character named Teiresias, who is blind.[36] Sophocles deliberately juxtaposes him with sighted characters in order to reveal the paradox of human vision. Those whose eyes function cannot see the tragic implications of the actions they choose. But the blind prophet Teiresias can see what the future holds and how that future is implicit in the present. For Teiresias sees with an inner eye, unimpaired by the tyranny of the obvious.

Our problem originates with the very nature of human sight, which is turned outwards. Our eyes deliver to us a dazzling and impressive array of stimuli. But we have no instrument of comparable power that automatically shows us what lies within. We are the ultimate benefactors of a biological tradition that aeons ago provided primordial creatures with eyes that helped them survive and thrive in the environment that surrounded them. But the reflective, inner-looking mind, capable of abstract conceptualization and self-evaluation, developed at a later time. The biological justification for this sequence of events is that physical survival has a higher priority than meditation. Bluntly put, the philosopher who cannot find food will be a dead philosopher.

Humanity, however, will need to draw upon its potential for self-examination in order to grow as a civilization. It will be insufficient in the future—indeed it will prove fatal—to become a species of observers entertained by stimuli. To realize the full potential of our minds we will need to oppose our biological inheritance and our very neurologic design, overriding the seductive stimulation of the optic nerve in order to look within.

We have now identified and explored the sources of now's power: technology, history, and the senses. The first source, technology, is actually an extension of the nervous system, for it facilitates the fulfillment of present needs and desires, converting "later" into "sooner" and "harder" into "easier." The second source, history, represents the geographical and political reality that is America, a new nation born in a New World and constitutionally dedicated to the pursuit of happiness. The third and most fundamental source is the human neurological system, which prefers pleasure to pain and assigns the highest priority to what it can see.

These three forces in combination have given to the present an elevated status higher than it has ever had before. The growth of America's power, combined with the enhanced role of technology in American society has gratified the senses of its citizens in ways the rest of the world has envied. And the American way, especially today, is the way of now.

It remains for us to examine how this immense power is, even now, transforming our personal lives and the world we know.

Chapter 3

The Transformation of
the Individual

THE CULTURAL TIME machine that is transporting us at warp speed is also transforming us as individuals. That transformation is being expressed in four ways: (1) through our subconscious acceptance of artificial flux as a natural part of reality, (2) through our hunger to experience the fleeting moment, (3) through the unnatural acceleration of our behavior and expectations, and, finally, (4) through the speed-driven metamorphosis of our outer and inner selves.

FLUX AND THE FLEETING MOMENT

The Invisible Ocean

Flux, or change, has always been characteristic of the natural world. Its dynamic presence was observed twenty-five centuries ago by the Greek philosopher Heraclitus. As Heraclitus put it: "Everything flows and nothing stays. . . . You can't step twice into the same river."[1] What Heraclitus meant was that the river of reality moves rapidly, changing in seconds from what it once was.

The flux Heraclitus described was a natural process, not an artificial one. Today, however, the flux inherent in the natural world has been augmented by human ingenuity, increasing the extent to which we are surrounded by motion. Today, we are immersed in an invisible ocean of change, a surging sea of electronic waves that flow around and even through us.[2]

As I type these words, sitting in my home near Detroit close to the Canadian border, radio waves unseen and unfelt course through my body, the transmissions of twenty-five AM and twenty-eight FM stations. The signals of four VHF and five UHF television channels simultaneously penetrate my skin. I—and you—are also awash in airwaves of still higher frequency: from cellular phones, radar devices for weather detection and flight, and satellites emitting microwaves from space.

To be sure, it is one thing to be enveloped in a medium, quite something else to absorb its substance or energy into ourselves. Though we swim through an electromagnetic sea, we need not let its waters soak into our souls. We can turn our radios and televisions off, closing our ears and eyes to their signals' presence.

But their Siren call is made difficult to resist by the sources of now's power. Our advanced technology grants us the opportunity to gratify our senses in ways formerly unknown. And our Constitution invites us to seek out these new experiences in an unending pursuit of happiness. Indeed, as will be discussed in chapter 5, we live in an electronically integrated society dependent upon instantaneous information for its daily existence. In such a society, *not* to listen and *not* to watch is equivalent to self-imposed exile. Thus, for practical reasons as well as for purposes of pleasure, the individual stays tuned, especially because doing so is as easy as pressing a button or flipping a switch. As a consequence, the invisible ocean lifts us on its tide.

Television: The Ocean Made Visible

Through the medium of television the electronic ocean that envelopes us is made visible. Today, the television set is an integral component of 98 out of 100 homes in America.[3] In 1990, for the first time, the average American home had two or more sets.[4] In each of those homes, at least one set was playing an average of seven hours a day.[5]

According to University of Maryland statisticians, "watching TV is the dominant leisure activity of Americans, consuming 40 percent of the average person's free time as a primary activity."[6] By "primary activity," the researchers mean the kind of activity to which people give their undivided attention. If we add to this those occasions when people are doing something else while their TV is on, "television takes up more than half our free time."[7] It does so because it gratifies our senses so readily and seems to ask so little of us in return.

Ironically, 20 percent of the time a TV is on, no one is even in the room watching.[8] Turning a set on and letting it play give many people a feeling of companionship even when they can't see the screen. The sound of television becomes a reassuring presence, not unlike the background sounds of nature—of birds singing, or of wind or surf—in a former, less technicized era. More than being just a friend, sharing our hours and the intimacy of our home, television has become tantamount to nature, a soothing environment into which the personality of the individual effortlessly blends. Such blending occurs because the viewing of television is an inherently passive activity.[9]

But how is the personality of the individual influenced by the medium into which it blends? The Bible tells us that when Lot's wife turned to look back at the dramatic destruction of Sodom and Gomorrah, she was transformed into a pillar of salt. Lot's wife is only the first example, albeit an ancient one, of a simple fact: rather than being separate from the events they observe, viewers can be transformed by the acts they witness.

In terms of our sense of time, then, how is a television viewer transformed? To begin to answer this question, we must first understand the nature of "television time."

The Dominance of the Present

Unlike works of art that are durable, television is by nature evanescent. Its auditory and visual images exist only in the dimension of the present, vanishing for all time (unless recorded) as instantaneously as they appear. Though the same might be said of real life, which consists of irretrievable moments, those moments are parts of an organic and living whole.

In the early days of television, it was easy to know when a performance was "live." The visual texture of films and the grainy quality of kinescopes betrayed their identity. But with the commercial introduction of the quadruplex videotape recorder in 1956, the nature of broadcasting was revolutionized. What radio had long before achieved by electronic transcription, television now possessed: the illusion of presentness.

Today the television viewer, no matter how experienced, cannot tell if a program is recorded or live. Except for a caption or voice-over announcing that a program was previously recorded, there is no way to determine this.

In one respect, videotape technology reveals with clarity the magical power of electronics to make the old seem new. But the blurring of past and present has deeper implications.

In actuality, the transmission of a videotaped program does not simply represent the blurring of the past and present, but something far more radical: the absorption of the past into the present, so seamlessly that the disappearance of the past into the all-consuming vortex of the present goes unnoticed. By their physical nature, books, records, tapes, and compact discs all disclose to their user that they embody the remembrance of a past event. But radio and television introduce themselves to us entirely in the dimension of now, because the mechanics of transmission are not evident to us.[10] To listen to radio, to watch television, is to be bathed in the present. This electronic immersion, accomplished first by the baptism of the child before the set, is sustained over our adult lives for decades and thereby reinforces the power of now that persists outside our homes.[11]

Fragmentation and Discontinuity

While the time available for television programming is finite, the desire to profit from its sale is infinite. The only way to satisfy the commercial appetite of multiple clients and at the same time increase advertising revenues is to accommodate as many advertisers as possible and profit maximally from their need. The net effect of this process is to fragment the experience of the viewer.

Since the relaxation of the National Association of Broadcasters code in 1982 and the abandonment of Federal Communications Commision regulations in 1984, neither industry nor government rules have existed to limit the number, length, and frequency of TV commercials.[12] On television, films are shown as a series of segments that are alternated with bunches of commercials; sporting events are restructured by time-outs to serve advertisers' needs; and even news stories are abbreviated and compressed to permit similar insertions. From 1983, when industry monitoring began, until 1993, nonprogram minutes in prime-time television (network commercials, local commercials, promos, and public service announcements) steadily increased to fifteen and one-half minutes per hour, an increase of 56 percent compared to 1983. More important even than the total number of minutes, however, is the total number of interruptions: an average of thirty-seven different messages per hour in prime time and a still higher number—fifty—in daytime. As a result of such practices, television watchers are subconsciously conditioned *not* to expect continuity in programming or, for that matter, in any other aspect of their lives.

Such features of programming are so common, we have grown oblivious to them. Indeed, only by deliberately counting the commercials we are shown per hour can we truly grasp their impact on our consciousness. In fact, it is precisely because we *are* oblivious to them that their influence is so potent. *All* television is educational, and this is true not only in terms of its often maligned content, but—more subtly and pervasively—in terms of its form. For the individual, commercial television is a cultural academy in which the dominance of the present is the basic doctrine and fragmentation, the curricular design.

Because television's content is so fragmented, the flux we experience in watching it does not resemble organic continuity. Instead, what we experience is the serial flow of disconnected realities, more like the disparate objects floating in a swift stream than the stream itself.

Transience

Without a picture, a television set is just a boring little box, like a wooden frame without a painting to fill it. But even with a single picture on its screen—unless that one picture is extraordinary—a television set can still be visually dull. To make us watch, the industry uses variety, changing the shapes, sizes, colors, and movement of its images to capture our attention and sustain our interest.[13] This is most evident in commercials, where viewer attention and interest are urgent priorities. In TV commercials, a single image is seldom held for more than three seconds. (To test how true this is, watch a commercial attentively and count out the seconds an image lasts. The quick, or "jump," cuts will soon be obvious.) Television depends for its commercial existence on short-lived sensations. It uses artificial flux for (our) fun and (its) profit. In turn, it conditions the individual always to expect something new.

Television's form is compatible with the products it advertises and the economic system it serves. New models, new styles, even new commercials, captivate us and help products sell. In fact, in a speeded-up society, the very newness of a product (a car, a movie) increases its appeal. Each new disposable product becomes the materialization of a fleeting moment—a look, a feel, a taste, a sound, a smell—that advertising and a commercialized society convince us we must experience in order to be happy, so we can be as new as the world around us. Thus, we find ourselves eagerly reaching for the moment before it slips away. We watch the now host interview the now guest about the now movie, and are nourished by their energizing immediacy.

To be sure, entertainment itself is nothing new. After all, the ancient Greeks invented theatre over 2,500 years ago. But never has any society, Greek included, devoted so much of its time to merely being entertained as our own.[14] It is for this reason that we began our discussion with television, the core of modern entertainment. For television fills an unprecedented proportion of our waking hours, filling them not simply with its content but with a definition of how consciousness should be spent. It is to this end—to shape individual consciousness—that advertisers spent almost $36 billion on television in 1996, more than the federal government spent on education during the same period.[15]

Cultures have always indoctrinated their members in preferred attitudes, behaviors, and values, shaping the individual to conform with the group. But never before in human history have desires been so rapidly and universally homogenized, nor has the dimension of the present been so cultivated to the exclusion of all other temporal realms. What we are witnessing is the ascendancy of now, a reign that, as individuals, we have been led to accept as natural with only minimal reflection. For in the fragmentary and fleeting images of the television screen we have found the familiar face of a friend whose name is transience.

The lessons we learn watching television are lessons we carry with us into life. Television has the power to make us subconsciously reinterpret the very definition of our selfhood: one in which life is viewed as a series of separate "programs" to be turned on or off at will, their options to be renewed or canceled at whim, their actors absent from our thoughts except when they entertain, with no continuity but the one a disposable paper guide provides. We distrust the permanent, having grown alien to anything that lasts, and look upon all relationships as inherently transitory. In such ways can TV script our lives. The very passivity with which we watch television has been found to spill over into the rest of our hours long after the set itself has cooled.[16]

But more insidious than any of these effects is the potential of television and the computer to distract us from other possible pursuits, pursuits more real, more active, more creative, and more personal.[17] Research has shown that as television viewing time increases, there is a compensatory decrease in time spent in interpersonal get-togethers involving conversation and socializing on a family or community level.[18] In a similar way, Internet use can become addictive and, paradoxically, can insulate us from true human contact. Thus, even as they nurture us, these electronic media isolate us as individuals from genuine sources of friendship and love.[19]

ACCELERATION AND METAMORPHOSIS

The artificial flux that surrounds us and the desire it breeds to experience the fleeting moment contribute to the acceleration of our behavior and expectations. In a culture based on high speed, the individual who "goes with the flow" in order to find happiness inevitably speeds up his life.[20] More than simply inducing stress, such acceleration—if prolonged—leads to marked changes in personality and character, changes evident in the external appearance of individuals and the nature of their inner sensibilities. In consequence, television and computer screens become symbolic mirrors, reflecting on their glass surfaces the images of viewers who are themselves perpetually transient.[21]

As we shall see, the very speed of our lives inhibits the possibility of self-discovery: first, because a life that is rushed provides few opportunities for critical reflection; and second, because a mind that is wired into the circuitry of its culture tends to lack the capacity and incentive for self-liberation.

While the analysis in this chapter draws upon features of our lives we may take as commonplace, such features—when viewed collectively—constitute compelling evidence of a radical change in our culture: a change in what it means to be an individual. The fact that we regard these things as commonplace merely demonstrates how pervasive their influence is and how much we have fallen under their spell.

The Outer Self

Fashion

The clothes people wear have changed from century to century. To appreciate the evolution of fashion we can take a chronological stroll down a museum gallery hung with portraits by American and European masters. Like a costume party, each century will introduce itself to us in turn in its customary dress.

Yet fashion, like almost everything else that is a product of human design, has accelerated its rate of change under the influence of modern mass communications and marketing techniques. The economic success of the garment industry depends upon the willingness of the individual to buy new clothes not because the old ones are worn out, but because they are simply old and therefore "out of date."[22] The profits of fashion are thus predicated upon change. The circulation of mass-market magazines targeted at particular consumer groups designated by sex, age, and class serves to excite the public's appetite. New issues every month combine commercialized features on fashion with glossy advertisements showing what it currently means to be in style. Indeed, these magazines themselves depend upon artificially stimulated change for their very existence, for if the wheel of fashion did not turn so quickly, there would be no need for readers to pick up a current issue. Thus, the garment industry and fashion magazines exist in a symbiotic relationship founded upon the concept of transience.

As a material embodiment of the present, fashion celebrates now. Justifying disposability, it glories in the ephemeral. Fashion clothes us in the moment, inviting us to treasure what is transitory and external.

Such an invitation is not evil; nor is yielding to it sinful. Surely, moments deserve to be treasured, and the response to beauty is one of humanity's most basic instincts. It is rather a question of proportionality. In a society that places so much emphasis upon the external and so little on the internal (viewing the latter as but an extension of the former—that we *are* what we *own*), each successive invitation to superficiality and transience becomes a further distraction, keeping us from pursuing the quest for deeper and more enduring truths.

Though fashion consciousness did exist in the past, it was generally a characteristic of the rich and effete, the leisured coterie of the imperial court, whether of Nero or Louis XVI. But thanks to the combined powers of democracy, mass production, and advertising, the many are now as style-conscious as were the few. Being sensitive to style today, however, is also a reflection of the times, fast times that have sensitized us to the present—and its demands—as never before. As designer Donna Karan mused one day: "Sometimes I wonder what we do here. . . . If women didn't go out and buy short last year, the whole thing passed them by, and now long is back again.

They have to realize they no longer have to buy what we tell them to. It all happens so fast. All they have to do is sit tight and their old clothes will be back in style." To which a colleague shrewdly replied, "Don't let them hear you say that."[23]

The colleague's remark underscores the fact that the fashion industry makes money by manipulating their customers' sense of time. By emphasizing what is current and by stressing that short is "in" and long is "out" a fortune can be made. Marketing psychology thereby succeeds in dressing us in the fabric of now.

To compete better with European manufacturers and with each other, American manufacturers have even advanced the traditional openings of the seasons.[24] In today's retail marketing, for example, spring blooms in January and fall/winter comes in May. Look for a bathing suit in July and you'll find nothing but tweed and cashmere. As a consequence, time-harried customers shop defensively, purchasing what they can't yet wear. Says one maker of designer clothes: "They think if they don't buy it now, it won't be around, and that's true."[25] Thus, the clothes we buy bear witness to an environment in which time has been distorted and nature's own seasons artificially accelerated.

Cosmetics

The transience of fashion applies also to the costuming of the face. The history of cosmetics can, in fact, be traced back to humanity's earliest days: cavemen and cavewomen may have applied blood-red pigment to their faces in prehistoric rituals; while in ancient Egypt black eyeliner was used by both females and males. The ancient use of cosmetics, however, pales before their consumption today. In America, cosmetics have become a $20-billion-a-year business.[26]

The putting on and taking off of makeup each day implies that personal identity is not permanent but transient and removable. The individual wears a temporary face, masking the durative effects of aging with an evanescent coating. The massive consumption of cosmetics in our country is but another indication of a society eager to cling to the present at any price.

Dieting

The power of now in our iives is also evident in our national compulsion to diet. It has been estimated that 48 million Americans, or 20 percent of the population, are on diets at any given time.[27] In fact, in 1992, 67 percent of American adults consumed diet foods or drinks.[28]

Dieting, in the best sense, should be motivated by understanding, by the realization that balanced nutrition contributes to health and longevity. But in America, the focus of dieting is generally not nutrition but weight loss. Indeed, in a survey conducted by the University of Cincinnati College of

Medicine, "thirty-three thousand American women told researchers that they would rather lose ten to fifteen pounds than achieve any other goal."[29]

Were the desire to achieve a certain weight the natural expression of free choice, it would be one thing. But it is not. Like the impulse to be in style, the compulsion to diet is driven by the engine of advertising, fueled by the profit motives of a $33-billion-a-year weight-loss industry.[30]

Says psychological counselor Dr. Anne Kearney-Cooke: "Many children and adults are more interested in developing an image rather than a self.... They live in a culture that says, 'Change your body, change your life.'"[31]

Given the priority our society assigns to material things and given the social impact of visual imagery, it is perhaps predictable that external appearance would be emphasized today to a degree unprecedented in history. Yet, it is not the role of the superficial that is as disturbing as its intensification by the power of now.

People don't merely want to lose weight. They want to lose it fast, and the faster the better. Popular supermarket magazines and tabloids (significantly displayed beside food checkout lanes) tempt shoppers with cover stories about quick weight-loss diets: "Drop Those Extra Holiday Pounds!," "Lose That Tummy and Enjoy That New Bathing Suit!," or "30 Days to a New You!" Nor are these subjects found only in newspapers and magazines. More than 500 different diet books cram bookstore shelves, many with painless, miracle cures—all this despite clinical tests and statistical evidence that have persistently demonstrated that crash diets and fad diets simply don't work, that rapid weight loss in radical dietary regimens is more than made up for by later gains. Lasting weight reduction requires, instead, a permanent change in eating behavior, often combined with an increase in regular exercise. But such advice will sell few books or magazines, because it flies in the face of an entire cultural outlook, one that wants results now.

Ironically, excessive eating is itself a reflex of the same principle that explains the popularity of crash diets, for gaining weight is usually the result of ignoring long-term consequences in exchange for instant gratification. Unrealistic eating and unrealistic dieting are, thus, parallel expressions of the same attitude, one that blinds people to everything but the urgings of the present.

Is it any wonder, then, that the young in such a society will come to suffer from eating disorders—from anorexia nervosa to bulimia—pathologically manipulating the very act of nourishing their lives? Or that antacids should figure so prominently in commercials and on drugstore shelves? Or that some should become addicted to diet pills or elect the potentially dangerous shortcut of liposuction to eliminate unwanted fat? All these things are alimentary by-products of a society moving too fast for its own good. The microwave oven and the fast-food restaurant—for all the convenience they provide—are simply more benign points on the same spectrum of speed.

Exercise

The microwave oven, like the electric and gas ranges before it, is a laborsaving device that saves us the effort of chopping wood or stoking coals to cook our food. When such laborsaving devices abound in our lives there is a biological consequence: the decline of physical fitness.

Out of a desire to achieve a sense of physical well-being, many people today have chosen to engage in a variety of nonwork-related exercise regimens, from jogging and swimming to weight lifting and aerobics. Thus, having first sought to reduce physical exertion through the introduction of laborsaving devices and then having recognized that decreased physical activity leads to diminished well-being, our culture has compensated by creating artificial devices and behaviors to expend the energy that was previously used.[32]

Such a sensible decision, however, contains a hidden cost. By freeing people for other higher activities, laborsaving devices end up making their lives more contrived. Put another way, the omnipresence of the machine serves to make man more machine-like in his behavior by inducing him to schedule even relaxation.

Furthermore, exercise activities also involve temporal compression. To achieve the same physiological results that would have come over a longer period of time from work, individuals compress the normal expenditure of muscular energy into a shorter period of time in the gym. On top of that, such accelerated motion is often squeezed into the tight framework of an already crowded workday. Ironically, then, the quality of leisure may actually come to reflect more and more the quality of the life people seek to escape.

The Hunger for Youth

Both exercise and diet are strategies Americans use to look and feel young.[33] America's love affair with being young is, in one sense, a natural reflection of its national history: by the chronological standards of world history, the United States *is* a young country, especially when compared to the older nations of Europe. In another sense, our love affair with youth is a product of technology: the possession of technological power tends to blur the line of demarcation between the possible and the impossible, suggesting, by inference, that we may even be able to retard or turn back the clock of aging. Lastly, our love-affair with youth is a product of sensory desire, of wanting always to experience maximum vitality and pleasure.

Not coincidentally, these three origins of our love affair with youth—history, technology, and the senses—are the very same as the origins of now's power.

In addition, the love of youthfulness, like now's own power, is related to the idea of speed. As the time of life with the greatest vigor, youth is the period most capable of motion. To put it simply, when we are young, we can "keep up" more readily than when we are old and slow. And "keeping up" is precisely what a fast-moving, synchronous society values. Because, however, aging implies slowing up and "falling behind," aging marks itself as an antisocial activity inimical to personal happiness and social fulfillment. Success, on the other hand, means staying young (or at least looking young) by whatever means possible: cosmetic, dietary, gymnastic, or—as will soon be discussed—surgical. The synchronous society, in turn, ideologically supports the concept of youthfulness as a mechanism of its own continuance and survival because youthfulness exemplifies what that society itself most needs and admires: speed and agility.

Conversely, the opposite qualities that characterize aging—slowness and deliberation—tend to be devalued. The long-term consequence of this devaluation may be that society self-destructs for want of those very qualities of mind and spirit—reflection and wisdom—that it has categorically rejected. Thus, like the addict hooked on amphetamines, an accelerated society may collapse from its ruinous addiction to speed.[34]

Meanwhile, age denial continues to be characteristic of our culture. *Modern Maturity*, the official magazine of the American Association of Retired Persons, features a euphemistic title and articles that continually celebrate the youthfulness of being old. What is more, the popularity of recent books like Deepak Chopra's *Ageless Body, Timeless Mind,* Jean Carper's *Stop Aging Now,* and Betty Friedan's *The Fountain of Age* reveal the need people have for reassurance that old age will not debilitate them. Indeed, in her book, Friedan avoided discussing the painful downside of aging and even shunned the use of the word "old," which she significantly omitted from her index.

More generally, the denial of aging represents the very rejection of life's own process. All organic life implies change, embodying, as it does, the flow of time. Therefore, the radical effort to resist such change means to swim against a natural current that courses through our very being.

Besieged by a hunger for youth, the individual remains trapped in a war-zone from which he or she cannot escape: the war zone of his or her own body. Unable to avoid the inevitability of aging, the spirit is pitted against the body that contains it. Nor can an armistice ever be declared in this war as long as the power of now reigns.

Plastic Surgery

To find temporal refuge, the self may seek out desperate measures, electing artificial rejuvenation and instant beautification beneath the surgeon's knife.[35] During the last decade, in fact, cosmetic surgery became America's fastest growing medical specialty.[36] By the early 1990s it was a $1.75 billion-a-year business.[37] Each year, 1.5 million Americans paid to have their bodies altered in this way, sometimes at the unexpected price of pain, disfigurement, and even death.[38] Besides the standard face-lift, newer procedures include facial liposuction, bone-sculpting, and the implantation of sculpted pieces of silicone to simulate muscle.

While the vast majority of cosmetic surgery patients have traditionally been female, male patients are visiting plastic surgeons in increasing numbers, seeking not only face-lifts, but also calf and pectoral implants to enhance their physiques.[39] Even more striking is the fact that people are getting face-lifts at younger ages. While surgeons just a decade ago would have thought it frivolous to operate in this way on patients under fifty, they have witnessed a huge increase in applicants between thirty-five and forty-five years of age. Thus, the power of now intensifies even the perception of aging, making individuals look increasingly older as they gaze into time's mirror.

Ancient cultures that believed in eternal life long ago tried to bestow youthful beauty permanently on the souls of the departed by depicting them as forever young in their tombs. Within the limits of their technology, they also sought to stay the passage of youth while they were alive by using aphrodisiacs, medicinal "cures" for wrinkles and baldness, and even surgery to correct pendulous breasts. But in both this world and the next it was the purity of the inner spirit that seems to have been the ancients' deepest concern, for upon it depended their entry into the afterlife. In our own manipulation of the external self, we differ from those ancients in two significant respects: we possess a level of technology far greater than theirs to accomplish our aims, and we serve a definition of selfhood less spiritual than the one they knew. Believing that beauty is primarily skin deep, Americans seek salvation by adjusting a subcutaneous, rather than a more inward, reality.

Growth Hormones

Cosmetic surgery can not only recapture the look of youth; it can also magnify it by amplifying the body's features. The amplification of the body, however, can also be achieved by chemical means.

Special eating regimens and dietary supplements (of vitamins, minerals, and proteins) have long been a staple of athletes in training. This was true as long ago as the days of the ancient Greeks, when heavyweight boxers ate large quantities of meat to increase their bulk while preparing for the Olympics.

No substitute, however, can produce results as dramatic or as rapid as anabolic steroids.[40] Manufactured synthetically to simulate the natural male hormone testosterone, these drugs were originally developed for medical needs. Indeed, every year some three million prescriptions for steroids are legitimately written to treat such conditions as growth delay, osteoporosis, and anemia.

It was soon discovered, however, that anabolic steroids can also enhance the muscles of healthy subjects. As far back as the 1950s, Soviet and East bloc athletes were using them before competitive events to give them an edge over their Western opponents that training alone could not provide. Such steroid use eventually became common in the Olympics and in professional sports and bodybuilding, as more and more competitors sought to gain a chemical advantage, or to equalize the unfair advantage they believed their opponents already possessed.

The victories won by anabolic athletes came, of course, with a price tag: the general undermining of fair play and the personal shame of discovery that came from testing. But there was also a biological price to be paid: short-term side effects such as premature hair loss and potentially violent mood swings, and severe long-term effects, including sterility, impotence, kidney disease, and liver cancer. Yet some dismissed the short-term effects as a price worth paying and the long-term effects as a trade-off too hypothetical or distant to worry about compared to the taste of experiencing victory now. Indeed, all too many continue to take these risks today. As Carlos, a bodybuilder from Queens, New York, put it: "We always have to take risks for whatever reason. Gamblers take it. I'm a gambler. . . . We don't really think about tomorrow because we want to see some results right now."[41]

The phenomenon of steroid abuse is all the more alarming today because it has entered America's senior and even junior high schools, involving an estimated 400,000 young people.[42] Nor is it only the football players and wrestlers who take these drugs. Users also include competitors in track-and-field, swimming, volleyball, and women's softball. In addition to athletes who take the drugs to enhance performance, male nonathletes are taking them as well to build confidence, to get noticed, and to attract girls. Thus, thanks to chemistry, the "98-pound weakling" at the beach, pictured in the old Charles Atlas ads, doesn't have to undergo as long a program of bodybuilding to stop a bully from kicking sand in his face. Popping oral steroids can achieve even more impressive results in an even shorter time. Said one highschool senior: "I was playing football and looking for a scholarship. I figured steroids would give me a better chance. I gained so much strength and weight it was incredible." Said another: "I put on 12 or 13 pounds, which is a lot for a guy my size. I could bench [press] 225 five or six reps for a couple of sets—before I couldn't do it even once."[43] Meanwhile, a study of high schoolers in Illinois showed two-thirds of those on steroids had started using them before age sixteen.[44]

As with quick weight-loss diets that emphasize speed, one of the appeals of steroids is the quick results they promise. But the philosophy of the short cut and the religion of the quick fix violate the temporal laws of the natural world. If we artificially speed things up, accelerating organic growth beyond its normal rate, Nature may demand we pay a price, not in money but in the currency of mind and flesh.

In response to this reality, the National Federation of State High School Associations in 1992 held a "steroid summit." Said one of its organizers, Dick Stickle: "I think this win-at-all-costs mentality could lead to an epidemic."[45]

The mentality Stickle referred to conflicts with an older sports philosophy: "It isn't whether you win or lose that counts, but how you play the game." Such a motto reflected a slower-paced culture than ours, one that understood and valued the role of process in building character. On the other hand, "Winning isn't the most important thing. It's the only thing!" reflects a different ethic and era, our own, an era in which the "bottom line" is what counts. According to the rules of now, in sports as in so much else, character is less important than victory.

Genetic Engineering

As the use and misuse of anabolic steroids show, chemistry gives individuals the ability to transform muscles. Another science, genetics, now gives the human race the ability to transform itself. In the words of anthropologists Kathy Schick and Nicholas Toth: "Through the technology of genetic engineering we are possibly entering a new phase of human evolution in which modifications of the human genome as an evolutionary tool may soon be a possibility."[46]

By the year 2005 and at a cost of more than $1 billion, the National Center for Genome Research will seek to map and functionally identify each of more than 100,000 genes that together constitute the biological blueprint of human identity. Already, scientists have identified the genes responsible for 200 of the 4,000 diseases known to be inherited and are aggressively pursuing their cure through experimental genetic engineering and therapy. Some day soon, it may be possible to intervene during or even before pregnancy to prevent such conditions from ever developing.

The future prospects for genetic engineering, however, include not only the prevention of disease but the deliberate designing of the future individual through the molecular manipulation of chromosomal parts and patterns. Referring to a tempting genetic menu, parents may be able to pick their babies' attributes, while society may be able to choose the talents of its future citizens in keeping with projected economic, scientific, and military needs.

With technological problems solved, the only obstructions to these efforts would be ethical. But if the actions taken are seemingly for the child's own good and society's well-being, on what grounds could one object, especially if the long-term implications of short-term genetic decisions will not be evident for generations?

Such technology may also grant human beings another unique power: the power to perpetuate their own individuality. Through cloning, an adult parent would be capable of duplicating his or her own physiological identity, minus any undesirable "flaws." Individuals could thereby narcissistically replicate themselves, corporeally projecting their perfected self-image into the future in order to achieve immortality. In such a scenario, biologic past would fuse with biologic future, and the organic power of now would itself become immortal.

While such topics might seem to lie in the realm of futurism, they are in now's domain. By accelerating our lives, the power of now makes the artificial compression of evolution seem perfectly natural. By conditioning us to see our desires instantly gratified, the power of now justifies the immediate fulfillment of our genetic dreams without overlong reflection on their ultimate consequences. And by teaching us that technology is always a faithful servant, the power of now validates its use. In all these ways, the power of now subconsciously trains and prepares us "to boldly go where no man has gone before." Indeed, without a nowist mind-set, the very practice of genetic engineering might be unthinkable.

Unlike other difficult decisions our civilization may face, the challenges posed by genetic engineering are not ones we can "sleep on." A nowist culture is always inclined to move rather than rest. Its momentum invites it to go forward rather than wait. But going forward into a territory filled with so many unknowns is an undertaking fraught with special peril. The impact of this new technology is potentially immense and unpredictable, and its use calls for the greatest caution. Yet, he who walks in giants' shoes cannot take small steps. As Jeremy Rifkin has wisely observed: "The question of whether we should embark on a long journey in which we become the architects of life is, along with the nuclear issue, the most important ever to face the human family."[47]

So far we have examined how the power of now affects the outer self of the individual. We have seen how contemporary fashion covers the body and how diet, exercise, plastic surgery, growth hormones, and genetic engineering can alter it. We must now explore the individual's inner self and the influence of nowism upon it.

The Inner Self

It is no easy matter to measure the power of now's effects upon the inner self. Unlike those already described, such changes are neither visible nor tangible. Yet, it is precisely because they go so deep that they are so important.

In chapter 1 we already observed how high speed can induce stress. In this chapter we will return to the inner self to examine the transformation of personal values caused by the power of now.

Time Pollution

Each of us is a time-traveler, journeying from past to future, oblivious as one melts into the other—like reveling passengers on a cruise ship unconscious in the moonlit night of the speed at which we cross the ocean swell. We surrender to time, yielding fluidly to its flow like silent marine creatures carried on by an underwater current. For time is our sea.

But like the ocean itself, the sea of time can be polluted. Cluttered with the flotsam and jetsam of hurried experience, fouled by the noxious effluents of haste, the sea of time can poison those who swim in its waters.

As Neil Postman has written:

> Changes in the symbolic environment are like changes in the natural environment; they are both gradual and additive at first, and then, all at once, a critical mass is achieved, as the physicists say. A river that has slowly been polluted suddenly becomes toxic; most of the fish perish; swimming becomes a danger to health. But even then, the river may look the same and one may still take a boat ride on it. In other words, even when life has been taken from it, the river does not disappear, nor do all of its uses, but its degraded condition will have harmful effects throughout the landscape.[48]

Like other organic creatures, our lives depend upon food, water, and air. If these vital elements are corrupted or denied, we grow weak and die. In much the same way, the element of time infuses our lives. Invisible as air, the atmosphere of time we inhale each day subtly influences how our body and mind function. Just as we may suffer from pollutants in the air we breathe or the water we drink, so can our health and thinking be damaged by the pollution of our temporal environment.

Such "time pollution" is caused by the sustained and unnatural acceleration of our lives, compounded by the multiplication of our activities and the demands they put upon us. Like pollution elsewhere in the environment, it is mainly the result not of a single incident that can be identified but of a potent accumulation of now forgotten events—a frustrating farrago of responsibilities, appointments, and deadlines that stretch back over weeks and months and years—reinforced by the rapid pace of our everyday existence. Its immediate effects include physiological and emotional tension; its secondary ones, health problems and frayed relationships. But time pollution, as we shall see, also affects and alters the basic values we live by.

The task of diagnosing this subtle environmental hazard is complicated by the fact that we are not independent and objective observers, insulated from and unmoved by the social forces we note; rather we are ourselves affected and transformed by the very phenomena we observe.

Even the self-proclaimed diagnostician is by no means immune to the disease he studies. The researcher who describes its behavior simultaneously stands as its victim. Because he is an inhabitant of the very community he strives to save, he risks losing the capacity to detect in himself the malady's most basic symptoms. For the most pernicious characteristic of this environmental disease is that it masks its own onset and colors its own progress, persuading its victims that its progressively chronic pathology is an altogether natural state. It spreads by barely perceptible increments, dispersing so widely in a population that the individual, surrounded by others similarly infected, concludes that his health is quite normal. The most treacherous hallucination of all is that there is no hallucination: that all is safe and well. As with hypothermia, the most fateful symptom of this temporal sickness is the seductive comfort of sleep, a numbing sleep in which we surrender our hold on life. We perish lacking the will to fight because illusion convinces us there is nothing to fight against.

Nor is death the main issue. Instead, the issue is how we shall live. For, as the sensory parameters of human experience shrink, the individual's definition of optimal experience shrinks as well, dependent as it is upon the measure of reality his culture conveys. Who will champion the deep blue of a nostalgic summer sky if he has grown up inured only to sulfurous yellow or grey? Without even realizing what he has surrendered, the individual accepts as normal a pallid heaven. Will he ever enjoy the personal satisfaction of a job well done if he has never been taught by his culture to take his time? Will he ever be able truly to give or receive love if he is, by cultural conditioning, alien to the intimate meaning of hours?

No sanctuary exists where we can be fully protected from the forces that are physically transmuting our fast-moving world. In separate experiments from Africa to the Arctic, eager scientists in quest of pure air have found only frustration. Circling the earth in global currents, streams of pollutants have paid their call on even the remotest of regions. Barely an Eden exists where an entrepreneur's boot, caked with contagion, has not trod, and even the cleanest of mountain brooks carries in its waters the invisible signature of commercial waste. In a similar way, time pollution has invaded our environment with its infection, altering the rhythms of the natural world with a life-style more aggressive than nature's own, deforesting and strip-mining the landscape of the human spirit.

The Pursuit of Happiness

Even as it harms the individual, the power of now intensifies the pursuit of happiness.

Curiously, the search for happiness has dominated man's thinking for only a tiny fraction of his planetary existence. From the emergence of early man down to the birth of civilization some 50,000 years later, most human energy was focused not on happiness but on simple survival. Even when the earliest civilizations arose, their concern was not for the happiness of the individual but for the prosperity of the community, a goal that was achieved by subordinating individual needs to the needs of the group by divine and royal command. Only with the coming of the Greeks centuries later did the notion of the autonomous individual arise.

All of this may seem strange to us. After all, we are members of a culture constitutionally founded upon the principle of unalienable individual rights and the pursuit of happiness, a culture that regards personal gratification as not merely one of a number of assorted social goals but as the essential purpose of civilization. But what our society has come to take for granted was, at humanity's inception, a novel and revolutionary idea.

While happiness was slow in arising as an articulated goal, its opposite was always a visceral reality. To ameliorate drudgery, sorrow, and pain, ancient cultures used potent substances to take the individual outside himself and give him comfort. Wine, beer, corn mash—all were developed to provide this release, and their use was often associated with religious ceremonies.

The desire for euphoria, and the use of catalysts to achieve it, is therefore nothing new. What is new is the way that desire has become an addiction and the way such catalysts have come to dominate people's lives. In short, the balance has shifted.

When ancient societies did contemplate the notion of happiness, they tended to view the fulfillment of the individual within a larger context of obligations, both sacred and secular. Some of their thinkers believed happiness could be found by following the road of reason; others, the way of revelation. Their concern was rarely the acquisition of instant and passing gratification, but rather the discovery of enduring truth through patient search and the struggle for self-mastery. Even Epicureanism, cheapened by the Romans into a hunger for orgies, began as a quest for life's most lasting pleasures, least of all the transitory ones met by the nerve endings of the flesh. Only through the rejection of the illusory temptations of the material world, taught sages both East and West, could the individual find true inner harmony and peace.

A nowist culture, however, does not cultivate patience as a virtue. Its emphasis, instead, is on speed and technical efficiency. As a result, endeavors that require large investments of time—the practice of a craft, the learning of a language, the study of music—tend to be viewed as anomalies and become unpopular. At the same time, mass marketing and advertising celebrate material possessions as the true source of happiness. As a consequence, nonmaterialistic endeavors are looked upon as insignificant. Instead, a nowist culture pursues happiness by embracing materialism and seeking the means to gratify its sensory appetites. One shortcut to happiness is electronic entertainment, especially in the form of television shows and computer games. Another is drugs.

Some pills speed people up so they can keep up the pace; others slow them down so they can escape it. Still other agents, like heroin, offer individuals synthetic warmth and love in a setting too cold to grant it on any other terms.

In a survey sponsored by the National Institute on Drug Abuse at the beginning of the 1990s, over 75 million Americans aged twelve and older admitted to having used an illegal drug at least once in their lifetimes, while more than 12.5 million said they had used such a drug in the last month. Because such a survey depends on honest replies, the real figures may well have been higher. The figures also do not take into account the frequency with which psychoactive drugs (analgesics, stimulants, tranquillizers, antidepressants, and sedatives) are legally prescribed in this country, and their abuse.[49] Nor do they reflect the abuse of alcohol, especially its rising incidence among the young.

What an indictment of our culture it is that millions of individuals should have to drug themselves into insensibility or artificially induce "highs" that neither self nor society can provide. And what an indictment it is also that just living in our culture is enough to give a person a headache.[50] But none of these facts seems that remarkable anymore, because we have come to accept them as normal. That alone is telling proof of our pathology.

The Search for Faith

In their search for faith and meaning, human beings have traditionally turned to religion. Traditional religious beliefs, however, are incompatible with the tenor of a nowist culture for two reasons.

First, traditional religion is rooted in the past. It directs the individual to a set of ethical standards and ritual practices hallowed by history and trains the individual to make his or her behavior in the present conform to its dictates. As such, traditional religion is authoritarian because it makes the present obey the past. The function of the power of now, however, is to melt down the icons of the past in the crucible of the present. Therefore, it is not the specific beliefs of religion that are incompatible with current sensibilities as much as it is their connection with the past.

Second, traditional religion is by nature conservative. Though it may invite commentary or undergo reform, its underlying tenets and scripture are non negotiable. A nowist society, on the other hand, lives by flux. Transience rather than permanence is its most essential characteristic. In its electronic eyes, no verity is eternal and unchanging.

These two fundamental types of incompatibility have created a dilemma for the individual and, in fact, for organized religion itself. For the individual, the dilemma can be expressed in the following terms: to believe or not to believe; for organized religion: to be or not to be.

It is significant that the Protestant denominations that suffered the greatest membership losses between 1965 and 1990 were the so-called "mainline" ones (United Methodist, 18%; Episcopal, 28%; and Presbyterian, 31%), while the most striking gains were posted by Evangelical ones (Southern Baptist Convention, 38%; Church of the Nazarene, 61%; and Assemblies of God, 122%).[51] This shift in "market share"[52] may be a result of the Evangelical emphasis upon emotional immediacy and the personal experiencing of spirituality—qualities that qualify it as a now religion despite the absolute authority it assigns to the Bible. Even though religious fundamentalism is by definition past-oriented, it may owe its recent popularity to these nowist qualities as well as to a tendency it shares with television, the simplification of what is complex.

As an organism with its own survival instincts, organized religion may inevitably try to modernize. But this survival strategy has its own built-in flaw. If religion modernizes too much, it may cease to be what it once was. With its foundation eroded, it may collapse; with its interior gutted, it may become hollow. By deliberately synchronizing itself with society in order to retain and increase congregational membership, a religious organization may become as amorphous as the society it seeks to win over. Having become a now religion instead of a traditional one, it may no longer be able to give its congregants what they most need—a steadfast anchor in a stormy sea.

In order to reach individuals more effectively today, some churches have turned to television. The phenomenon of televangelism represents not simply the use of the medium as an instrument of communication but the very conversion of electronics into a sacrament. "Now touch your TV screen and be HEALED," the minister proclaims, and tens of thousands lean forward. Whereas the early Christians huddled in dark catacombs, electronic Christians huddle by their sets.[53]

That televangelists have suffered falls from glory is due less to their own human failings than to the very nature of the medium, which thrives on what is superficial and transient. Though Jesus himself acknowledged the electrifying effect of miracles, he feared they would distract his audience from his true message. Television offers a shallow religion, because TV deals not in commitment but in sensation, not in eternity but in evanescence. But in that very immediacy lies its power to christen its viewers creatures of a nowist society and comfort them at the same time.

Besides organized religion, there are other sources of faith and comfort for individuals in a society like our own. They may, for example, turn to materialism and its shrines—the First Church of Walmart and the Cathedral in the Mall—reading the gospel of the coupon, joining fellow congregants at Sunday sales, carrying not crosses but credit cards.[54]

Even if traditional religion strikes individuals as dated and unappealing, they will still have spiritual needs that cry out to be met. Just because all the restaurants are closed doesn't mean hungry travelers will cease being hungry. Instead, they will seek to satisfy their appetite in other ways.

One recourse is to call or visit a psychic; another, to use crystals or health nostrums that offer tangible hope in a confusing world. Some people with crowded schedules have turned to single-session therapy programs[55] or counseling-by-phone.[56] Meanwhile, mass-marketed products can be found in bookstores—from faddish trends in pop psychology and spiritualism to the latest concepts in feel-good self-help, each with a remarkably short shelf life. Such books constitute the secular equivalent of sacred scripture, except for the fact that they grant only temporary salvation. As critic Wendy Kaminer has observed: "Self-help books market authority in a culture that idealizes individualism but not thinking and fears the isolation of being free. 'A book must be the axe for the frozen sea within us,' Kafka wrote. Self-help is how we skate."[57]

The fact that the individual today must resort to *self*-help also demonstrates the fragmented state of society and the failure of traditional support systems for the human spirit.

In his quest for meaning, the individual may have found a friend in the computer. Dr. Roger Gould, a clinical psychologist at University College of Los Angeles, has designed a ten-session therapy program for corporate employees.[58] One corporate client even said that three-quarters of its employees preferred to be counseled by a computer than by a person. The computer, in fact, may someday provide enough stimulation and diversion to make the individual forget he has any inner life at all. [59] Because of its addictive appeal, logging on may offer not only a popular substitute for flesh-and-blood relationships but even the basis for quasireligious experience.

"Virtual reality," now in an early stage, may ultimately permit the average individual to step into, as easily as one's own home, an imaginary realm of stereoscopic cyberspace, the three-dimensional illusion of an alternate world in which one can move and with which one can electronically interact, a world more realistic than that of film or television because it can be entered.[60] It will be a world with its own experiential past and future. Moreover, it will be a world in which all things imaginable are instantly accessible and—because they are—become more desirable than the frustrating outer world of physical reality. "Why bother with phone sex, or an inflatable rubber doll, if you could interface with a hot digital partner, wearing a full-body Data Suit with strategically located tactile feedback? The safest sex imaginable!"[61] Through technology, all wishes and fantasies—intellectual, material, sexual—may someday be granted instantaneously. For, as psychotherapist Norman Liberman has observed: "The new intimacy is electronic."[62]

Fulfilling the need to feel a certain way, satisfying the desire to look a certain way, the power of now shapes the individual within and without. Like a chameleon, whose colors change to match the background against which it moves, the individual fluidly glides across the landscape of time, continually altered in body and spirit by the energy of the present.

THE MYTH OF PROTEUS

This chapter began with the image of an invisible ocean, an ocean of perpetual change. Though the ancient Greeks did not live in an electronic world, they understood the challenge posed by change.

According to one of their legends, a hero named Menelaus, while sailing home from war, was marooned on a desert island for want of winds to carry him back.[63] To get the winds to blow again he had to extract a secret from divine Proteus, the "old man of the sea." Getting Proteus to talk, however, was no easy matter. Menelaus had to catch Proteus and wrestle him into submission. This task was made all the harder because Proteus could change his form at will, assuming the shape of any living creature on earth, of flowing water, and of blazing fire. As the story goes, Menelaus caught Proteus and grappled with him, holding him fast through all his terrifying metamorphoses, until finally the god resumed his original shape and surrendered, yielding up his secret.

In his book, *The Protean Self*, psychologist Robert Jay Lifton has taken the image of Proteus as a symbol of healthy adjustment and hope.[64] Adapting and having a "protean" self, Lifton argues, is a survival skill in a rapidly changing world.

Though he readily admits the limitations of using a myth as a metaphor, Lifton's central argument is based on a deceptive misreading of Homer's tale. In the epic, Menelaus is the hero, not Proteus. And Menelaus is heroic precisely because he refuses to surrender to circumstance and change—however rapid or frightening that change might be. Proteus, for his part, does not trade one personality for another. Ultimately, he returns to an identity he had never lost, only disguised. Indeed, in order to find his homeward way, Menelaus must both retain his own identity and compel Proteus to resume his as well.

The computer-imaging technique known as "morphing" allows one object on a screen to change seamlessly into another before our very eyes. In a similar sense, the high-speed electronic currents of change that flow through our everyday lives collaborate to transform us as individuals. If we are to hold on to our fundamental selfhood and find our way home again, we will need to struggle like Menelaus of old against the seductive forces of flux.

Our identities as individuals, however, are also a function of the roles we play as members of families and of society at large. These entities too are being transformed by the power of now, and with them our own wider identities as well. It is time, then, to study the power of now's impact on these institutions and, through them, its further effects on us.

Chapter 4

The Transformation of
the Family

LIKE A PASSENGERED spaceship traveling through the dimension of time, a family makes a wondrous voyage. To trace that voyage and see how it is affected by society's speed, we will need to study each stage in the human life cycle, exploring how the interrelationships among family members have been transformed by the power of now.

The family constitutes one of the most complex laboratories in which to study the action of time. This is true for three main reasons. First, and most fundamentally, a family is comprised of interacting individuals of different ages. Moreover, as family members grow older with the passage of time, they assume different roles—child, adolescent, single adult, spouse, parent, grandparent—some roles played out sequentially, others simultaneously, as aging advances. Furthermore, as each family constitutes a living entity in its own right, it is influenced by time not only in respect to its parts but also in terms of its totality, especially when it regenerates and helps to bring yet another family into being.

In designing space stations for long-term occupation in a weightless environment, scientists have proposed the creation of artificial gravity using mechanically generated centrifugal force. Such gravity would supply astronauts with the illusion of a familiar earth-like environment. In terms of our own experience, however, the very opposite has come to pass. The symbolic gravity that originally let families keep their feet on the ground has been replaced by a new, whirling social momentum. Instead of holding the family together, the momentum of change has torn it asunder, confusing old identities and straining traditional relationships. As a result, the "centrifugal family" has become one of the most characteristic features of our rapidly spinning society.

LOVE AND MARRIAGE

Nature and Love

From the earliest days of which we have record, lovers measured the depth and breadth of their feelings against the background of the natural world. Their love poems—some over three thousand years old—show how they used imagery drawn from the familiar world of nature to communicate their emotions graphically.[1] The limited personal experience of the poet could be magnified and glorified by comparing it to the larger elements and events of the cosmos—the sea, the desert, the stars. At the same time, the poet could find solace in the realization that personal loss and pain is not an isolated phenomenon—and harder to bear because of that—but part of an all-embracing natural cycle of birth and death.

Though ancient, the love poems of the past express an acute sense of the present: the fire of passion blazing in the now. The poet may even forswear thinking about the future, consumed as he or she is by the urgent need to reap the moment, to "seize the day."[2] But nature also gave poet-lovers a height from which to survey the broader landscape of time and to sense the place of their own travail within that landscape. The regularity of nature, evident in the changing but eternally returning seasons, offered a stable foundation for personal hope.

The tempo of ancient culture was similar to the regular tempo of nature. In large measure, this was true because ancient economies were essentially agrarian, and their periods of activity and rest were synchronous with the cycle of events in the natural world around them. The pace of history was normally slow as well. Kings might come and kings might go, but everyday life tended to go on much as it had before.

Technology and Love

The velocity of life has accelerated, fueled by technological innovation. More and more, the present has become the only time to cling to, the only source from which to draw pleasure and satisfaction. Like frenzied lovers, we feverishly seize the day.

Given the insistent demands of the present upon our sensibilities, it is only natural that the way we view love would also change.

When we think of definitions, we tend to think of descriptions in a thick and dusty Webster's dictionary, descriptions established ages ago and fixed in tradition. Einstein's theory of relativity, however, proposed that what we regard as reality is not, in fact, absolute. When the factor of time is changed, the nature of physical reality itself undergoes alteration, for time is a factor in the equation of existence.

While the word "love" may be defined in the abstract, the human reality of love is always conditioned by time. The rushing first love of youth, for example, is not the same as the enduring love of old age. But love's quality is conditioned not merely by the age of lovers but by the times in which they live. Fast times, as we shall see, breed a special kind of love.[3]

Our everyday expectations are in fact governed by the technology that surrounds us. As its efficiency increases, the time that once was required to perform conventional tasks shrinks. The obstinate potato, for example, that once took a whole hour to bake can now be microwaved in only a few minutes. But as we grow accustomed to such devices and the progressive efficiency they offer, our expectations—and our frustrations—may rise. We wait by the microwave, impatiently watching its digital clock count down. A few minutes now seem intolerably long.

Psychologists tell us that the brain is an "associative memory processor." What that means is that we remember things by associating them with other things. As we recall that special night with a loved one, for example, we may also remember the song the band played. Upon hearing that same song years later, the memory of that night will return. But the brain's associative tendency is not limited to souvenirs of romance. As our everyday experiences and their associations enter our brain, linkages are created between the actions we take and their consequences. Such linkages stored in our memory may then consciously inform or subconsciously condition our later behavior. Remembering the pain of putting our hand in fire, we deliberately stand back from a flame. Remembering the pain from passion's fire, we may hesitate to love again.

Our personal relationships are affected by our constant conditioning in other realms and the associations we have made there. Living in an environment suffused with rapid technology, we transfer our technological expectations to situations that are not technological at all. Immersed in immediacy, in a culture of quick turn-around time and instant results, we look to life to express-deliver the love we need, and grow restive when it does not, ironically giving less of ourselves to others even as we expect more of them in return. Thus, as the tempo of our lives quickens, the parameters of our temporal relationships with others artificially contract.[4] Short on patience, we hurry the sun.

To be sure, our impatience is not due to our having microwaved one potato too many! That would be too simplistic an explanation with an all too simplistic remedy. Rather, it is the result of our living in a microwave culture that conditions us to expect electronic speed in all things.

The fact that our material culture is also characterized by the making and buying of things that do not last, indeed that were never intended to last, transfers the expectation of impermanence to human relationships as well. Thus the profit-driven motives of our material culture warp the nonmaterial values of our lives. As fewer lasting things abound, the durative aspect of society recedes and, with it, our very expectation of durability. Instead, flux and transience prevail and color our attitudes.

Even anniversary gifts have been redefined by technology and speed. The traditional gift for a first wedding anniversary used to be paper, but now it is clocks. The traditional fourth anniversary present used to be fruit or flowers; now it is appliances. The fourteenth anniversary was once commemorated with crystal; today it is celebrated with watches.[5]

Living Together

The cosmic decision of two fragile human beings to share their lives as long as life itself will last may seem romantically appealing, but it is alien to our times. While couples may find the concept of marital permanence wistfully nostalgic, an increasing number are either deferring marriage or are approaching it already preconditioned to anticipate the likelihood of divorce.

Strikingly, most marriages today end not in the death of a partner but in divorce. Since 1960, the divorce rate in America has, in fact, doubled. Not only have the rate and sheer number of divorces increased, but so has the speed with which they take place. For example, 30 percent of those who married back in 1957 were divorced twenty years later. For the same percentage of those who married in 1962, however, divorce took only fifteen years. By 1967, for that same percentage, divorce took place in ten. By the mid-1980s, 25 percent of those who married had already been divorced. Currently, the odds of a new marriage succeeding are only about one in two.[6]

The acceleration of divorce in America can be attributed in large measure to a lowering of legal and social barriers. "No-fault" divorce laws make divorces easier to get, and being divorced no longer bears the social stigma it once did. But rather than simply being contributing causes, such changes can also be viewed as society's formal acknowledgment of a new and undeniable reality—the unprecedented erosion of permanence in human affairs.

Increasingly, more and more Americans are refraining from entering into the bonds of marriage and are living together instead. As Ronald Rindfuss, a population specialist at the University of North Carolina–Chapel Hill notes, cohabitation was relatively rare until the late 1960s, became popular during the 1970s, and is today common practice.[7] According to James Sweet, professor of sociology at the University of Wisconsin-Madison's Center for Demography and Ecology, 25 percent of all American adults have lived unmarried with a sexual partner at least once in their lives. Such cohabitations are relatively short-lived—most last about twelve months.[8] About half of such cohabitations lead to marriage,[9] though these marriages are 33 percent more likely to end in divorce than marriages where couples had not lived together first.[10] In 1990, the number of couples living together numbered almost 3 million, six times what it had been in 1960.[11] Indeed, the number of couples choosing to cohabit rather than marry has been responsible for an apparent leveling in the number of divorces since 1980: it's not that marriages are getting stronger; instead, fewer couples are getting married in the first place.[12]

There are many obvious explanations for the rise in cohabitation: the everpresent power of sexual attraction combined with more liberal attitudes toward premarital sex; the fear of contracting AIDS from multiple sex partners; the existence of birth control as a means of preventing unwanted pregnancies; the economic benefits of sharing expenses like rent; and the desire to try out a relationship before risking the potential emotional, legal, and financial consequences of marital breakdown.

But underlying all these explanations is the ideological acceptance of transience as a life-style. Marriage is, after all, a "diachronic" pursuit, one that implies a commitment of energy, effort, and emotion that reaches across time itself. But in a short-term society like our own, long-term endeavors of any sort seem increasingly incomprehensible and even unattractive. Abiding commitment is inherently inconsistent with a high-speed society whose trademark is the temporary and whose verities thrive only in the now. Instead, short-term marriages to a series of partners or nonbinding live-in relationships more accurately mirror our societal consciousness. That people choose to divorce or cohabit is not so much evidence of public immorality as it is additional proof of the pervasive power of now.

This power has engendered a redefinition of marriage itself. Nena and George O'Neill's *Open Marriage*, published just three years after Toffler's *Future Shock*, offered just such a redefinition.[13] An "open marriage," as the authors originally defined it, was a marriage open to change, one that continually and fluidly reshaped itself in response to the needs and desires of husband and wife. Most significantly, this "new life style for couples" was infused with a heightened sensitivity to now, one that viewed the marriage "contract" as only a working draft.

The power of the O'Neills' argument transcends the decades that have passed since its first publication. That power is based on the obvious fact that we can only live in the present, that all our experience takes place in the here and now, and that, as people, we change over the course of time.

The weakness of their argument, however, is its lack of balance. What we experience in the present—indeed, what we *are* in the present—is conditioned by our memories of the past and our hopes for the future. It is perhaps for this reason that families whose homes are destroyed by fire mourn most the loss of objects like treasured photos and cherished dolls, objects that have little commercial value but are the priceless tokens of human remembrance and continuity.

The fact is that at any one time an individual's life is not an isolated moment but a point on a vital continuum. Looking forward and back need not detract from a couple's life together; it can, in fact, be a source of strength, for shared memories and shared dreams give a marriage meaning and purpose.

Like memories and dreams, commitments color who we are—the deeper the commitment, the richer the color. To say this is not to dismiss the human capacity to make mistakes or the painful need to undo them by ending a marriage. Nevertheless, the fact remains that living in the flux of a superficial present, where contracts exist only to be rewritten and commitments are regularly broken, leads people to underestimate the value of an enduring vow. It is symptomatic of our times that the word "character" is conspicuously absent from contemporary conversations. More often than not, the word we hear is "personality," a far more flexible term that denotes how much the pliancy of psychology has replaced the firmness of religion as the gauge of current diction and thought.

The values of *Open Marriage* are still very much with us today not because of the direct influence of the O'Neills' book but because this book was and continues to be a reflection of a fluid society in which the old solids of tradition keep dissolving in the ever-moving currents of change.

Erotic Time-Travel

Two people who share a life move through time together. But it may also be said that, through these people, time itself moves, transforming them by its process.

Marriage solemnizes not a state but a journey, a journey through time in which those who end the journey are not the very same as those who began it. No wonder then that marriage is such a precarious voyage as those who undertake it risk being separated not only from each other but from their very own selves.

Each partner in a marriage inevitably changes physically and psychologically because of the effects of aging. But these effects represent the workings of essentially internal mechanisms. Each of us, however, is moving not against a static backdrop, but against one that is also in motion, because time and change affect not only human beings themselves but also their world. Thus, it is not only the observer that changes, but the observed.

If the background against which a life is lived is fixed, or moves very slowly, the observer's sense of change will be simple and basically internal. But should the background move more rapidly, the experiencing of change will become complex, as it will reflect a compounding of inner and outer events. The more rapid the movement of outer events, and the more unexpected their inception and direction, the greater will be the impression of change.

Nature's world tends to follow predictable cycles. Except for aberrations of weather or climate, the behavior of nature is generally patterned, for the cosmos obeys unwritten, but universal, physical laws. The inanimate aspect of the cosmos is dominated by such laws and by chance; its animate aspect, by law, chance, and instinct. But human affairs are shaped by the peculiar interaction of all these in combination with another potent element, the element of choice. Human affairs are therefore less predictable than the workings of the natural world, and, accordingly, civilization can take unexpected twists and turns that outnumber those of nature.

Just as human beings can adjust to changes in their natural environment, so can they adapt to changes in their cultural one, especially if those changes are not too sudden or strong. It is one thing, however, to adapt to the consequences of a single event or group of events. It is another to adapt to change as a perpetual condition. An unexpected event may initially induce stress but ultimately produce perspective as the person affected comes to terms with what has happened: thus the sudden death of a loved one may lead the heart from overwhelming grief to final resignation. Yet, if painful changes persist and are sustained over a long period, the individual may retreat into emotional numbness, like that born of repeated rejection.

In its own way, duration can be more devastating than the impact of any single incident. Despite its apparent solidity, even a boulder can be eroded by the persistent flow of a stream. And in a stream of time that flows swiftly, the rate of marital erosion is certain to be rapid.

In trying to explain why so many modern marriages fail, experts and pseudoexperts point to a number of frequently cited factors, from financial problems and interfering in-laws to sexual incompatibility and verbal noncommunication. But perhaps the greatest factor today is the fast pace of life. Traditional marriage is vulnerable to wear precisely because it stands as an affirmation of constancy in an inconstant world.

Speed-induced stress, discussed earlier in chapter 1, takes a special toll on two-career couples, in particular those with children. As Martha Farnsworth Riche, director of policy studies at the Population Reference Bureau in Washington, D.C., has noted: "Today, only 22 percent of married-couple households contain a male breadwinner and a female homemaker, a dramatic decline from 61 percent in 1960."[14] "It's very hard for two-career couples to juggle all their responsibilities," comments Paul J. Rosch, president of the American Institute of Stress. "Women often feel they have to be Supermom, getting ahead at work, getting the kids to and from Little League and ballet, and still having dinner on the table at 6 every night. And men who were raised to see themselves only as breadwinners often have trouble taking on housework, family and nurturing responsibilities."[15]

Allen Elkin, director of the Stress Management and Counseling Center in New York, points to studies that show two-career couples talking with each other as little as fifteen minutes a day, and then mostly about bills, house-work, and child care. Says Elkin: "They're so exhausted they become apathetic. They stop planning the things that make their relationship fun. Instead they just veg out in front of the TV."[16]

The television set, the electronic organizing principle of living-room furniture, then shows them what life should be. Through its commercials, it teaches them it is better to relate to things through possession than to people through sharing. It demonstrates that self-gratification is preferable to self-sacrifice. It educates them in impatience, programming them to expect the resolution of all problems in an hour or less. And, through its soap operas, it continually dangles before them the sensual allure of infi-delity. Servant of now, television deifies the secular moment even as it desanctifies the vow.

Though the television set brings a couple into physical proximity, it conveys attitudes conducive to their spiritual separation. Transmitting images of transience, it projects nothing less than a temporal reformulation of love itself.

All the while, the old world of nature, that for millennia offered through the certainty of its cycles the reassurance of permanence, retreats—ob-scured, obliterated, and ultimately displaced by the evanescent works of man. All the while the TV set plays, the season of love grows shorter.

PARENTHOOD AND CHILDHOOD

Besides hastening the process of marital breakdown, the power of now also accelerates a deterioration in the meaning of parenthood and child-hood.

Parenthood and Responsibility

Being a parent, like being married, is a diachronic activity, an activity that extends through time. The commitment of spouse to spouse that an enduring marriage demands is paralleled by the dedication of parent to child—and often with less immediate return. In today's hurried society, however, with its emphasis on short-term gain, any activity that requires such long-term involvement may seem like a bad investment.

Dominated by the senses and their gratification, our society does not cultivate the capacity for self-sacrifice. Yet self-sacrifice is an integral part of being a good parent. In a similar way, in a fast-moving society like ours, the virtue of patience, so needed by parents, becomes rare.

The very naturalness of being a parent is contradicted by the technologi-cal premises of our culture, because what is natural is everywhere being supplanted by what is artificial. Moreover, as nowism by definition diminishes the relevance of and respect for the past, it undermines the foundation of parental authority: those unquestioned convictions, passed on from generation to generation, of right and wrong, including the most fundamental conviction of all, that it is a parent's duty to exercise authority over a child. In a society so fixated on youth, the benefit of the doubt is often given to the young, an act of deference that can also be an act of default. As a result, many parents no longer act simply and spontaneously but continually question their own judgment. Consequently, a neologism known as "parenting" has become a popular subject for self-help books and seminars.

There is no doubt that parents are imperfect and often wrong; many times they hurt their children because of the authority they exercise. But taking all of this into account, children still need parents to help them grow, especially in a society where there are no fixed verities and everything is in constant flux. They also need good parents, but—as we have seen—the very dynamics of our society work against the development of those qualities of character—dedication, self-sacrifice, and patience—essential to the making of a good parent. One of the most telling statistics is offered by University of Maryland surveys: in 1990, parents spent 40 percent less time with their children than they did in 1965,[17] a fact supported by the growth of child day-care into the $5 billion-a-year business it is today.[18] Parents cannot teach by example if they are not physically present in their children's lives, and no amount of artificial "quality time" can make up for their absence when they are truly needed.

Not surprisingly, many couples have deferred or rejected the prospect of parenthood, not simply for financial reasons but because what once seemed natural has become alien to America's life-style. Instead, with the technological help of contraception, the intense and immediate pleasure of the sex act is deliberately uncoupled from its otherwise natural consequences, procreation and childrearing. In a nowist culture that dwells on sensory stimulation and the pleasures of the moment, sexual gratification becomes a central goal.

Because of the cultural centrality of sex and the widespread tendency to act on impulse, the rate of illegitimate births in the United States has climbed rapidly. Between 1960 and 1991, it rose more than 400 percent[19]—in fact, more than 70 percent between 1983 and 1993.[20] Indeed, in ten major American cities during 1991, more than half the births were out of wedlock.[21] In 1992, one out of three babies born in America was born to a single mother, compared to one out of five in 1980.[22] Illegitimacy, moreover, cannot be regarded as a problem of inner-city blacks; it has risen even more rapidly among whites.[23] Reflecting both illegitimacy and divorce, the percentage of single-parent families in America more than tripled between 1960 and 1991.[24] According to the Census Bureau, 27 percent of all children under eighteen today are living with a single parent who never married.[25]

In America the rise in illegitimate births is paralleled by a rise in abortions. 1.7 million abortions were recorded in 1991, almost triple the number in 1972. In fact, since 1972, a total of 35 million abortions are known to have been performed. For nearly every three babies born today, a fourth birth is aborted.[26]

Though family planning may be motivated by necessity and even love, it is given added impetus by the power of now. From the standpoint of the individual, "family planning" may in reality be a euphemism for self-interest. Likewise, from a social standpoint, such measures as government-funded abortion counseling and the legalization of the morning-after pill represent not simply benevolent responses to public health needs but society's way to helping itself enjoy the moment. Such measures constitute the means by which a now-centered culture makes living for the present more easy.

The Transmission of Values

The capacity to procreate is something human beings share with other living creatures. Human beings are distinct, however, because they perpetuate themselves not only biologically but also culturally. The transmission of physical traits and instincts is automatic, but the transmission of culture is not. To pass on principles of conduct from one generation to the next often requires deliberate and committed effort, for the mere physical replication of the human race does not guarantee the survival of its ideals.

Translated to the personal level, this means merely having children won't give them the values they ought to have. Hence, the critical social importance of education, both formal and informal, as the transmitter not of just knowledge and skills, but of moral sensibility. For without the transmission of such values a culture dies from within.

The technology of television exerts a formative influence on the personalities of children. The preschool child watches television more than twenty-seven hours a week,[27] while teenagers spend more time alone with their TV sets than with their parents.[28] According to a study conducted in 1992 by the Carnegie Council on Adolescent Development, teenagers on average spent three hours a day watching television, but only twenty minutes alone with their mothers and only five minutes with their fathers.

The very nature of television repudiates the notion of a heritage. Its forte is showcasing the present, and directors of programming, knowing novelty's appeal, hasten to serve up the new. At the same time, commercials indoctrinate the young in the values of materialism and consumerism, in the purchase and consumption of expendable products in the here and now as the essence of human happiness. Children between four and twelve years old are especially targeted because they represent the demographic group with the greatest sales potential, spending $9 billion of their own money every year and influencing $130 billion of adult purchases.[29] Through visually stimulating commercials and programs that continually change, children are educated in the positive value of flux.

Meanwhile, computerized video games teach children the virtues of speed.[30] "Pong," introduced as America's first video game in 1972, sold only 6000 units in its initial year. "Super Mario Bros. 3," introduced in 1989, sold 7 million. From 1990 to 1993 alone, the home video-game industry grew 35 percent and generated $5.5 billion in annual sales. By 1993, 85 percent of American families with boys eight to sixteen years of age owned video-game players, and by 1994 the first interactive game channel was introduced on television by Sega.

Such games are sometimes praised because they are said to speed up hand-eye coordination.[31] Indeed, such games reward speed like no others in the entire history of play. But by challenging young players to keep pace with electronic impulses, they artificially condition the young to the art of living fast. Because children have quicker reflexes than their parents and have fewer ties to the past, they are even freer to jump on the spinning merry-go-round of time.

The Acceleration of Childhood

Through time-lapse photography the entire growing season of a flowering plant can be compressed into a film lasting but a minute. During every minute of daylight a single frame of film is exposed. When the film is later projected at regular speed, buds burst into bloom and, just as rapidly, fade away. Such a photographic technique is merely a way of recording reality; it does not alter reality itself. The real rose bush continues to bloom at its own natural rate, for its accelerated development is but an artifice.

But what if life should imitate art? If their development could be accelerated, would the roses that then bloom be different in any way from those that grew more naturally?

Such a question should not be of interest only to horticulturalists and weekend gardeners. It must be a question of vital concern to us all. For we are all involved in a grand experiment that will demonstrate whether human culture and human nature itself change when subjected to chronological compression. And in this experiment we are not detached observers, but the very objects being experimented upon.

Even those too young to comprehend the full meaning of such compression can suffer its effects. Children born into an accelerated society absorb its pace internally and, in consequence, "mature" too fast, precociously experimenting with behaviors from spending to sex, while at the same time being deprived of the judgment that only more gradual maturation could have provided.[32] For in life some things simply cannot be rushed, least of all growing to responsible adulthood, or a heavy psychological and emotional price will be paid.

In *The Hurried Child: Growing Up Too Fast Too Soon*, Tufts University psychologist David Elkind explains how this price is paid out.

> Hurried children are forced to take on the physical, psychological, and social trappings of adulthood before they are prepared to deal with them. We dress our children in miniature adult costumes (often with designer labels), we expose them to gratuitous sex and violence, and we expect them to cope with an increasingly bewildering social environment—divorce, single parenthood, homosexuality. Through all these pressures the child senses that it is important for him or her to cope without admitting the confusion and pain that accompany such changes. Like adults, they are made to feel they must be survivors, and surviving means adjusting—even if the survivor is only four or six or eight years old. This pressure to cope without cracking is a stress in itself, the effects of which must be tallied with all the other effects of hurrying our children.
>
> Hurried children seem to make up a large portion of the troubled children seen by clinicians today; they constitute many of the young people experiencing school failure, those involved in delinquency and drugs, and those who are committing suicide. They also include many of the children who have chronic psychosomatic complaints such as headaches and stomach-aches, who are chronically unhappy, hyperactive, or lethargic and unmotivated. These diseases and problems have long been recognized as stress related in adults, and it is time we looked at children and stress in the same light.[33]

Peg Heiney, a suburban kindergarten teacher now approaching retirement, has observed in over 30 years of teaching a marked change in her students. Though today's four–to–six–year-olds are more sophisticated (from experience with computers, for example, or travel), they are also more tense. Today's kindergarteners, she notes, bite more pencils and are more verbally and physically aggressive than in the past. "It's not the kids," she says, "It's the times. It's what they're being subjected to on TV, and all the activities that are out there that parents feel pressured to put them into."[34]

Communications scholars Joshua Meyrowitz and Neil Postman would agree with Heiney about television's impact on the very young. Both have pointed out the medium's propensity to dissolve the barrier that once separated childhood from adulthood. By dissolving that barrier, Meyrowitz argues, television leaves children with "no sense of place" they can call their own.[35] As Postman explains:

> Television erodes the dividing line between childhood and adulthood in three ways, all having to do with undifferentiated accessibility: first, because it requires no instruction to grasp its form; second, because it does not make complex demands on either mind or behavior; and third, because it does not segregate its audience.
>
> Television . . . is the consummate egalitarian medium of communication, surpassing oral language itself. For in speaking, we may whisper so that the children will not hear. Or we may use words they may not understand. But television cannot whisper, and its pictures are both concrete and self-explanatory. The children see everything it shows.[36]

By letting young children see and hear things that only adults were once privy to, television contributes to the disappearance of a more innocent childhood. By giving information to those not yet equipped to handle it, television unnaturally and harmfully hastens the process of growing up. Yet in doing so, the television industry is not acting maliciously. As Postman points out, television's leveling tendencies are intrinsic to its very nature as a mass medium. In addition, when television accelerates growing up, it is only faithfully expressing the dynamics of the speeded-up society it serves.

The acceleration of childhood is particularly evident in the sexual behavior of the young. Young people on average are having sex at an earlier age than ever before, and they are having children before marriage at an increasing rate.[37] As the stages of life are speeded up, children are having children. According to the Alan Guttmacher Institute of New York, twenty years ago one out of two boys and one out of three girls had sexual intercourse by the time they were eighteen. Today, the figures have increased to three-quarters of all boys and half of all girls. In addition, according to the National Center for Health Statistics, since 1960, births to unmarried teenagers have nearly doubled.[38]

Certain types of acceleration are, in fact, encouraged by well-meaning parents who help their children adapt to society's new pace out of a desire to see them succeed. Infants, for example, are given "educational" toys to play with and are later enrolled in preschool programs to "prepare" them for kindergarten.[39] Advanced curriculums in elementary and middle school and advanced placement courses in high school complete the students' preparation for college.[40] Long before high school graduation, affluent students are already vying for admission to the most prestigious colleges to assure themselves of rapid financial advancement later in life. The traditional four years of college are eagerly compressed into three and a half. Indeed, even before they have finished all their final exams as seniors, many will have already participated in their own commencement exercises. Trained in this academic regimen, they can hit the ground running as adults and shift into high gear without even breaking a sweat. Of course, whether they (or anyone) should be running this fast, or whether treadmills really lead to anywhere except to hurried but empty lives, are questions they were never trained to ask.

One of the most insidious aspects of this acceleration is that parental aims are paved with such seemingly good intentions. Who, after all, would criticize conscientious, car-pooling parents who simply want their child to "fit in," to "succeed," and thus to "be happy"? Indeed, isn't the "pursuit of happiness" a natural right of all Americans? Indeed, it is. But the exercise of any right can be carried to an unhealthy extreme.

In schools, the need to advance has also spawned an epidemic of academic expediency. More so than ever before, cheating on exams and plagiarism have become common behavior in high schools and colleges.[41] Material success is a powerful incentive for the young, especially when the time saved by cheating and plagiarizing can be devoted to pleasure. In a sensory society that measures time by its tangible results, learning for its own sake fast becomes an anachronistic value.

An unnaturally high rate of acceleration, as we have seen, does not simply speed up those who are young. More significantly, it changes the very nature of youth.

THE CENTRIFUGAL FAMILY

Society's high speed affects the cohesiveness of a family as well as the personal lives of its members. Divorce is, in a narrow sense, merely the legal consequence of powerful but unrecognized centrifugal forces that daily pull at the integrity of American family life.

To understand these forces better, let us imagine the turntable of a phonograph. Standing on the turntable in our analogy are some chess pieces placed at different intervals and distances from the turntable's center. If we let the turntable rotate at a slow speed—say 16½ revolutions per minute—the chess pieces will still remain in place. At 33⅓ r.p.m. they may still be standing. But at 78 r.p.m. they may topple and tumble from the turntable's surface. As their plane of reference spins faster and faster, the pieces respond by leaving their pre-set "orbits," especially if they are jolted by a sudden increase in speed.

This principle, in fact, is the very one that underlies the operation of a centrifuge, a mechanical device that employs centrifugal force. A washing machine, for example, during its spin cycle presses wet clothes outward against the inner surface of its drum, squeezing out the water they contain. Though in reality people are not chess pieces and the world is not a washing machine, the transformation of today's family is caused by speed-related social phenomena similar to centrifugal force. At first glance, it may seem inappropriate to apply analogies from the sphere of physics to the sphere of sociology. But when an essential physical characteristic of a society is altered, consequent alterations may occur in the structure of human relationships within it. Thus, for example, when the mass or size of a population greatly increases, as in a big city, the potential for a depersonalization of experience also grows.

In the 1960s, sudden acceleration jolted the human playing pieces out of their fixed positions on the turntable of American society. The radical movements of the '60s can be viewed not simply as separate causes of social advancement but also as mutually intensifying consequences of fundamental and deep but less visible forms of change already taking place in American culture, forms that were perhaps more traceable to the overwhelming impact of an accelerated technology than to the particular influence of any one social issue. The politicizing of the young in the '60s and early '70s put added stress on the already polarized structure of the average family as two generations of Americans became strangers in each other's eyes. The media proclaimed the existence of a "generation gap," oblivious to the fact that such gaps had occurred previously in history when the natural separation of age-based points of view was widened by the force of radical social change.[42]

The high speed we have experienced ever since makes it impossible to stand the pieces up again in a way that will make them stay. It is simply not possible to reestablish the original stability of the family and the traditional orbital locations of its members without the existence of a centripetal force powerful enough to override the speed-driven tendency toward centrifugal disintegration. Love and respect are the only forces capable of preserving or restoring a family's integrity, yet they are impossible to regenerate artificially in one family let alone in society as a whole.

One social critic, Judith Stacey, has even argued that the family itself should be dispensed with on democratic grounds because it is innately inimical to "the diverse means by which people organize their intimate relationships."[43] As Stacey says in *Brave New Families*: "The 'family' is not here to stay. Nor should we wish it were. On the contrary, I believe that all democratic people, whatever their kinship preferences, should work to hasten its demise."[44] In such a statement, the factor of egalitarianism is exponentially raised in order philosophically to justify the effects of centrifugality.

In a less militant way, Stephanie Coontz has addressed the same issue, proposing that the traditional family embodies a comforting but misleading myth. In *The Way We Never Were: Families and the Nostalgia Trap*, she writes:

To handle social obligations and interdependency in the 21st Century, we must abandon any illusion that we can or should revive some largely mythical traditional family. We need to invent new family traditions and find ways of reviving older community ones, not wallow in nostalgia for the past or heap contempt on people whose family values do not live up to ours. There are good grounds for hope that we can develop such new traditions, but only if we discard simplistic solutions based on romanticization of the past.[45]

In one basic sense, both writers agree. While Stacey says we shouldn't go back, Coontz says we couldn't even if we wanted to.

Meanwhile, the turntable continues to spin ever faster. In 1960, fewer than 1 percent of children under eighteen had experienced the divorce of their parents. Today, almost 50 percent have.[46] The divorce of parents when children are young, moreover, significantly increases the likelihood of their own divorce or separation by as much as 60 percent.[47] Ironically, the fragmentation of the family has itself become a tradition, a tradition that perpetuates itself through the children of divorce.

If centrifugality hasn't proven the truth of Thomas Wolfe's dictum, "You can't go home again," it certainly has made the return trip enormously more difficult.

THE ELDERLY

The troubled acceleration of childhood is matched by turbulent change at the other end of the biological spectrum.

Thanks to medical science, adults can now look forward to longer lives. Indeed, as gerontologists Alan Pifer and Lydia Bronte point out, "What is startling about the aging trend today is the rapid pace at which it is proceeding."[48] Back in 1950, only 10 percent of all Americans were over 65. In only two generations, however, the percentage doubled.[49] The number of those over 85 has, in fact, quadrupled, making it the fastest growing age group in our population.[50]

The Problems of Aging

Many of the elderly do not know what to do with the extra years science has given them. For many, forced retirement becomes an economic and psychological burden. Compelled to live with the insecurity of an eroding income, they struggle to survive. Some, racked with illness and impatient that death has not come soon enough, may elect assisted suicide or choose the termination of prolonged life-support.

More and more of the elderly, in fact, are being indirectly penalized by society for living too long. Just as social acceleration causes the compression of childhood at one generational extreme, it brings about the isolation of the elderly at the other. The comfort of growing old in familiar surroundings and ultimately dying in one's own home and bed, surrounded by loved ones, is a gift today's centrifugal family seldom gives. Indeed, artificial "homes" for the aged and impersonal long-term care facilities are expected to witness nearly a doubling of their populations by the year 2010.[51]

Despite the needs it will serve, long-term health care for the elderly is threatened by the financial expense it represents. In the twenty-first century we may witness a new type of generational conflict as young and old clash over costs. As biomedical ethicist Daniel Callahan argues:

> Should the young come to believe they are penalized by the aging society's commitment to the health needs and demands of the elderly, their sympathy could well evaporate. Why should the young harm their present prospects, and their own prospects as the next generation of the aged, to make heavy sacrifices for a generation of elderly people who have become able, through the blessings of affluence and medicine, to live for themselves only, and are content to do so?[52]

The only thing that may prevent this from happening is the continuing growth in the numbers of older Americans, who, out of self-interest, will politically advocate the fulfillment of their own needs. But to pay for those needs, someone will undoubtedly have to sacrifice. Children, a demographically shrinking advocacy group, may end up being short-changed in education or elsewhere in order to pay for the lives and life-styles of those who are older. Any selfishness in such a debate will have been exacerbated by the rapid disintegration of the traditional family and its bonds of loyalty and love. Ultimately, the common denominator uniting the generations may turn out to be not mutual commitment and respect but shared selfishness and expediency.

The Obsolescence of the Old

The elderly in any era are the biologic embodiment of the past tense.[53] To the extent that the past is devalued, to that extent also will the elderly be devalued and deemed socially irrelevant. In a society governed by the pull of the present, the elderly are bound to seem more and more irrelevant—even to themselves—as they continue to lose touch with the rapidly shifting topography of a land they once knew as their own.

Traditionally, elders have been regarded as the living repositories of wisdom, a wisdom built up from their having experienced life over the course of many decades. A number of factors, however, are conspiring to strip the elderly of such credentials. First, the speed with which society is changing tends to make knowledge based on past experience seem obsolete. Though the obsolescence is mostly a technological one, the dominance of technology in contemporary society casts a long shadow over all other kinds of knowledge as well and obscures their value. Secondly, the reliance upon data in such a society and their growing accumulation tend to make objective facts overshadow subjective wisdom. As a result, we tend to respect the "judgment" of a computer more than we would the judgment of a person.

Once valued as guides for a long journey, the elderly in such a society become the trivialized guardians of an empty suitcase—the impotent, grown-up version of a culturally illiterate younger generation. As a class the elderly come to constitute the social equivalent of the Alzheimer's victim, paradoxically oblivious to the past at the very time when their collective store of memories is the greatest.

Denied their special role as defenders of age-old tradition by a society that worships the new, and treated as anachronisms by the families of which they were a part, the elderly either lose self-respect or, in a socially commended gesture, increasingly imitate the young. Either way, long-term memories are displaced by short-term ones as antiquated experience slips down the slick memory-chute to oblivion, to be retrieved and exhibited only in brief moments of nostalgic reminiscence. In the nowist society of the future, where history itself will be an anachronism, few moral traditions or permanent ethical standards are likely to survive, especially as newer, even more now-centered generations replace those of former times. As a result, the family will have lost one of its most valuable possessions, a sense of continuity that, like a gyroscope, can stabilize it in turbulent times.

THE ENDANGERED FAMILY

It is no accident that the life of the family is in such danger today. Diachronic commitment, so necessary for family survival, is a concept alien to our society. Alien also is the concept of continuity. Continuity is different from mere transience, for continuity emphasizes not moment but meaning, the meaningful connection of parts—female and male, young and old—into a living whole bonded by common purpose, a whole in which energy (for the family, the energy of love) is given and shared. The increased incidence of family breakdown today permeates the environment in which people live with an atmosphere of impermanence that seeps into the interstices of every human relationship. Family fragmentation, rather than being an exception, has become the rule.

One thing is certain: never before in history has a civilization been so deprived of the cohesiveness of family as a defense against the centrifugal force of change.

Chapter 5

The Transformation of Society

BESIDES AFFECTING the individual and the family directly, the power of now influences them indirectly through the medium of society. This indirect influence is profound because the attitudes and beliefs of society define for its members the very nature of reality, including the meaning and purposes of time. The society we live in teaches us what is worth doing fast and what is worth doing slowly and what is worth spending any time on at all. Time, in this sense, is like currency, and society sets its value.

To derive benefits from society the individual obeys its dictates. In exchange, society meets the individual's needs. But in serving those needs, society becomes an accessory to the power of now by expediting the gratification of its members' desires. The rate at which it does so, in fact, is the most common measure of social progress.

This chapter will examine two facets of contemporary society: the way it satisfies basic desires (Section 1) and the speed at which it does so (Section 2). As we will see, popular gratification has become the ruling principle of contemporary society, and materialism its guiding philosophy. As greater and greater efforts have been expended to make the gratification of the senses faster and faster, the mechanisms of society have speeded up. Ongoing technological advances have accelerated three types of activity in particular: the movement of things (through commerce), the movement of ideas (through communications), and the movement of people (through transportation). The combined acceleration of these separate but related activities has generated a swirling vortex that today sucks into itself all elements of individual experience, thought, and emotion. In its whirling, fluid funnel all times cease to matter except now.

Section 1:
MATERIALISM AND GRATIFICATION

THE ASCENT OF MATERIALISM
Biological Beginnings

As long as living creatures have striven to survive, life has centered on now. Biological needs can only be met in the present; for the body there is no other time but now. Hunger and thirst can be deferred, but remain insistent and demanding. Heat and cold can be endured, but continue to oppress. Our nerve endings speak only one language, the language of the present.

In the beginning, matter was insensate. Later, when sentient, it knew need. Later still, when it comprehended the reality of its need, it became self-aware. The earliest human creatures no longer simply felt their needs. As thinking beings, they became cognizant of their need as fact.

Yet there is more than one kind of need, more than one kind of hunger. There are needs of the physical self, but there are also needs that transcend the purely physical. Beyond basic biological cravings, there are other yearnings that stem from an aching sense of deeper incompleteness.

To fulfill their nonphysical longings, human beings from prehistory have reached out to the physical. On the walls of caves they uttered through Stone Age art their earliest prayers. Such an approach was only natural, as their primordial origins lay in matter, and matter had gratified their earliest desires. In the beginning, therefore, human beings were governed by tangibility's power.

The Mediation of Society

One of society's first functions was to aid the individual in meeting urgent needs. In prehistoric times, for example, the concerted efforts of the tribe in sharing both work and danger helped to insure the survival of its members. The cumulative acts of the tribal group were enhanced, moreover, by the strength that was born of its unity. Yet, beyond serving the immediate needs of its members, primitive society also acknowledged a wider framework of time.

Through its ceremonies, it invoked the power of future and past. Society did this because its consciousness represented a fusion of the consciousness of its members. While the individual looked forward and back from the present, from the vantage point of personal experience, society drew upon a collective sense of a shared future and a shared past, stretching out in both directions for successive generations.

Without the broad temporal foundation laid by one's culture, the life of the individual would have been constructed on the narrower base of the present. Through its collective memories, however, culture reminded individuals of the past and offered them its guidance. Through its collective dreams, moreover, it inspired them with goals. Thus, past and future lent the present their structural support.

This principle of temporal interdependence is evident in the etymology of the word "religion." "Religion" is derived from a Latin root that means "to tie or bind," for religion binds us to others outside ourselves and to other times outside our own. Through its teachings, religion defines the moral implications of "long ago" and "yet to be," instructing us to make our current actions compatible with an invisible but nevertheless real continuum of time.

As human beings struggled individually and collectively to meet their basic needs, those who succeeded eventually rose from a level of mere subsistence to a level of comfort in which they enjoyed a surplus of material possessions. In a simple society, such wealth might be a cow or a string of ceramic beads; in a richer one, a herd or a necklace of gold. Indeed, different levels of wealth might coexist within the same society. In such cases, the concentration of wealth could have symbolic as well as real value, denoting the social status of the possessor.

For most of human history material wealth tended to be concentrated in the hands of numerically small but powerful classes, who exulted in the splendor radiated by their possessions. As in the pyramid, the resplendent apex was usually carried on the backs of thousands of baser blocks. As an institution, religion affirmed such social architecture and reveled in its rewards. What arose was an edifice of aristocratic privilege, reinforced by a static ideology of time that declared the sovereignty of the past and the subordination of the people to the task of perpetuating tradition into the future.

The Materialistic Revolution

The architecture of rigid aristocratic dominion was first cracked by tremors that shook the Mediterranean in the seventh and sixth centuries B.C., when a series of Greek revolutions replaced royalty with popular government. By the fifth century B.C., democracy had fully emerged in Athens. Five centuries later, after gaining military mastery over the Mediterranean, the Romans introduced a perversion of democracy on a worldwide scale: a society dedicated to raising people's standard of living at the price of their freedom. Shrewdly combining hedonism with power, the

Roman elite kept the masses in Rome happy by guaranteeing them security and comfort. More than the swords of Roman legions, materialistic plenty and satisfaction were the true tools that kept the Roman Empire together for half a millennium. Eventually, economic weakness, the appetite of hungry barbarian tribes, and the moral emptiness of Rome's own leadership brought about the system's collapse.

Amid the poverty and chaos that followed the Empire's fall, the old class structure reasserted itself, assuming the form of feudalism in the Middle Ages. After the Crusades, the rise of a merchant class in Italy set into motion, like widening ripples, notions of the individual's right to lay humanistic claim to his or her own material betterment. This Renaissance dynamic would be affirmed by the reasoned arguments of the seventeenth century and would culminate in the philosophical Enlightenment and revolutionary movements of the eighteenth. Though it often exploited the masses, the Industrial Revolution of the nineteenth century, coupled with democracy in Europe and America, laid the foundation for the widest distribution of material goods the world had ever known.

To be sure, across that world, elite nations and classes would continue to monopolize wealth, but the mechanisms for its redistribution had already been forged. The materialistic revolution had begun, a revolution that would socially reestablish the primacy of the present and its demands.

From Ants to Grasshoppers

The materialistic revolution laid the basis for a consumer society. Harsh necessity had compelled the most primitive societies to dwell almost exclusively on consumption. Whenever possible, however, surpluses were stored to insure survival. When prosperity grew, surpluses permitted wealth to be amassed by those whom society honored as its leaders. In such cases, productivity was translated into the accumulation of wealth as the economic symbol of prestige. Though wealthy individuals and classes persisted under democracy, production was increasingly redirected toward the manufacture and distribution of material goods for society at large. Productivity thus shifted from narrowly focused accumulation (acknowledging and honoring the past) to broad-based consumption (responding to and satisfying the present).

After the basic needs of people were met, their nonessential wants could also be addressed. With time, of course, habitually satisfied wants came to be perceived as additional needs. As the circle of popular need expanded and was fulfilled, consumption continued to grow, limited only by society's resources, the structural capabilities of its economy, and the responsiveness of its leaders.

Eventually, capitalists realized that profits could be enhanced not merely by cultivating existing wants but by inventing new ones. The development of advertising in the late nineteenth century not only accentuated the appetite for material goods; it also became the instrument for publicly generating appetites that previously had not been known.

Though more people than ever before could now accumulate wealth, the unprecedented degree of consumption in the twentieth century constituted a fundamental change in the nature of human activity and human values.

The accumulation of wealth had always implied process. In keeping with the symbolic logic of accumulation, goods were created whose actual use was often never intended. Instead, time was invested in their development, their presentation, their acquisition, their storage, their preservation, and their display as symbols of status. Consumption, however, implied a different frame of temporal reference. While it might take time to make the goods that were to be consumed, their essential purpose was served by their spontaneous use.

The conversion from an economy of accumulation to an economy of consumption thus involves a change from duration to immediacy. The temporal values implicit in such an economic transformation educate a populace in a new type of behavior—one that emphasizes short-term gratification over long-term appreciation.

The contrast between such attitudes is illustrated by the fable of the grasshopper and the ant, told by the ancient Greek storyteller Aesop. As the story goes, a profligate grasshopper had spent the summer amusing itself by making music. The industrious ant, however, had spent the summer gathering food for the coming winter. As winter approached, the hungry grasshopper came to the ant and appealed for food. "If you sang in the summer," responded the ant sarcastically, "why don't you dance in the winter?"

More than teaching that we should prepare for the future, the fable also depicts two different attitudes toward time. Only decades ago our culture could have been compared to a colony of ants, laboring to build a store that could be drawn upon in later times. Today, however, our culture increasingly resembles an aggregation of grasshoppers who only live for the present.

The New Primitivism

By widening consumption, contemporary materialism creates the impression of social progress. In actuality, however, by reducing the public to feverish consumers, it paradoxically returns society to its most primitive state, a time when the human animal lived hand-to-mouth and from moment to moment. Simpler and earlier cultures supplied their members with the means to counterbalance what might otherwise have been an exclusive preoccupation with the present by instructing them in the meaning of the past and the future. Contemporary society, however, by renouncing these times in exchange for instancy, abandons its members to the impulses of now. Whereas traditional religion embodied symbols that lent comfort by reason of their immutability, the new consumer society makes a religion out of transience and disposability. Onto its dumpster altars the masses hurl the oblations of their secular faith.

As more and more material goods fill up society's intellectual space, they crowd out the significance of nonmaterial concerns. In this respect also, society reverts to its primitive state, to a time when meeting physical needs left little occasion for anything else. In this new primitivism, matter reclaims its place as the consummate source of human satisfaction.

All the while, the ethic of materialism soaks subconsciously into the nonmaterial layers of consumers' lives, permeating the tissue of their values. All things come to be judged by the degree to which they facilitate the acquisition and enjoyment of material goods.

A public mood of insecurity is bred by seemingly separate phenomena that collaborate in creating a climate of impermanence. However, they are not merely the causes of this climate, but its consequences as well, the connected and interrelated expressions of a pervasive temporal atmosphere that makes durability universally wither and impermanence thrive.

The Failure of Success

The materialistic success of a society can, in fact, set the stage for its eventual failure. Long ago, as the ancient Greeks were entering their Golden Age, their playwrights tried to warn them of hidden dangers that lay ahead.

Despite the common assumption that we are most at risk when we are weak, the Greeks concluded that we are, paradoxically, more vulnerable when we are strong. In their philosophy, they identified a causal linkage between four concepts: *olbos* (prosperity), *hybris* (presumptuousness), *ate* (folly), and *nemesis* (divine vengeance). In this chain, prosperity leads to presumptuousness, presumptuousness inspires folly, and folly invites divine vengeance. Acted out on the stage, the pattern was personified by a powerful figure (the tragic hero), who, blinded by his imagined invincibility, sets into motion forces that ultimately bring great suffering to himself and those he loves. For, when man presumes to act like god—unaccountable to anyone but himself—the jealous gods (so the Greeks believed) teach us who we really are by painfully reminding us of our human limitations.

The Greeks, who always possessed a keen sense of irony, saw man as a creature seduced and betrayed by his own hunger for greatness. Aching to fulfill his potentialities, he was destroyed by his own deepest desires. Even success, they noted, rather than being an occasion for unmixed celebration, was in fact a time fraught with peril.

Notwithstanding the warnings issued by their playwrights, the fifth century B.C. Athenians proceeded to act out their own political tragedy on the stage of history. In an era when every Greek city-state was autonomous, civic pride and materialistic plenty whetted the Athenians' appetite for even greater glory. Their imperialistic ambitions and arrogance eventually provoked a twenty-seven-year-long war that ended with the fall of Athens.

In a similar vein, many have argued that the fall of Imperial Rome was due to the corruptive influences of a materialistic creed that transformed a people of hardy farmer-soldiers into a passive race corrupted by luxury. The irony was that, in trying to better their lot materialistically, earlier generations of Roman peasants had paved the road to their nation's downfall.

Centuries before the fall of Rome, the Hebrew prophets had denounced the shallowness of their own society, an affluent urban society that had put greed ahead of compassion and exploitation ahead of social justice. For such sins, the prophets charged, God would destroy Jerusalem and chastise his chosen people. In each historic instance, materialistic success contributed to tragic national failure.

Predictably, the external differences between these ancient worlds and our own tend to obscure the existence of internal similarities. Yet, if human weakness is a universal common denominator, the lesson for America is clear: our materialistic success may pose the gravest dangers to our survival as a society, especially if we are moving too fast to calculate our moral trajectory.

In Praise of Poverty

We can, of course, simplistically argue that our best national hope lies in the prospect of sustained poverty. After all, that way we will at least avoid the corruptive influences of wealth and the tragic pitfalls of materialistic plenty.

Unfortunately, the first people to object to such a romanticized version of low-income living will be the very people trying to survive on just such a budget. It is, alas, a luxury of the well-heeled to celebrate the barefoot life.

In our current society, there are millions who are denied even the basic necessities of life and millions more who, unable to save anything, struggle on a day-to-day basis just to make ends meet. To argue that we'd all be better off if we just became less rich is hardly a source of comfort to those who can't make it now on what they've got.

What are we talking about, then, when we speak of materialism and its dangers? For if this argument appeals only to those insulated by affluence, it will have failed.

Materialism, first of all, doesn't refer to meeting people's basic material needs. That is a goal we should all wish to see met, a goal that our nation has still not succeeded in achieving. Nor does materialism even refer to the enjoyment of luxuries. It would be mean-spirited to deny ourselves or others the pleasures that effort has earned.

Materialism, as used in this book, refers to an attitude toward life which holds that owning and using things is our highest human calling, that it should be our main goal in life, above all others. Socially, it implies an arrangement designed to fulfil these purposes, at least for those with the appropriate ways and means to achieve them.

The inherent flaw of materialism is that it distracts us from discovering and realizing other levels of our being—that our lives can mean more than the sum total of what we possess, that in the end "getting and spending"[1] will not satisfy our deepest needs. Translated socially, materialism's flaw is that it distracts people from discovering their potential together, from realizing that self-serving wealth is not the fullest measure of a nation's success.

These flaws of materialism are exacerbated by the power of now, which—like the rushing torrent of a river in flood eating away at its banks—washes away the soil-like stability of community and erodes the last tangible shore of a people's hope. For those denied its rewards, the temptations of a consumerist society can only breed a heightened sense of urgency and desperation.

The longing for material possessions has always been a theme in humankind's story. From earliest times, possessions came to signify an individual's position in society. Over the course of history, ancestral wealth and power crystallized into the formation of privileged groups. In such societies, rich and poor came to be polarized as the components of a rigid class structure. Like ragtag spectators viewing a glittering procession of royal carriages, the poor could only humbly behold wealth from afar, and then only on rare ceremonial occasions.

A materialistic society, however, neutralizes that polarity by establishing a marketplace open to all regardless of their birth or former economic status. The materialistic economy implies, inspires, and, indeed, thrives upon a social mobility energized by consumption.

Today, the have-nots, as never before in history, can see the "good life" every day and night of the year in their very own kitchens, living rooms, and bedrooms thanks to the omnipresence of television. Television levels society further by persuading the haves that they are, in fact, have-nots—convincing them through commercials that there are still some essential experiences and possessions they lack.

The consumerist impulses stirred by television become even more perverse, however, when viewers discover they are incapable of gratifying all their desires. Like a bizarre Pavlovian machine, the persistent ringing of the bell produces only a tempting *picture* of dog food, totally inedible in itself. In fact, the very multiplicity of competing commercials and their mutual exclusivity (how many brands can we simultaneously buy?) inevitably leads to the conviction that we will never be able to satisfy all our wants. On the one hand, television holds out to viewers an open invitation to participate in the abundance of society; yet, on the other hand, economic reality forbids them fully to partake. And so they become resigned, not to their social class as much as to their own inherent and personal inadequacy.

In short, the materialistic principles of our society lead us to define our worth in terms of our possessions. But, at the same time, our society's chief instrument of communication makes it impossible for us to feel materially secure. In this no-win situation, repeated economic frustrations add up to a sense of inner failure.

Such frustrations can lead to crime, especially when have-nots are continually exposed to taunting electronic images of material wealth, images that signify self-worth and success. Even the poorest of homes will have a color TV to remind a family daily of its deficiency.

Indeed, when examined within the context of materialism and now-centered ethics, so-called deviant social behavior (including violent and criminal acts) turns out to be paradoxically consistent with contemporary society's highest goal: to get as much as you can as fast as you can.[2] While theft provides the goods, drugs supply the illusion. To be properly understood, then, crime in our society must be viewed not as deviance but rather as consistency.

This is not to assert that crime is purely a contemporary phenomenon. Near the Roman Forum, the subterranean chambers of the Carcer (from which we get our word "incarceration") clearly testify to the existence of prisons in the ancient world.

Peculiar to our day, however, is the radical expansion of criminal behavior, an expansion that cannot be explained on the grounds of population growth alone. Contributing to this increase in crime is the power of now. Nowism devalues anything that smacks of the past, including the traditional respect for old-fashioned laws and old-fangled authority. Secondly, it sanctions impulsive acts meant to gratify current wishes. Thirdly, by focusing on the present, it obscures the reality of the future and the consequences it contains. The drug addict and the thief live for now, not because they reject society's values, but because they respond more automatically to its subliminal call.[3]

COMMERCE AND COMMUNICATIONS

The Pervasiveness of Commerce

Escaping the influence of nowism would be easier if commerce did not so comprehensively pervade our lives. Materialism and consumption however, have become so emblematic of American society that we can confidently say: today, society *is* commerce. It is only natural that the GNP (gross national product) and the GDP (gross domestic product), which measure purely economic activity, are regularly held up as the truest standards of America's success as a nation.

The commercialization of American society is evident in the role business plays in our daily lives. Indeed, that role is more dominant in our culture today than it has been in any previous era of human history. This dominance is due, first of all, to the sheer number of commercial events in everyday life, a number that is the product of decades of exponential multiplication, so much so that the very texture of our lives equals the sum total of our transactions.

But the dominance of commerce can also be illustrated by its subtle invasion of once inviolate zones. Slowly but inexorably, aspects of our culture that were originally noncommercial are being absorbed into the domain of business.

For most of history, a dichotomy existed between market and home. Humanity's earliest economies were essentially self-sufficient. The few commodities that family or village could not produce for themselves were acquired by trading with others, often by traveling to the places where they were available. In agrarian societies, markets arose for common convenience, operating in central locations on customary days. Market days became great social occasions, accompanied by entertainment and festivities.

With the development of urban life and its concentration of population and need, craftsmen and merchants took up permanent locations to sell their wares. The urban marketplace that grew up frequently became the center of civic life, replete with government buildings and religious shrines.

Except for the activities of itinerant merchants, it was centralization that characterized commerce until the era of modern communications. Beginning in the mid seventeenth century, however, advertisements in newspapers reached potential consumers in their very own homes. In the twentieth century, first radio (in the early 1920s) and then television (from the early 1950s) reached even wider audiences through commercial announcements. It was the Sears and Roebuck catalogue, however, first introduced in 1893, that radically transformed commerce by allowing customers to buy goods from their homes, by mail or telephone, using a book filled with pictures of merchandise, descriptions, and fixed prices. What radio and television later did electronically, printed advertisements and mail-order catalogues did typographically: breaking down the traditional wall between the sanctity and tranquility of the home and the hustle and bustle of the marketplace.

Recent innovations in electronic technology may well serve to remove all traces of that wall. In only a decade, a new concept, video retail, has become a $2.5 billion-a-year industry.[4] By the end of the century, it may in fact be a $25 billion-a-year business.

Dominated by two cable giants, the Florida-based Home Shopping Network and Pennsylvania-based QVC ("Quality, Value, Convenience"), video retail permits cable viewers, or "members," to see and buy merchandise at home using their television screens and touch-tone phones.[5] Both networks operate round-the-clock, showing nothing but commercials. Unlike the usual TV commercial, however, these are not simply persuasive messages but highly focused pitches designed to elicit a high volume of sales within a specific time. The Home Shopping Network creates a "buy-it-now-or-you'll-never-be-able-to-get-it-again" psychology by permitting viewers to place orders only as long as the merchandise is being shown on their screens. For its part, QVC shows a digital clock that counts down the seconds till the commercial will end. Meanwhile, thousands of operators take orders—HSN's partly automated system can take 20,000 calls a minute—as sophisticated sales screens post each pitch's second-by-second effectiveness.

> Displayed prominently in most executive offices [of HSN] and in every corner of the broadcast studios and control rooms, the sales screens reset every 15 seconds, updating the item offered, the number of buyers calling, units sold per minute, total units sold and the remaining inventory. The screen counts the money collected, dividing it into dollars per minute for the last three minutes, dollars per hour and dollars per show. . . .
>
> As [the salesman] casually introduces a 20-piece set of china at the top of his three-hour shift, he has one eye glued on the sales screen hidden in his desk. By comparing the viewers' response to various sales pitches, he knows in a matter of seconds that buyers are more interested in the plates' discount price than in their lovely design and changes his pitch accordingly.[6]

According to Barry Diller, former head of Paramount Pictures and the Fox Network and now chairman of QVC, video retail constitutes "part of the architecture of a new world."[7] Others agree it may be "the biggest telecommunications prize of the early 21st century,"[8] earning as much as 55 percent of all retail business within 15 years.[9]

Apart from the profits the video-retail industry earns for its owners, it provides convenience, stimulation, and entertainment for hundreds of thousands of loyal subscribers. Moreover, it provides a sense of community and participation that brightens many lives. The Home Shopping Network, in particular, presents itself as a club. Members who call are greeted as friends and are even sent greeting cards on their birthdays and anniversaries. The process of ordering gives members, especially the lonely, something to do and someone to talk to. In addition, offering on-air testimonials for products (as members are invited to do) gives callers the affirmation that their choices and opinions are valued.

The "friendship" these networks offer, however, is a purely financial arrangement. Stop buying long enough and you stop being a friend. Like the business of prostitution, video retail gives "love" only in exchange for dollars.

That some should feel a desperate need to seek out such a sense of community on commercial terms is a measure of how barren of real caring our society may be. Yet their response is natural in a society such as ours that long ago confused the idea of being with the idea of having, and that has already commodified so much.

By breaking down the final barrier between marketplace and home, video retail (like telemarketing before it) has opened the floodgates to a commercialism that abounds elsewhere in our society, allowing it to inundate the sanctuary of the home, flooding whatever was left of people's private activities and values. That it does so effortlessly, and with public cooperation and enthusiasm, is its most worrisome feature.

Ultimately, the convenience of going to an electronic mall may well save people time that they can then devote to other, less materialistic pursuits. But television is an inherently seductive medium that can draw viewers in. With home shopping as an added feature, viewers are conditioned to act on impulse in a "*have*-to-have-it-now," "*can*-have-it-now" setting that only reinforces the tendencies toward instant gratification that already exist elsewhere. In addition, the Internet's World Wide Web is rapidly being exploited through the creation of retail home-pages and on-line "stores."[10]

The commercialization of America is also evident in other facets of society: in religion, in sports, and in education.

In the area of religion, holidays are sources of immense profit. Christmas, to take one glittering example, has become an industry. Down through history to meet its legitimate needs, organized religion has sought contributions from its congregants. At times, the acquisition of such wealth became an end in itself, obscuring religion's spiritual mission. The commercialization of Christmas, however, and the consequent commercialization of Hanukkah, are blatant examples of the mass conversion of the sacred into the secular. It is a conversion performed not by church or synagogue, but by society upon itself. With the eager complicity of the consuming public, businesses turn timeless messages into short-term profit.

In sports, the nostalgic bond of loyalty between athlete and team, and between team and fans, has been corroded by financial calculation. Almost every sensible professional player of standing now uses a business agent to negotiate a lucrative contract, and owners have been known to move whole teams to find more profitable venues. As a result, the ardor of fans has been cooled by the same kind of cynicism that now infects so many other parts of the American spirit. Even collegiate $port$ have been corrupted front end and back by coaches, athletic directors, and governing boards, who realize the impact a winning football or basketball team can have on alumni giving.[11] Meanwhile, America's participation in the Olympic Games is exploited on an international scale, as networks bid against one another for coverage rights and corporate sponsors compete for airtime and athletic endorsements.

Commercialization has also made major inroads in the field of education. Some 7 million students from grades six to twelve (over 40 percent of America's teenage population) see Channel One, a satellite network for schools that broadcasts three minutes of commercials intermixed with twelve minutes of current events.[12] Over 10,000 schools hungry for free TV sets and VCRs subscribe to this illuminating service that pumps commercialism right into the classroom, mixing what's happening (in MTV style) with what you can buy.

Students, thoroughly indoctrinated into materialism in school and out, can then go on to college, where getting a degree is viewed as a boring means to a money-making end and where academic consumers are all too willing to sue professor and institution alike if they don't get the diploma they paid for.

In each of these once sacrosanct areas—religion, sports, and education—commerce and its underlying monetary principle have come to characterize more and more of the American experience.

Besides injecting materialism into our lives, commercialism distorts our sense of time. This is most evident in a strategy used by the greeting card industry, a strategy that is all the more subversive because this industry sells on paper the very symbols of time. No sooner is Christmas past than Valentine's Day cards fill the shelves. As for Christmas cards themselves, they appear well before Thanksgiving. Indeed, the Thanksgiving Day parade held in major cities is in actuality a commercial ceremony designed to stimulate the buying of toys for a holiday not to be celebrated for another month.

Such marketing strategies tear the seasons from their age-old, traditional moorings. No longer anchored in the security of cosmic order, they become the playthings of commerce, manipulated to maximize earnings. Likewise, in recent times, historic American holidays have been chronologically uprooted to make way for the three-day weekend: hence Memorial Day is now "observed" on the most secularly convenient Monday, and Washington's and Lincoln's birthdays are jointly noted on depersonalized Presidents' Day.

Communications

The acceleration of society is evident not only in commerce but also in communications—the movement not of things but of their images. Indeed, communications—*electronic* communications—radically transcends the mechanical limitations of traditional commerce, for through electronic communications the speed of light becomes the standard at which society functions. It is instantaneous and integrated communications that has made possible the emergence of a new form of society about which we will soon learn more—a synchronous society—a type of society that even now is reshaping the way we think and feel.

Neural Networks

What individual organs are to the human body, the separate media of communication are to the body of society. Indeed, the latter are, in essence, technological extensions of the former.[13] Thus, historically, the ear became the telephone, the mouth became radio, the eye became television. Each invention arose not because the individual exists as an individual, but because the individual exists as part of a group. *Social* necessity is the mother of invention, for without the existence of others to hear, speak to, or see, there would have been no incentive to invent.

Over the course of time, each communicational technology has increased in versatility and sophistication. The aural dimension of the telephone has been enhanced by fiber-optic digital transmission for clarity; wireless, cellular, and satellite transmission for distance; and a variety of features for convenience—conference calling, caller ID, call waiting, call forwarding, the personal answering machine, and voice mail. The oral dimension of the radio has been increased by wave-length, frequency modulation, and stereophonic sound; the visual dimension of television, by the development of color, high-definition digital transmission, and the large screen.

Certain technologies have already served more than one human faculty (the telephone: hearing and speech; television: sight and hearing). But current technological developments promise to revolutionize traditional communications by fusing once separate devices into integrated multimedia systems in which individual technologies merge, systems with which the user can creatively interact.

As Robert E. Allen, board chairman of AT&T, has said: "We envision a seamless web of competing but interconnected networks—both wire and wireless—that will enable people to have easy access to each other and the information they want and need at any time, anywhere and in any form."[14]

What Allen and others envision is the technological equivalent of the human nervous system but on a social scale. By virtue of this neural network, the consciousness of the individual will meld into the consciousness of society as never before.[15]

Such technological sophistication is, in fact, an organic reflex of society's current size and complexity. In order to survive and thrive as an organism, a society is compelled—almost by biologic necessity—to invent new systems that enable it to adapt to the challenge of changing circumstance.

In the primitive village, the integration of consciousness was spontaneous. No elaborate system of telecommunications was needed because the villager's world was small and his life simple and comprehensible. A large and diversified society, however, requires artificial devices to hold it together and help it function efficiently.

The behavior of society in such circumstances resembles the operation of systems, both living and nonliving, in which energy is exchanged. According to a theory developed by Nobel Prize–winning chemist Ilya Prigogine:

> The more complex the . . . structure, the more integrated and connected it is and thus the more energy flow-through it requires to maintain itself. [If] fluctuations become too great for the system to absorb, it will be forced to reorganize. . . . [T]he reorganization always tends toward a higher order of complexity, integration, and connectedness and greater energy flow-through. Each successive reordering, because it is more complex than the one preceding it, is even more vulnerable to fluctuations and reordering. Thus complexity creates the condition for greater reordering and a speedup of evolutionary development and energy flow-through.[16]

History offers proof of Prigogine's theory, for the larger political entities became, the more elaborate became their systems of communication.

In his fifth century B.C. account, the Greek writer Herodotus told how the ancient rulers of Persia possessed a highly organized and efficient system of sending official communiques to the far-flung corners of their vast empire.

> Nothing mortal travels so fast as these Persian messengers. The entire plan is a Persian invention; and this is the method of it. Along the whole line of road there are men (they say) stationed with horses, in number equal to the number of days the journey takes, allowing a man and horse to each day; and these men will not be hindered from accomplishing at their best speed the distance which they have to go, either by snow, or rain, or heat, or by the darkness of night. The first rider delivers his dispatch to the second, and the second passes it to the third; and so it is borne from hand to hand along the whole line, like the light in

the torch-race, which the Greeks celebrate to Hephaestus [the
ancient god of technology].[17]

This ancient communications system was necessitated by the expanse the
Persians ruled, a territory that stretched from Egypt to India. Without such
rapid communication, their hold over their empire would have slipped
away.

In a later era, the ancient Romans built all-weather paved roads to
achieve the same purpose and facilitate the movement and logistical support of their legions. Like the sea-lanes of the Mediterranean which the
Romans patrolled, these roads homogenized cultures by circulating commodities, people, and ideas. Indeed, it was the existence of this network of
communications that allowed the small Near Eastern cult of Christianity to
spread, despite official persecution, across the Roman world. At the height
of the Empire, the total length of Rome's roads was 50,000 miles, a total that
still exceeds the combined mileage of all of America's interstate highways.

In U.S. history, the closest analogy to the Persian postal system was the
Pony Express. Using a relay system of horses and riders, the Pony Express
provided rapid mail delivery between Missouri and California.[18] Begun in
1860, the experiment ended only 18 months later, replaced by an even more
rapid system of transmission—the telegraph.

The difference between the Pony Express and the telegraph, however,
was not merely one of speed. While the Pony Express physically trans-
ported actual letters, the telegraph electrically transmitted only their messages. The transportation of the letter was bound by the limitation of the
horse and rider's speed, but the message itself was unbridled and could
race nearly at the speed of light.

Since 1860, these two systems of delivery—the delivery of actual objects
and of their analogues—have increased in speed, capacity, and complexity.
Mail service has been enhanced by air mail and same-day delivery; message transmission, by wire, fiber-optic, and wireless systems. Words, numbers, voices, and faces can today travel instantaneously across mere miles
or across an entire nation or world fused into simultaneity by sophisticated
global networks of humming satellites and glowing screens. Indeed, the
fact that we have come to take all of this for granted is the most convincing
evidence of technology's power to change how we think.

Visual messages moving at the speed of light are, of course, nothing new.
The fifth century B.C. playwright Aeschylus tells how beacon-fires were
used to send news of Troy's fall across the Aegean to Greece. In the third
century B.C., watchtowers along the Great Wall of China used similar
beacons to send military messages from the Pacific Ocean to the Gobi
Desert in twenty-four hours or less. And in America, Indian tribes used
smoke signals with similar effect. But all these were exceptional messages
used only by a people's leaders in times of great urgency. Today, on the

other hand, systems of communication operating at the speed of light literally constitute the very fiber of our everyday existence.

By virtue of their great speed, electronic communications set the pace of our culture. But their influence goes far beyond their simple capacity to transmit messages.

By closing the time-gap between transmission and reception, between expectation and delivery, electronics contracts the temporal interval between "before" and "after." In addition to reducing the interval's length, it minimizes the very notion of an interval. By linking "what was" with "what will be" more directly, an electronic connection serves to eliminate the perceptible difference between a distinct and separate past and a distinct and separate future, replacing that continuum with the preeminence of now. In essence, the speed of electronics rewires the traditional circuitry of both human and mechanical reality, streamlining experience even as it contracts our perspective on events.

In the electronic convergence of the future, the television set as we know it will have ceased to exist, as will the traditional telephone, fax machine, and personal computer. Taking their place will be innovative systems already being marketed in which various components, like the organs of the human body, are organically connected and collaborate. The "brain" of the system will be the domestic computer linked to external data banks by a national neurological network of fiber-optic cables—the celebrated "information superhighway" that will lead from centers of knowledge and research by lesser electronic streets and byways to individual schools and homes, with full capability for two-way communication.

Existing consumer-oriented on-line computer services like America Online (with more than 4 million subscribers) as well as movies-on-demand services already available by touch-tone phone give us only a hint of what electronic entrepreneurs are already constructing: a home environment in which high-definition television screens offer us personalized entertainment and information in keeping with our own individual interests and tastes, or become the video display terminals (VDTs) for home computers that let family members shop, bank, pay their bills, vote, play, or grow intellectually with the help of CD-ROMs and an Internet connection.[19] The global computer network known as the Internet is in fact doubling its size annually and currently may have more than 25 million users worldwide.[20]

Communications is also being revolutionized by portability, featuring a new generation of telephone that will create "a totally in-touch society with a phone in every pocket—and wow what a phone,"[21] a cellular device that permits a user to hear, speak to, and see (thanks to its screen) anyone in the world, a phone complete with its own voice-activated, computerized directory; a phone whose screen can show you the world by giving you access to televised programs transmitted by satellite from every country on earth; a phone whose screen becomes a VDT linked not only to your computer at home but to the entire national and international data network, and whose miniature keyboard puts knowledge in your hand; a phone capable of sending and receiving faxes, and of transforming your handwritten notes into precisely formatted letters; a phone capable of calling your physician and simultaneously conveying your complete medical history encoded on a microchip; of ordering a carry-out dinner with the help of a scanning light-pen; of showing you the want ads and instantly transmitting your resume!

Such dazzling domestic and mobile technologies may attract many customers because they seem to offer stress-reducing convenience: shopping at home instead of at a market or store; "going" to work with the help of E-mail and fax;[22] replacing the four walls of an office with the four wheels of a car;[23] and even ordering gifts and souvenirs by phone from an airplane 30,000 feet in the air.[24] Many will certainly be attracted because of the devices' initial novelty; still others will be repelled by their unfamiliarity.

Notes social historian Claude Fischer: "New technologies always get a rise out of people who object for various reasons. But once you get past [the] novelty stage it tends to get absorbed into everyday life. We may wonder 10 years from now what all the fuss was about."[25]

Arno Penzias of Bell Laboratories recognizes, but at the same time dismisses, whatever initial public resistance there might be to such new information technologies.

> People are frightened by the thought of getting too much information, which just shows we're not in the Information Age yet. Are you frightened by the thought of getting too much money? Too much happiness?
>
> On one side, you still have the Age of Paper Work. On the other side you have something I like to think of as information transparency.
>
> And when will you know you're in the Age of Information Transparency? I will tell you. If somebody says I can get you 10 times as much information as you have now, if that makes you feel good, you're in the Age of Information Transparency. When people relish the thought that the information that flows to them can become bigger, then you're in the Age of Information Transparency. And until then we're in the Age of Paper Work.[26]

Some, in fact, see communicational convergence as a force that can unify society, but others disagree.

At one time, it is argued, network television programming served that function by making all America a common family that shared the same television experiences together at night. The multiplication of cable channels, however, and their popularity fragmented that audience, leading many to wonder what the social fallout might be. One such critic is Michael Tracy, director of the University of Colorado's Center for Mass Media Research. Observes Tracy: "TV is a unifying force. I think it's important for society to have that sense of cohesion. The question is then what happens when new technology destroys that common experience."[27]

The linking of computers would address Tracy's concerns by providing individuals the means to identify one another and communicate with one another as friends across great distances by electronic bulletin boards and E-mail, building "virtual communities" united by common interests and concerns.[28] But such communities, we must recognize, would never have the breadth and depth of a national audience. Indeed, Ralph Nader has argued that an elite information highway could serve to create a two-class society made up of those who can afford to travel it and gain knowledge and those who can't.[29]

Of course, the projections about how society will be transformed by multimedia technologies should be tempered by realism about society's own eventual preferences. Commenting on interactive media, Olafur J. Olafsson, former president of Sony Electronic Publishing Co., remarked: "Most people when they come home and plop in front of a television don't want to interact with anything but the refrigerator."[30] Sociologist S. Robert Lichter, director of the Center for Media and Policy in Washington, DC, agrees: "People don't necessarily want to have their lives rearranged. These designers are precisely the wrong ones to ask. They are the most excited about what they are doing and are the least likely to know how it's going to change people."[31]

Lichter may well be correct. But many of the men who have spoken on this issue, like Apple Computer's John Sculley and Tele-Communications, Inc.'s, John Malone, are not designers but businessmen, "data merchants" who recognize the tremendous profits that can be made from converting the technology of an entire nation.[32] After all, buying and using electronic technologies will not be free. As George Fisher, chairman of Motorola, Inc., notes: "By the year 2010, telecommunications could be a $3 trillion market in equipment and services."[33] Significantly also, Vice President Al Gore has termed the data superhighway the "most important marketplace of the 21st century."[34] Because of the profit and power at stake, the organic convergence of electronic devices is certain to be aggressively promoted and controlled by commercial interests and supported by the political parties and leaders they bankroll.

However, drowned out by the cheerleading for more and more access to more and more information is the quiet voice of reason. Access is not the same as wise use—or even use. To imagine an efflorescence of intellectual enlightenment across the nation because young and old have access to vast stores of knowledge ignores two facts: (1) our human rate of absorption is limited, and (2) tens of thousands of library books have already been gathering dust for generations.

People must first want to learn. They must be intellectually, emotionally, and spiritually motivated. Second, they must be guided, especially if they are entering an information jungle without machete. They must be helped to distinguish what is significant from what is not. Third, they must be helped to integrate what they learn with what they already know in order to reach a new level of understanding.

It is marvelous that a student can "read" a manuscript housed in a library continents away. But the equipment itself will not motivate the student to do so. If access alone could inspire students, university libraries on campuses across America would be crowded to overflowing every day. But they are not—not so much because books are dusty or typography is inherently dull, but because students must first passionately want to learn more than they already know.[35]

What is certain is that the organic convergence of media will radically accelerate the flow-rate of information and thereby foster the acceleration of those instruments of society that thrive on data: business, industry, and government. But this is a far different thing from fostering human perspective, which does not depend upon speed and for which speed can even be counterproductive.

A century and a half ago, from his wooded perspective above Walden Pond, Henry David Thoreau speculated on the strides and shortcomings of technology, and America's love affair with it. Speaking of what he called "modern improvements," he said:

> There is an illusion about them; there is not always a positive advance. . . . Our inventions are wont to be pretty toys, which distract our attention from serious things. They are but improved means to an unimproved end, an end which it was already but too easy to arrive at. . . . We are in great haste to construct a magnetic telegraph from Maine to Texas; but Maine and Texas, it may be, have nothing important to communicate. Either is in such a predicament as the man who was earnest to be introduced to a distinguished deaf woman, but when he was presented, and one end of her ear trumpet was put into his hand, had nothing to say. As if the main object were to talk fast and not to talk sensibly. We are eager to tunnel under the Atlantic and bring the Old World some weeks nearer the New; but perchance the first news that will leak through into the broad, flapping American ear will be that Princess Adelaide has the whooping cough. After all, the man whose horse trots a mile in a minute does not carry the most important messages.[36]

As Thoreau noted elsewhere: "In the long run men hit only what they aim at."[37] If our society aims for data under the delusion that data—even organized data—is synonymous with wisdom, it will get data and not much wisdom. The social result of this practice will be what Robert K. Merton, echoing Thoreau, once called "a civilization committed to the quest for continually improved means to carelessly examined ends."[38] Yet so bright is the glare of material progress, so technicized our mentality, that such a characterization appears to many not simply mistaken but virtually incomprehensible.

Section 2:
SOCIETY AND SPEED

THE ACCELERATION OF SOCIETY

Technology helps us get what we want by granting us artificial power. In some cases this power reduces the amount of physical effort we would otherwise have expended. In other cases such power shortens the time it would otherwise have taken to perform the same task.

Such speed may, in fact, be one of the least recognized, but most telling expressions of a civilization's values. The essential beliefs of a culture are in many ways related to motion: those societies that move rapidly seem to embody certain traits, while those that move more slowly tend to exhibit others. Slower societies, for example, may be more inclined to cling to tradition; faster ones, more prone to leave it behind. But besides expressing a society's values, speed may also shape them.

Sensing Speed

For the most part, sensing speed requires a spatial frame of reference. As long as he is perusing an in-flight magazine, the passenger on a jet plane will be oblivious to the great velocity at which he is traveling. Only the runway lights rushing by at touch-down or, more gradually, the miniature, glistening lakes gliding by far below will inform him—as he glances out his window—of the actual speed at which he flies.

Societal speed likewise requires a frame of reference if it is to be perceived. But here the frame of reference resides not in space but in the mind, in the memory of the historic pace at which life once was lived. The quality of the perception is thus relative to the remembered experience of the observer. From a contemporary perspective, the rhythm of an earlier culture may seem nostalgically languid; yet, to someone entering that culture from a still earlier and slower time, that same pace might seem rushed.

Take these words, for example: "The mass of men lead lives of quiet desperation. . . . From the desperate city you go into the desperate country. . . . A stereotyped but unconscious despair is concealed even under what are called the games and amusements of mankind. . . . Men have become the tools of their tools."[39] These lines were written not in our own technologically-driven day, but a century and a half ago. They are the perceptions of Henry David Thoreau, who had taken refuge in a lakeside cabin in 1845 to rediscover his selfhood in nature's solitude in an era many might think was actually less harried than our own.

Indeed, forty-three years earlier, the oppressive weight of the Industrial Revolution and the materialism it had spread led William Wordsworth to proclaim:

> The world is too much with us; late and soon;
> Getting and spending, we lay waste our powers.[40]

To these two nineteenth century thinkers, Wordsworth and Thoreau, despair was engendered by a way of life that had lost touch with the older rhythms of a world attuned to nature.

But we can go back farther still—to the world of ancient Rome. Reflecting on the installation of the city's first sundial, the third to second century B.C. comedy writer Plautus cursed the stress and regimentation it had brought:

> God damn the man who invented hours, who first set up a sundial in this city, and who divided up my day into miserable little bits! When I was a little lad my belly was my sun-dial— much the best and most reliable of the lot! When he said it was time, you ate, if there was any food in the house. Now, even if there is anything, it don't get eaten, unless the Sun gives the word. Nowadays the whole town is full of sun-dials, and most people are crawling around half dead with hunger.[41]

By the first century B.C., the poet Horace was comparing citified life to a rat race.[42] With increased urbanization, the first century A.D. philosopher Seneca bemoaned Rome's noise pollution, and the satirist Juvenal its traffic jams.

Wrote Seneca, who lived near a bathhouse:

> Just imagine some of those "sonic booms." When the muscle men lift their bar-bells (really going at it or just showing off), I get their grunts, hear 'em sucking it in or blowing it out. Or take the flabby type getting a two-bit rub-down—when he gets slapped (cupped-hand or flat), it's a percussion symphony! "Anyone wanna play ball?"—that's all I need! Then throw in a brawler and a pickpocket who's just been pinched and a chorus

of shower room tenors. And how about the fat guys that hit the pool with a whomp![43]

Meanwhile, Juvenal battled chariot-style gridlock:

The wheels creak by on the narrow
Streets of the wards, the drivers squabble and brawl when they're
    stopped,
More than enough to frustrate the drowsiest son of a sea cow.
When his business calls, the crowd makes way, as the rich man,
Carried high in his car, rides over them, reading or writing,
Even taking a snooze, perhaps, for the motion's composing,
Still, he gets where he wants before we do; for all of our hurry,
Traffic gets in our way, in front, around and behind us.
Somebody gives me a shove with an elbow, or two-by-four scantling.
One clunks my head with a beam, another cracks down with a beer keg.
Mud is thick on my shins, I am trampled by somebody's big feet.
Now what?—a soldier grinds his hobnails into my toes.[44]

Ancient testimonies like these persuade us that urban frustrations, and the tensions they induce, are by no means an exclusively modern phenomenon. After all, to those who recalled Republican Rome, even Imperial Rome could seem stressful! And to those who lived in nineteenth-century England or New England (romantically sylvan in *our* mental landscape) the hold of technology over nature could seem overpowering.[45]

Are we then justified in dismissing most social criticism as myopic? Can we rightly refer to a theory of social relativity that says: "Things aren't really getting worse. They just *seem* that way"? Or are there grounds for arguing that change has been taking place in absolute terms as well? Is there long-term evidence for a progressive transformation of our psychosocial environment?

Transportation

To begin with, let us take the matter of speed. While the perception of speed may be relative, speed itself can be objectively gauged. Its progress can be plotted on the graph of human history as a continuously ascending line.

From the dawn of civilization, human beings have invented artificial means to increase the speed at which they could travel. At first, animal-powered devices enabled man to use another creature's speed to enhance his own. Later, inanimate machines were created to accomplish the same purpose. Such machines had major advantages over animals. They did not tire; therefore their speed could be sustained over longer periods. Furthermore, they could be designed to exceed the speed of animals and carry greater loads. From the wheeled cart of the third millennium B.C. to the chariot of Juvenal's day to the railroad Wordsworth and Thoreau knew, the speed of human transport has grown steadily.

The railroad, however, represented a restrictive form of travel. The train could not move freely but had to follow a rigid and predetermined track. Furthermore, the passenger was not free to determine his or her own direction but had to travel as part of a group along a preset course in keeping with a preset schedule determined by a company.

The invention and mass production of the automobile and the building of multiple roads and highways democratized American transportation by allowing people to travel freely and individually.

Today, the car has become an extension of the human personality. Its ownership represents a cultural rite of passage from childhood to adulthood, and personal activity would almost be unthinkable without it. To some degree, in fact, it may be argued that the human personality (and human culture) has become an extension of the car.

Such a transformation was prophesied as far back as 1918 by novelist Booth Tarkington. In *The Magnificent Ambersons,* one of his characters reflects on the social and psychological impact of cars:

> With all their speed forward they may be a step backward in civilization—that is, in spiritual civilization. It may be that they will not add to the beauty of the world, nor to the life of men's souls. I am not sure. But automobiles have come, and they bring a greater change in our life than most of us suspect. They are here, and almost all outward things are going to be different because of what they bring. They are going to alter war, and they are going to alter peace. I think men's minds are going to be changed in subtle ways because of automobiles; just how, though, I could hardly guess. But you can't have the immense outward changes that they will cause without some inward ones, and it may be. . . that the spiritual alteration will be bad for us.[46]

Today, about one out of every three adult Americans travels by air each year.[47] Even so, the automobile persists as the more dominant force in our lives because its use is more common. An intricate and pervasive network of roadways, resembling the circulatory system of the human body, directs the flow of our everyday lives. In addition, the automobile has altered our spatial and temporal perception of our physical environment. By enabling us to cover greater distances than by foot, it has brought familiar points closer together. And, by shortening the time between our origin and our desired destination, it has accelerated the speed at which we live on a daily basis.

A novel invention a century ago, the "horseless carriage" is today an integral component of American life. Nine out of ten American households have at least one automobile; five out of ten have two or more. In the thirty years between 1960 and 1990, the number of registered passenger cars and taxis in America more than doubled. Meanwhile, during the same period, the mileage covered by passenger cars in America nearly tripled. Today, approximately 88 percent of America's work force drives to work, 76 percent of them alone.[48]

In the light of these quantitative changes, we must ask whether our lives have been changed qualitatively as well. And, if so, whether for good or ill.

Have we, for example, surrendered something of value in exchange for moving at this greater speed and accepting its rate as natural to our existence? To be sure, the quality of our air has deteriorated because of auto emissions; but what of the quality of our lives? Certainly, expressways have made the abandonment of inner cities easier; but what else, of a personal nature, have we abandoned in the process. In short, do the values of a person used to traveling at 65 m.p.h. or more differ from those of a person whose life moves much more slowly? Such a question may seem foolish, but only if we assume our perceptions—unlike our bodies—are exempt from the long-term effects of time.

The effect of motion on equilibrium can be potent and long lasting. The seasick passenger on a rolling boat will suffer symptoms of seasickness even after he or she has stepped onto dry land. And riders on roller coasters carry with them the rush of the last plunge even after they have stepped off the car. We delude ourselves into thinking modes of transportation are merely instruments we employ. In actuality, we are participants in a psychological journey, at times turbulent, at times smooth, that affects us long after physical motion itself has ceased.

As drivers commuting in cars, we soon learn to ignore the boring "in between," the space intervening between the here and there of our lives. We tune out proximate reality, listening instead to drive-time radio, our minds literally attuned to a reality that is remote. We drive automatically, cultivating the skill of dissociation. As Jerry Mander has described it: "Humans who use cars sit in fixed positions for long hours following a narrow strip of gray pavement, with eyes fixed forward, engaged in the task of driving. As long as they are driving, they are living within what we might call roadform. Slowly they evolve into car-people."[49]

Some would argue that covering more ground exposes the speeding driver to more of what is real. But, ironically, the faster we go, the less we truly see. Speed insulates us from organic detail, and space becomes not homes, neighborhoods, and individual lives, but a disembodied medium through which we move. Though more is seen, less is observed, for the depth of our understanding is inversely proportionate to our velocity. Life itself in turn becomes one big "commute," devoid of that density that only caring and commitment can yield. Indeed, we become so inured to motion that our greatest stresses occur when our movement is impeded against our will—by a long check-out line, a traffic jam, a delayed flight—each a blunted by-product of society's quest for speed. Meanwhile, those who love to live in the fast lane curse the impediments in their path, never realizing that those impediments would never have existed if only they had chosen a lower speed.

Just as motion becomes its own justification, so its absence provokes a strange unease, leading many to feel restless when they are, in fact, at rest. As a result, some have recourse to journeys without destination, running—when they are not driving—just to keep on moving, even on an endless track.

As it turns out, Robert Frost's road "less traveled by" is the very one Americans habitually use.[50] As mobile journalist Charles Kuralt once put it: "The Interstate Highway System is a wonderful thing. It makes it possible to go from coast to coast without seeing anything or meeting anybody."[51]

The Rate of Exchange

Our society is characterized not only by the movement of people, but also by the movement of things. Motion is implicit in the notion of commerce, for motion takes place when things are exchanged. As the extent of commerce increases in a society, movement and change intensify. As a consequence, the tempo of a society quickens as its members respond, consciously or subconsciously, to the accelerated pace of commercial activity around them.

A series of inventions, both ancient and modern, have progressively speeded up the process of commercial exchange and with it the overall speed of society.

The system of exchange used for most of antiquity was barter, a cumbersome method of trading one object or commodity for another—cumbersome because each trading partner must not only have something the other wants, but must also have something he or she is willing to give up. Not only that, but these "somethings" must be portable and of equivalent worth. For example, my wanting your sheep will be of no use if there is not something else I possess that you would give it up for. Likewise, your wanting my bracelet will be of no use if I do not want what you can offer in trade.

However, as most families were self-sufficient and as few luxuries existed for common folk, there was no widespread need for a more efficient method of exchange. Except for the activities of traveling merchants who traded in commodities, economic exchanges tended to be few. The commercial pace of civilization was characteristically slow. Indeed, by its very nature, bartering inhibited a faster tempo.

The first steps in streamlining exchange were taken by merchants who realized that commerce could be speeded up by using portable tokens with universally accepted values. Such tokens could be made of precious metal, but some might be suspicious of how precious the metal really was. Consequently, the merchants stamped the lumps of metal with their seals to guarantee the tokens' weight and purity.

This system, however, had its own limitations, as a given merchant's reliability and reputation might only go so far. It is at this point in history—around 700 B.C.—that government took on the joint roles of manufacturer and guarantor, stamping the coins (for that is what we may now call them) with its own uniform seal.

Though coinage was first invented in the Turkish kingdom of Lydia, its power to quicken exchange and profit was soon recognized by the enterprising Greek merchants of the Turkish coast and Aegean islands. Greek city-states that were united by political alliance adopted similar denominations to make trading easier. Later, Alexander the Great's conquests helped to spread the concept of coinage through the Near Eastern world. Eventually, the Romans manufactured sufficient coins in mints worldwide to satisfy the economic needs of their imperial common market. All of these changes served to accelerate the pace of ancient commerce and, in turn, of ancient society.

Two later events heightened this acceleration: the manufacture of coins by machine (in the sixteenth century) and the introduction of paper money (in the seventeenth). These two relatively modern developments increased the amount of money in circulation, lubricating the engine of commerce and enabling it to run faster. Before this time, money had consisted almost exclusively of metal coins, struck by hand from dies, coins whose worth generally reflected the value of the metal they contained. Indeed, without the mass production of money, the materialistic revolution would not have been possible.

Today, commerce continues to accelerate because of developments in electronics. Though the invention of the cash register in 1879 shortened the time required to make a purchase, universal product-code (UPC) scanners contract it even more. Debit cards further expedite transactions by instantly arranging for the transfer of funds between buyer and seller. Another innovation, the stored-value card—already used at copying machines and pay phones—eliminates the need for taking out cash or getting change. Instead, a magnetic strip in the wallet-sized card is encoded with an initial cash balance that declines as purchases are made. Some day, in fact, the very idea of cash may be an anachronism.

These developments, however, come with a psychological price tag attached.

The more changes there are in our lives, the more our lives are characterized by change. But change does not simply mean getting married or starting a new job or moving to a different city. Change also exists on a microcosmic level, in small, everyday events that are so common we take them for granted and cease to notice them.

In a materialistic society like ours, commerce is a dominant activity. Every commercial transaction, no matter how small, involves exchanging one thing for another. To the extent that such exchanges fill up our lives, to that extent also are our lives influenced by them, for hidden in the word "exchange" is the concept of "change."

The greater the number of exchanges we make, the more inured to change we become. And the faster the rate of exchange, the more we perceive life as flux. Even the instruments of exchange have undergone progressive metamorphosis (from commodity to coin, from dollar bill to electronic impulse), losing more and more mass at each step.

Though matter itself continues to prevail in our lives, the physical nature of economic transactions is fading. Like a color wheel spinning faster and faster, colors that were once distinct blur into the extinguishing whiteness of now.

The credit card, first introduced in the 1950s and now used by 80 percent of America's families, compounds our disorientation by creating and sustaining the illusion that our income is elastic rather than finite.[52] The credit card is the ultimate passkey to materialistic pleasure, a key that ends all need to wait by granting instant entry to the kingdom of now.

Adaptive Commercial Strategies

Faced with a radical increase in the speed of commerce, business leaders have responded by devising new strategies to help them adapt to a world of rapid change. In some cases the strategies have meant acquiring new types of equipment and personnel. In other cases, entirely new products and services have rapidly evolved to meet the new needs of a fast-moving society. In many instances, circumstances have led to a fundamental rethinking of how business must be structured and conducted. Indeed, as the speedometer of social activity continues to climb, it becomes more and more certain that only those businesses geared to high speed and change will succeed. As Boston business consultant George Stalk, Jr., points out:

> Like competition itself, competitive advantage is a constantly moving target. . . . The best competitors, the most successful ones, know how to keep moving and always stay on the cutting edge.

Today, *time* is on the cutting edge. The ways leading companies manage time—in production, in new product development and introduction, in sales and distribution—represent the most powerful new sources of competitive advantage. . . .

In fact, as a strategic weapon, time is the equivalent of money, productivity, quality, even innovation.[53]

Management consultant Christopher Meyer, creator of the California Institute of Technology's public seminar on time-based competition, puts it more succinctly: Says Meyer: "Be fast or be last."[54]

High-speed commerce demands quick reflexes. Equipment must be state-of-the-art and swift; human resources, flexible and agile.

In manufacturing, the time-span between new-product design and production is being dramatically reduced through the use of 3–D computer simulations that eliminate the need for modeling and testing prototypes. Automotive and aeronautical parts, for example, can be tested for fit, stress, and vibration before they are ever made, thanks to innovative software. Meanwhile, virtual reality techniques permit car designers to "get inside" a new model and experience its interior layout before a single one is ever built. On the assembly line, computer-programmed robots can spot-weld faster than any human. Outside the factory, electronic data interchange has become critical for assembling facts, spotting trends, and transmitting orders. In fact, in retailing, says consultant Tom Peters, the three most important keys to success are "rapidly changing from location, location, location, to database, database, database."[55]

But because technologies themselves are undergoing rapid metamorphosis, hardware and software must be continually upgraded and changed. These technological developments, combined with tax advantages, have persuaded many companies to lease rather than own. Today, for example, expenditures for equipment leasing are approaching $200 billion a year.[56]

Human resources are likewise increasingly being leased. Today, across the nation, there are more than a million temporary employees on management as well as clerical payrolls. "Temps" are not just filling in for absent regulars; they are being called upon for tactical support to meet specialized needs. Says business consultant William Bridges: "As the pace of change accelerates, [permanent] jobs are becoming more and more dysfunctional. . . . That is why they are going away. We say that companies outsource work to save money. . . . But money's only part of the reason. Smart companies are doing these things to become more flexible and responsive."[57]

At the same time, companies are spinning off a panoply of time-sensitive products and services. Most of these have become so commonplace—cellular phones and pagers, microwave ovens and meals—that we fail to recognize how much our material culture has changed in just a few short years and how, in turn, our everyday lives have been speeded up.

Nothing may seem more ordinary than today's supermarket; yet every time we go into one we are entering a time machine for consumers crammed with a myriad of pre-picked, pre-washed, pre-cooked, pre-cut, and pre-wrapped products designed to save us time.[58] Outside the market with its instant food products, fast-food franchises abound. Indeed, the number of outlets has grown at four times the growth rate of America's population—from 90,000 restaurants in 1973 to over 180,000 in 1993.[59] Wendy's aims for accurate counter service in fifteen seconds, and another chain will give you your meal free if it takes more than a minute. Even traditional sit-down restaurants are joining the race, attracting lunch traffic by promising a free lunch if an order isn't served in fifteen minutes.

America is increasingly a society on the move, and what was once drive-*in* is increasingly becoming drive-*thru*. One funeral parlor even offers drive-thru visitation,[60] with the corpse laid out behind a glass window and a handy sign-in book within reach of the mobile bereaved.[61] A New Jersey church even offers express worship: a quick greeting, a short apology for sins, a brief statement of faith, a mini prayer, a little song, an abridged selection from Scripture, and a two-minute sermon. Says the pastor: "You give us 22 minutes and we'll show you the Kingdom of God."[62] Drive-thru banks, one-hour cleaners, half-hour film drops, overnight mail, quick oil-change stations, and express checkout at hotels are simply further testimonies to a culture on the go.[63]

Twenty million Americans—almost 20 percent of the country's full-time work force—now work at night.[64] To serve their needs and the needs of 9–to–5'ers who still can't find enough hours in the day for shopping and other errands, many businesses we frequent now offer their goods and services around the clock: from 24-hour restaurants and markets to all-night gas stations, pharmacies, photocopy centers, and automated banks. All these businesses not only profit from our shortage of time; at the same time they enable us to pack more into the time we have. And when we might otherwise have fallen asleep, round-the-clock TV programming—from comedy shows and old movies to late-breaking news—conspires to keep us awake.

In terms of equipment and personnel as well as products and services, time pressure is transforming commerce. But speed is also transforming the very way business does business. Two theories in particular have made an impact on business today: just-in-time (JIT) manufacturing and delivery and fast cycle time (FCT).[65] Inspired by a Japanese system called *kanban*, just-in-time manufacturing means "producing the minimum number of units in the smallest possible quantities at the latest possible time."[66] The immediate aim of JIT is to reduce inventories and, thereby, reduce any unnecessary investment in capital and labor in excess of actual demand. By efficiently making goods as needed and only as needed, a manufacturer can cut expenses and maximize profit. But in order to achieve such efficiency, a company must be acutely sensitive to consumer demand and be capable of immediately responding to its call. Low inventory also frees a company to modify its models quickly to make them more appealing. But once again, the company must be capable of instant response. Because of this, electronic communications are critical to the success of any JIT operation.

Fast cycle time, for its part, aims to increase a company's overall efficiency by eliminating time-wasting steps.[67] As FCT expert Christopher Meyer defines it: "Fast cycle time is achieved not by working faster, but by aligning the organization's purpose, strategy, and structure."[68] Increased speed is the inevitable by-product, however, once the form of an organization more efficiently expresses its proper function. And in a world short on time, potential customers will gladly pay a premium to get faster service. In keeping with this objective, outdoor clothier L.L. Bean recently awarded a multiyear contract to Federal Express to deliver 80 percent of its 10 million annual package shipments. To encourage efficiency, Federal Express itself has funded a Cycle Time Research Institute that is currently exploring further ways companies can economize on time.[69]

Improving efficiency in the workplace was espoused at the beginning of this century by Frederick W. Taylor.[70] Taylor believed that productivity could be increased by precisely measuring the optimal time it took to perform a task and then holding workers to this arbitrary standard. Taylor's philosophy of scientific management has been updated today with the help of the computer. Not only can computers perform certain tasks faster than humans; they can also compel humans to keep pace with them: the very word processors some operators use are designed to monitor and report their keystrokes covertly.[71]

Computerization is also being used to speed up operations in the pizza industry. Pizza Hut's goal, for example, is to take a new customer's phone order in a minute; a repeat customer's in thirty seconds. To achieve this goal, order-takers are instructed to control the conversation by using a prepared script. All the while, the order-taker's efficiency is being electronically timed. Meanwhile, the efficiency of drivers is gauged by their ability to deliver pizzas in a maximum of thirty minutes and return to the store in another eight. They clock out when they leave with orders and log back in when they return. Throughout, data from point-of-sale to delivery is being instantly fed to Pizza Hut's computerized national headquarters in Wichita, Kansas.[72]

Contemporary business practices are also being shaped by the very ideas of newness and speed. New products and services are not simply the result of progress; their very newness can serve as the basis for a sales campaign. In a society that is under the spell of now, newness has a magical appeal, for the new is the embodiment of the present. In a society where so much is evanescent, what's "in" is what counts. Advertisements may not even need to point out the advantages (if any) a new model has over an old. In a culture that lives by consuming the present, newness is one of an advertiser's most persuasive arguments. And if a product or service also embodies speed, the argument is even more compelling. Here are some examples of how contemporary advertising copy expresses the persuasive power of now.

"What's the Fastest Way to Get from Point A - to - Point B?" (Microsoft)

"Keeping the World Up to Speed" (McGraw-Hill)

"In the Time It Takes to Read this Headline, Intrepid Can Do 10 Million Things." (Dodge)

"You Have 12 Minutes to Make Changes on a Thousand Copies. Is Now a Good Time to Talk Copying Systems?" (Canon)

"I Want It On Time." (Federal Express)

"Double Time" (Hewlett Packard)

"NONSTOP" (South African Airways)

"Moving at the Speed of Business" (UPS)

"Moving at the Speed of Life" (Shell Oil)

"Of Course I'll Find Time to Think about Our Investments. As Soon As I Find Time To Think." (Fidelity)

"This Just Might Be the World's Fastest Shaver." (Wahl U.S.A.)

"Most moms don't have a lot of time in the morning. But it only takes 90 seconds to make Instant Quaker Oatmeal—so it's just as quick and easy as cold cereal." (Quaker Oats)

"Look This Great The Quick, Easy Way." (Fitness USA)

"O.K. Let's get down to business.[tm] 24 hours. That's all we get. And still for some, it's just not enough.... Make the call. Because after all, it's about time." (GTE)

"She Has Time for One Career, One Family, One Business Magazine." (*Business Week*)

"Steven Jacobs Just Had 12 Meetings in 5 Cities." (SkyTel)

"What Are *You* Waiting For? Life in the Fast Lane.... Enjoy All the Breathtaking Speed, Upgradability and Performance You'd Expect from a U.S. Robotics Courier. Courier.[tm] The Business Modem." (USRobotics)

"Today in business, fast is no longer fast enough. Even faster is still too slow to keep pace with the incredible demands placed on people and the computers they work with. That's one reason why IBM developed a Pentium chip computer so fast, so powerful, it makes today's conventional computers seem like they're moving at a snail's pace." (IBM)

"We Help Sell a Home Every Minute of Every Day." (Century 21)

"FORTUNE Magazine's 100 Fastest Growing Companies" (NASDAQ)

"How to Accelerate Your Job Search! FasTrak Connects You Directly with Top Employers Faster, Easier, and at Less Cost than Ever Before." (*The New York Times*)

"It's a Fast Paced World. Better Keep Up." (Audi)

"We Don't Want to Pressure You, but the World's Waiting." (Putnam Investments)

"The Future Is Erupting around Us. Seize It." (*Hardwired*)

"How Fast Are You Going?" (Chrysler)

If you felt your pulse rate increase as you read through these ads, you've already experienced one of the effects of exposure to such advertising: it revs us up, previewing for us the overstimulation the products and services themselves deliver.

Collectively, they overstimulate us not only because of their speed but also because of their multiplicity and mutability. As a consequence, our material culture is in constant flux, and we are psychologically caught up in its swift current. This situation is attributable in large part to the acceleration of manufacturing processes that have radically shortened the time needed for product development.[73] The shortening of product-development time has, in turn, radically shortened the life expectancy of new products entering the marketplace, in some cases from six years to only six months or less. Thus, as new products tumble off the assembly line, they push old products off the shelves, changing what Tom Peters calls "the whole metabolism of the economy."[74]

Going to our neighborhood supermarket, we find 49 separate varieties of juice; 105 kinds of bottled salad dressing; 190 kinds of cereal; and 253 kinds of cookies.[75] One year alone saw the introduction of 574 new salty snacks.[76] In the forthright words of one stressed-out shopper: "And they want to know why people have their brains scrambled? You're just bombarded with so many things that you can't even think."[77]

Which is exactly what many shoppers can't do, or choose not to. Faced with a multiplicity of options, many go with the products they're used to. While shopping, they learn to close their eyes. There are just too many breakfast cereals, too many cookies, too many everything. They have become victims of "choice anxiety," or what David Heim, managing editor of *Consumer Reports* has called "panic in the potato chip aisle."[78] Paradoxically, they are also the victims of plenty. And while the failure rate for new grocery products is high (about 85 percent), just because products fail doesn't mean they weren't seen. Their very appearance and disappearance reinforces in the mind of shoppers the nagging sense of transience that oozes from all the other corners of their lives. Indeed, some valuable products are never given the chance to succeed if they don't "catch on" fast.[79]

Nor is it any better for managers or entrepreneurs. Like greyhounds in pursuit of a mechanical rabbit, they chase the tails of JIT and FCT, so focused on short-term gains that they may lose sight of a more distant goal, so driven by speed that they can lose their capacity for long-term planning. It is to this danger that Barry Diller referred when he warned fellow executives of "this unthinking pursuit of the magic formula that clouds our very ability to think clearly. . . . It used to be that there was a cadence, a rhythm to things. . . . I do believe the acceleration of daily life, this confusing mad rush to get ahead of the future, is eroding our ability at the most critical time to gather together the building blocks to do the real and necessary work of new product creation."[80]

People in business, after all, are not immune to the power of now and its ability to distort a person's judgment, least of all those who trade in speed every day. Nor is the environment of business likely to slow down. As John R. Walter, president of AT&T says: "We used to make changes in business according to this command: Ready. Aim. Fire! Today, the command has to be: Fire. Aim. Fire. Aim. Fire. Aim! You Fire in order to aim. Fire a burst. See what happens. Make corrections. Fire another burst. Build speed into everything you do and measure yourself against the speed of the world around you."[81]

Adds Tom Peters:

> The pace of commerce is, in my opinion, going to continue to move in the direction it is moving in now—that is, faster and faster. And so the issue is not do we *choose* to be faster; the issue is the genies are only barely out [of the bottle] and you ain't going to stuff them back in. That's your competitive world, ladies and gentlemen, like it or lump it. . . . I'm advocating speed not because I think it is a good idea. I'm advocating speed because all the forces at work seem to be pushing in that direction and how can you escape it?[82]

As we have seen, speed has become the sole value that justifies the existence of whole products, services, industries—the defining value that makes people turn to them and depend upon them. The most important question for the future will be whether speed should also become the sole value that defines our social existence. If we accept its inevitability, as Peters does, we will have acceded to its right to rule our lives.

THE SYNCHRONOUS SOCIETY

A new type of society is emerging under the influence of electronic interconnectivity and instancy, a synchronous society.[83] In such a society, people are not separated from one another by barriers of space and time, but coexist synergistically and achieve their effectiveness by intimate collaboration. The synchronous society is a mass society whose component parts are integrated, like those of an electronic circuit, by neural networks of communication that link marketplace to home and home to workplace. Mass communication in such a society does not simply provide information; it is the necessary product of a connected mentality that requires instantaneous information to sustain itself.

To get a mental picture of such a society and its operation, the reader might imagine what a metropolitan expressway system would look like from high in the air when traffic is flowing smoothly and efficiently. This imaginary view can be enhanced by picturing the scene again from the air, but at evening, when the cars would appear in the growing darkness as smoothly and regularly moving dots of light tracing luminous patterns— now straight, now gracefully curving—on the earth's surface below.

There is an undeniable beauty in such a sight (more real, perhaps, for the spectator who can see the whole than for the participant), a beauty that—along with synchronism's inductive pull—may account for its seductive appeal. It is a beauty perhaps not unlike that of glowing impulses of light coursing through the glass filaments of fiber-optic cable, or of electrons speeding silently through a silicon maze.

At the same time, however, the synchronous highway offers no off-ramps to the weary traveler, no shoulders for emergency stops. For its speed and flow make it intolerant of delay. After we have bidden farewell to the dirt roads, narrow streets, and stoplights of an earlier and slower world, the synchronous highway carries us along but requires a higher spiritual toll than we may someday be willing to pay.

The Erosion of Privacy

The rise of instantaneous mass communications by dissolving borders of space and time promotes the growth of a unified societal consciousness.

But the existence of such a consciousness, though it facilitates the life of a society, constitutes a profound threat to the privacy of the individual.

On purely physical grounds, the establishment of an electronic network diminishes the possibility of isolation, for the interconnection of society's various components eliminates the barriers that kept them apart. As walls of separation, visible and invisible, yield to social fusion, the potential for solitude is diminished. As identities are universally linked, privacy—"the right to be let alone, the most comprehensive of rights"[84]—tends to shrivel, not only for celebrities, whose private lives automatically become public property, but for the rest of us as well.

Today, innovative instruments and services, growing in sophistication and popularity, permit more and more people to stay in contact. The cellular phone, whether in a car or on the street, symbolically breaks down walls and gives total mobility to communication. E-mail dissolves the distance that once separated office from home. Personal 800-number service now offers callers free access to our ear, while personal 900-number service provides a universal lifetime telephone number at which we can be reached no matter where we move. Combined with globally accessible pocket pagers and electronic transmitters that constantly monitor and signal our whereabouts, we need never be out of touch—or out of reach.[85]

Privacy does not refer only to the physical isolation of the individual, however; it refers also to the inner sanctum of an individual's personal feelings, preferences, thoughts, and experiences. This intangible sanctuary can likewise be violated by electronic linkage. As the technology becomes ever more penetrating and intrusive, it becomes possible to gather information with laserlike specificity and with spongelike absorbency.[86]

As systems of intercommunication draw upon reservoirs of personal information and interact, facts that were once discreet are digested, assimilated, and synthesized by the social organism to help it perpetuate its life. Like some science fiction monster that feeds on electricity, society thrives on such synergy, and invites us to give it more.

Economic convenience is society's most seductive inducement. To make our lives easier, we become accomplices in our own betrayal, dutifully surrendering our privacy in order to participate fully in society's system of economic rewards. Indeed, the commercial requirements of society present major disincentives to functioning in any other way. To obtain credit, we must disclose our lives. Without established credit, we are looked upon as poor risks. And in a society that lives by credit, poor credit is tantamount to death.

The net effect is that we create "datashadow":[87] "the trail each of us leaves behind in our computer-recorded actions and transactions, electronic footfalls that are then combined with others and stored for future use and sale, often by direct marketers and often without our consent and knowledge."[88] Separate databases already exist (in government agencies, schools, libraries, hospitals, doctor's offices, manufacturing companies [remember those friendly warrantee cards?], credit companies, and banks) that reflect almost every aspect of our everyday lives, and continuous efforts are being made to combine them into more comprehensive, nation-wide systems. As an electronic expression of the power of now, these databases are instantly responsive (and vulnerable) to requests for infor-mation about almost every aspect of our personal lives—from our gross annual income and how many TV sets we own to the diseases we've had and the books we tend to read. Though database networks currently exist by category only ("health" or "credit," for example), efforts are under way to integrate them into a single, nationwide supernetwork.

Unlike a number of European countries, the United States has no gov-ernment agency mandated to guard against the unauthorized accessing and use of computerized records. Though the Fourth Amendment in the Bill of Rights ("the right of the people to be secure in their persons, houses, *papers*, and effects, against unreasonable searches and seizures. . . ") could be construed as guaranteeing this protection, its phrasing is an anachro-nism from a pre-electronic age. "It protects the places where private infor-mation used to be, but not the places where it is today."[89]

We thus risk losing control over our private lives, not because of the malevolent policies of a dictator, or even (more realistically) because of the mercenary interests of computer spies, but because of the fundamental structure of a mass society that demands the existence of an advanced, instantaneously responsive neurological system to insure its efficient op-eration and survival.

As we bob up and down in these dangerous waters, some warn us of schools of database parañas that will nibble our privacy away. Still others, fearing that political waters can change from fresh to salt, warn us of the bite of the totalitarian shark. But few discern the long-term danger of exposure itself, of that prolonged exhaustion that comes to welcome the billows as comforting arms and death as a surcease from struggle. As a result, we may die not from assault but from acquiescence.

The whole issue of privacy assumes far less importance, however, if we assume people will have little to be private about. If the widespread dominance of materialism and mass-media imagery produces a leveling of consciousness and aspiration, individualized thinking will decline, and, to that degree, the need to discover it will become redundant. Just as credit was once localized (in the downtown department store or the corner grocery) but ultimately became both centralized and national (in Visa, Mastercard, and Discover), so may opinion in an electronic age tend toward uniformity. This is not to say there will not be differences of opinion. But they will all represent mere varieties of the same universal premise, not unlike the varied colors, designs, and logos of the credit card itself.

Meanwhile, throughout the societal landscape, a creeping electrolysis will suffuse former sanctuaries of the self as cell phones chirp in dining rooms and pagers beep in the concert hall, reminding us we can never be alone.

Conformity

Connectedness is the most essential feature of a synchronous system, for only if things work together and at the same time, will synchronism be achieved. As a corollary, whatever is incongruous to the system and its efficient operation will be discouraged or rejected. In society, therefore, synchronism tends to produce conformity, but it is a conformity of structure rather than of substance. Since mutability is at the very core of a synchronous system, popular beliefs and behaviors will not necessarily remain constant. For, in a synchronous society, the specifics of what people think and do is less critical than the fact that they think and do them simultaneously.

Because incongruity is fundamentally alien to such a society, synchronism tends to have a leveling effect. This leveling applies not only to what people will think but to the very nature of reality itself, as society controls— by inclusion or exclusion—the content of what people regard as real. Ethnic uniqueness will be tolerated, but only to the degree that its vestiges lend superficial variety to an otherwise uniform landscape. Meanwhile, politically correct changes in language will be enforced in order to create the egalitarian illusion that actual differences between people have ceased to exist. Day and night, television will transmit the same commercial images nationwide, while radio will broadcast voices purified of regional accent.

Because a nowist culture always appreciates the evanescent, public fascination with mass-marketed novelties (human or otherwise) will always be socially acceptable. But these will only distract the audience from contemplating society's deeper premises. Instead, the faces of celebrities will abound, only to be replaced later by others who are equally ephemeral.[90]

Conformism itself is no invention of our own times. What is new is the temporal dynamics of conformism today. For it is not anchored in a finite set of socially sanctioned beliefs and values, but drifts and spins from one curving emotional current to another; not enforced by rigid and arbitrary authority, but induced by the seductions of solipsistic pleasure through an electronic linkage of thoughts and sensibilities that instantly reaches into the most private parts of people's lives, transforming their very notion of the limits and contours of reality.

It is a conformism that precludes rebellion, because in order to rebel one must know what one is rebelling against. The prisoner who does not know he is in prison will not seek to escape. All that is necessary to dissuade him is sufficient comfort and the illusion of free choice.

Anything, however, that truly resists absorption into the synchronous whole will be called subversive. The old neighborhood that blocks the building of a new manufacturing plant, the wilderness tract that forestalls the spread of condominiums—each is a spatially and temporally subversive entity that, by holding steadfast to the past, challenges the authority of now. Marked for demolition also are America's traditional institutions— of government, religion, and school—because they embody the durative aspect of human experience as opposed to the instantaneous. Such institutions have historically measured contemporary behavior against the fixed standards of the past, whether those standards are enshrined in a constitution, a Bible, or a grammar. The authority of these institutions, however, is weak and suspect today not because of the specific beliefs they embody as much as because they embody specificity itself. As such, and because they smack of the past, they have become alien to popular taste. In effect, the quicksilver flux of our culture, electrified by technology, has degaussed what Antoine de Saint-Exupéry once termed the invisible "lines of force" without which our lives cease to have magnetic definition and formal direction.[91]

The fate that has befallen traditional institutions has of course befallen tradition itself. The attacks of multiculturalists against Western culture are motivated not only by the perceived narrowness of academic canons but also by the temporal exclusivity of a curriculum that assigns a higher value to the past than the present. To contemporist eyes, all works that are not of the present blend together into a single meaningless anachronistic mass. Thus, Don Quixote joins Aeneas and Faust in the same common melting pot of time.

Ironically, teachers of modern languages now face a problem once known only to teachers of Latin and ancient Greek: the accusation that literature is irrelevant. Once restaurant French and tourist Spanish are left behind, teachers of modern languages must admit that the writings of their older authors are as antiquated to their students as those of Homer and Vergil. Those who teach "living" languages and those who teach "dead" languages now find themselves standing together on a common battleground as the circle of conflict and temporal devastation grows wider. For it is tradition itself that has become alien, and the past has become a foreign language.

HYPERCULTURE

Accelerated by an expanding electronic technology, society's velocity grows ever faster. As more and more of its instruments approximate the speed of light, society itself is drawn into light's higher speed, as though obedient on a social level to that principle of fluid dynamics known as Bernoulli's Law.

Seeking to understand the behavior of fluids, the eighteenth century Swiss mathematician Daniel Bernoulli found that as the speed of a moving fluid increases, it tends to attract or draw to itself an adjacent fluid that is stationary or moving more slowly. Transferred from the world of fluid mechanics to the world of social dynamics, Bernoulli's Law helps to explain the origin and behavior of a synchronous society. A rapidly moving social phenomenon, for example, would tend to draw into its stream other phenomena that move more slowly. Thus, an acceleration in the rate of one societal activity would tend to induce acceleration in tangent activities. In instances of such contact, the greater speed would tend to prevail. Faster transportation would tend to raise the speed of transportation elsewhere; faster communication, the speed of communication overall; and both in collaboration, the average speed of everyday life.

To those in a society who yield to such speed, who "go with the flow," would come the peace of belonging. To those who resist, or who are incapable of moving faster, would go unremitting stress.

As more and more people are drawn into the electronic stream, they become assimilated into a modality of time characteristic neither of the organic world (with its cycles of renewal and death) nor of the mechanical one (with its linear progression from assembly to disintegration). Instead, they take on the characteristics of suborganic matter, the atomic world of electrons, protons, and neutrons, a world with no perceptible future or past, whose particles mindlessly whirl at the speed of light in a luminous now that is everlasting.

The societal change we are witnessing is the prelude to an act of mutation made possible by advanced technology: the mating of humankind with the primal essence of the subatomic world. This mutation may represent the back-sweeping arc of a great orbit, an orbit that began with atoms yielding primordially to life and self-awareness, life that later organized itself into civilization, ultimately inventing the very mechanisms that now cause it to return to its timeless source—like a comet that, having arced around the sun, now swings homeward back into the darkness of outer space.

Compared to this hypnotic act of self-immolation, our scientific efforts to split and fuse the atom may seem as primitive and naive as prehistoric man's first attempts to make fire. For our nuclear manipulations were always predicated on the assumption that the atom was an entity separate from ourselves. But the electronic world we now play with is one that magnetically leads us into its own logic and its own temporal law, drawing us into oneness with its inner nature.

For decades, two historic lines have been converging: the line on which man is becoming more like the machine and the line on which the machine is becoming more like man. In physical terms, the first line reflects achievements in bionics and prosthetics (the artificial heart, the artificial limb—each incorporated into a living being). The second reflects achievements in robotics and artificial intelligence, which implant patterns of human action and thought into devices made by man. Eventually, when these two lines intersect, it will be difficult to distinguish man from machine—and machine from man.

The realization that bodily systems operate electrochemically long ago led to the use of external current to renew or regularize the rhythm of the human heart or, more crudely, to shock the emotions into harmony. In the future, the organic integration of human brain and computer (not unlike the integration of heart and pacemaker) may lead to a new level of intellectual power. Today, in fact, such critical evolutionary changes are already taking place as humanity adapts socially to the superhuman velocity of the technology it has implanted in its soul.[92]

Until a true bionic metamorphosis takes place, society will race ever faster, more and more compulsively focused on the moment. Because of its hyperactivity, we may speak of it as a hyperculture, a pathological cultural state induced by high speed.

A hyperculture is a culture that is easily bored and readily distracted, one in which entertainment is transformed from an occasional personal and group diversion to a way of life, occupying all the interstices between periods of work. Quickly exhausting its energy reserves, a hyperculture continually demands refuelling. Rejecting the acquisition of perspective as necessarily too time-intensive an activity, it craves instead to be injected with doses of short-term stimulation. For the hyperculture is a society of "busy bodies," frenetically striving to keep up, not simply out of economic necessity but out of psychological preference.[93] Time—unstructured, unused—hangs heavily on its head. It may demand relief from specific tasks, but soon fills the vacuum of inertia with even more activity.

Strikingly, these behavioral characteristics recall those of the "type A" personality, described in the 1960s and 1970s by cardiologists Meyer Friedman and Ray H. Rosenman.[94] The "Type A Behavior Pattern" is "a particular complex of personality traits, including excessive competitive drive, aggressiveness, impatience, and a harrying sense of time urgency. Individuals displaying this pattern seem to be engaged in a chronic, ceaseless, and often fruitless struggle—with themselves, with others, with circumstances, with time, sometimes with life itself. They also frequently exhibit a free-floating but well-rationalized form of hostility, and almost always a deep-seated insecurity."[95] In short, type As are victims of what Friedman and Rosenman call "hurry sickness," a condition statistically linked to a higher than normal incidence of heart disease.

Significantly, "type A individuals both seek and create time-urgent environments."[96] Not only do they feel at home in fast-paced cities, they deliberately sustain the pace. Research suggests that "the temporal expectations of fast-paced cities demand time-urgent behavior in all people—type A's and [the more relaxed] type B's. The result is that type B individuals come to act more like type A's, while type A's strive to accelerate the pace still more."[97] As though obedient to Bernoulli's Law, those who are slower are sucked into the faster stream, even as the stream itself picks up momentum.

There is a marked difference, however, between type As and the hyperculture they inhabit. We live in a society where high speed is reinforced by a pervasive technology. Because a synchronous society chiefly rewards those who "go with the flow," true type As stand out as anomalies. Though they share a love of speed with the rest of society, their very individualism puts them at cross-purposes with their culture. As a result, they suffer a sense of personal entrapment. As psychiatrist Lawrence Van Egeren observes, "It is precisely the poor fit of Type A behavior to the current reward system that makes it behaviorally maladaptive and psychologically damaging."[98] Thus, even as type As struggle to speed things up—and speed up others in the process, they pay a premium price in body and mind.

The rest of us pay a price too—simply because of our membership in a high-speed society—a price measured out in stress and the breakdown of human relationships. There is a human cost to speed, and it is a cost none of us can escape. The centrifugal force that is disintegrating the American family is also disintegrating the very structure of American society. The higher the speed, the harder it will be to stop.

Chapter 6

The Transformation of Democracy

THE TRANSFORMATION of American society as a whole is evident in the progressive transformation of its institutions. In chapter 4 we observed how the American family is changing under the influence of high speed. Such change is also evident in another American institution, democracy.

Government has always been a creature of time. Though its laws may attempt to concretize time by establishing fixed standards of conduct, those very laws are frequently revised in response to new circumstances and events. The face of government also changes as new leaders arise. Indeed, over the long course of history, the very forms of government have changed by evolution or revolution.

While all forms of government embody some degree of change, democracy is peculiarly vulnerable to its influences because democracy reflects the potentially unstable moods and variable sentiments of a large populace, especially in a country where democracy itself is relatively new.

This susceptibility was detected by an acutely observant French tourist named Alexis de Tocqueville, who visited America over a century and a half ago. In *Democracy in America* he wrote:

> Nothing is less suited to meditation than the structure of democratic society. . . . Everyone is in motion, some in quest of power, others of gain. In the midst of this universal tumult, this inces-

sant conflict of jarring interests, this continual striving of men after fortune, where is that calm to be found which is necessary for the deeper combinations of the intellect? How can the mind dwell on any single point when everything whirls around it, and man himself is swept and beaten onwards by the heady current that rolls all things in its course?

A democratic state of society and democratic institutions keep the greater part of men in constant activity. . . . The man of action is frequently obliged to content himself with the best he can get because he would never accomplish his purpose if he chose to carry every detail to perfection. He has occasion perpetually to rely on ideas that he has not had leisure to search to the bottom . . . and in the long run he risks less in making use of some false principles than in spending his time in establishing his principles on the basis of truth. The world is not led by long and learned demonstrations; a rapid glance at particular incidents, the daily study of the fleeting passions of the multitude, the accidents of the moment, and the art of turning them to account decide all its affairs.[1]

Tocqueville recognized that democracy encourages mobility because it gives its citizens political and economic freedom. In a democratic society, he noted, "everyone is in motion." But as he also noted, this very mobility tends to weaken democracy. Because a hurried life leaves little time for thoughtful reflection, citizens in a hurried society may lack the knowledge and perspective they need to make wise political decisions.

What Tocqueville sensed in the America of the 1830s is all the more true today because of the increased speed at which our lives are moving. Some would argue, however, that this apparent weakness is more than made up for by today's communications systems whose range and speed give citizens the information they need to act responsibly. In this chapter we will examine this argument as we explore the nature of citizenship in an electronic commonwealth.[2]

INFORMATIONAL DEPENDENCY

"Sunny today," declares the radio announcer, ensconced in his windowless broadcast booth. But outside, even as he speaks, the rain falls.

Even if the weather report does not mirror the weather, it does reflect the script the announcer holds in his hand. If only he had stepped outside for a moment, he could have saved himself the embarrassment of telling his audience what most of them could see was untrue. But his perception of the weather was limited to the periphery of his own sensory experience. Because he had no window to look through, he had to depend on second-hand information, information all the more convincing because he held it in his hand. The announcer's problem, however, is a problem all of us face as members of a large and complex society.

In the dim mists of prehistory when the earliest human societies arose, human needs were basic and simple, and most were met by the individual himself or the small group to which he belonged, the family or tribe: hunting, fishing, and gathering edible plants; making shelter and clothing; building a campfire. Hundreds of thousands of years later, the earliest civilizations arose in fertile river valleys, where the richness of the environment and its bounty created a surplus of food. This surplus promoted a specialization of labor in which individuals, no longer struggling to meet the needs of their own personal survival, exchanged the products of their special talents for the essentials of life.

Such complex societies were characterized not so much by self-reliance as by interdependence. In large settlements, whole classes of specialists arose: priests and poets, soldiers and shoemakers, potters and musicians. Out of such specialization were born civilizations of great variety that offered their members new sources of stimulation and the benefits of a rich material culture.

Over the course of thousands of years, more technologically advanced cultures arose in which vocational specialization was even more pronounced. In our own culture, for example, there exists a myriad of occupational categories and subcategories. The technological power we possess as a civilization may well lead us to conclude that our culture is stronger than any that has ever existed. While that may be true on the national level, it is not true on the individual one. The very interdependence that explains the strength of our economy makes the security of our personal lives more fragile. To the degree that we are economically dependent upon others, to that degree our personal future is at risk.

The prehistoric cave man could survive against great natural odds. To be sure, our sports cars and big screen color televisions would put his primitive life-style to shame. But thrust into the same situation, alone for example in an icy wilderness, we would not know how to survive. Should the sustaining structure of our civilization collapse, we would not be able to produce for ourselves the necessary things we daily take for granted.[3] We could not make gasoline to run our car, generate power for heat and light, or secure enough food and clean water to provide for our most basic needs. We would, in short, die, specialized out of existence like creatures so refined by breeding that they lack the stamina and resilience to sustain themselves.

But our dependency as members of a civilization is not limited only to the requirements for our physical survival. It applies also to the requirements for our intellectual survival. For, like the announcer trapped in the windowless studio, we depend upon others for the information we need.

The more complex the life of a society, the greater the need of its members for information. But the very size of that society means most of that information will come second-hand.

To be sure, we know far more about the world than did the cave man. But what he knew, he knew first-hand.

The abundant information we receive is purchased at a price: the price of dependency upon others for the truth. As a society expands, it becomes less and less possible for its members to know first-hand all the things essential to their lives. Hence, they depend upon others.

As first-hand experience diminishes in proportion to second-hand information, the sense of reality becomes less an integer and more a fraction. Ages ago it may have been a thousand elements of personal experience to one element of information; eventually it became one of personal experience to a thousand of information. As a consequence of fractionated experience, the individual loses what was once a firm grip on his life. Information replaces actuality.

Thus, the age of communication is also paradoxically an age of vulnerability. In a society highly dependent upon communication, the individual is more than ever before susceptible to the quality of information he receives and, thus, can be more readily managed by others than in a society where less needs to be communicated. In short, our life comes down to this: we are what we are told and shown. For it is mostly from the data we are presented with that we construct our mental picture of reality.

The questions a society asks will ultimately depend upon the reality it acknowledges. In short, before any problem can be addressed, people must first realize it exists.

Selective Data

It is not simply the accuracy of society's sources that is at issue, for implicit in every source of information there is also an unseen process of selection. Though the masthead of *The New York Times* proudly proclaims "All the news that's fit to print," it is an empty boast, for no newspaper would ever have enough space to narrate all the events that took place on a given day, assuming it even knew they happened. Instead, a selection must be made by editors whose job it is to decide what is "newsworthy" and what is not. But newsworthy to whom? And for what reason? Indeed, what does it truly mean to say something is "fit to print?" An event you or I might regard as important might be of no interest to someone else. Should a story then be printed only if it will appeal to a wide audience? Should a story of narrower interest be excluded? Such questions are not merely academic since the selection of data can be as significant as factual accuracy in shaping a society's consciousness. A nation, for example, may be willing to go to war if it is informed its territory has been attacked or its vital interests threatened. It may be less willing, however, if it learns that its own forces provoked the attack. However accurate a particular piece of information may be, it can be misleading if the full story is not told.

But how "full" should a story be? Certainly, full enough so we are not misled. And who should decide? Certainly, any reasonable person and, in the case of the media, the reporter and/or editor. It is, we might say, a matter of editorial judgment.

And so it would be if all media were the same. But each medium has its own special strengths and its own weaknesses. Television, by bringing us instantly to the scene of breaking news, gives us visual immediacy. Newspapers, by gathering facts and opinions, give us grounds for reflection. Ideally, in a society, the strength of one medium should complement the weakness of the other.

A synchronous society, however, thrives not on reflection but on stimulation; not on the past tense but the vivid present. It is for this reason more than any other that newspaper after newspaper have merged for survival or simply shut down. For in an electronic cultural environment, print media operate at a distinct psychological disadvantage.[4]

After tracking newspaper readership, a University of Maryland study concluded: "The decline in newspaper reading over the last three decades has been one of the steadiest and most pronounced trends in the free-time behavior of the American public." In 1946, before the age of television, 85 percent of American adults said they had "read a newspaper yesterday." By 1965 the percentage had fallen to 73 percent. By 1985 it had dropped to 55 percent.[5] Though daily newspaper circulation has remained fairly constant ever since, another critical change has taken place: a decrease in the number of newspapers in existence. While at the turn of the century there were more than two newspapers in most major American cities, today only forty U.S. cities have competing papers.[6] Such a decrease in competitive journalism means a decrease in opposing editorial viewpoints and story angles and a consequent decrease in the perspective they could provide to readers in a democracy.

Journalism and Now

In today's media world, it is the power of now rather than perspective that is all-pervasive. Comments journalist Mark Hertsgaard: "So much of what is problematic about our news media coverage comes from its insistent focus on now, now, now. If something happened two days ago the media do not care about it."[7]

Essayist Sven Birkerts agrees:

> One of the most telling effects of the electronic media has been
> the creation of a persuasive sense of an eternal present, a now.

So powerful is the hold of the image and the rapid-shift sequence, so mesmerizing the juxtaposition of contents, that the
watcher is gradually seduced away from causal/historical habits of mind. The structure of programming allows absolutely no
time for absorption or reflection. Hour after hour the world's
montage is rushed past our eyes. . . .

With a steady collage of the past flowing by us on our screens,
we find ourselves planted—marooned—in the now. We have not
only lost our grip on real history, on the past shaping the present,
but we have also lost any vital sense of the future. The possibili-
ties are so unnerving, our awareness of our lack of control so
paralysing, and the diet of present-tense stimulus so addicting
that we look no further into the calendar than the time we have
circled for our next vacation.[8]

Birkerts' remarks are those of a television observer, but his perceptions
match those of journalists working in television. Commenting on TV's
coverage of political campaigns, NBC news anchor Tom Brokaw says:

The news cycle has become a 24-hour-a-day thing, and it moves
very fast all the time now. What happens is that a fragment of
information, true or false, gets sucked into the cycle early in the
morning, and once it gets into the cycle it gets whipped round
to the point that it has gravitas by the end of the day. And,
unfortunately, people are so busy chasing that fragment of information that they treat it as a fact, forgetting about whether it
is true or not.[9]

Like a whirlwind, then, television draws all things into its vortex,
blurring the line between fact and fiction.

Reporter Lesley Stahl agrees. Electronic speed, she believes, can lead to
irresponsible journalism.

Journalism hasn't caught up with the technology we're using.
You can throw a guy on the air live. You haven't any thought, in
your own mind, about what you're going to do once he opens
his mouth. We don't check anything out until it's out there. And
once it's out there, the talk show hosts get it and the tabloids get
it and then we say, "Oh my God, we're being forced to run
that."[10]

Such speed, however, characterizes the television industry as a whole,
as NBC president, Robert C. Wright, points out: "We have tried to stay

ahead of the curve to make changes we anticipated we need to make before we are banged over the head. But the world is moving very quickly. If we are running at 8 miles an hour, the world is running at 12. That's very tricky."[11]

Comparing print with electronic media, critic Neil Postman persuasively argues that electronic media in general and television in particular create a "decontextualized information environment."[12] By facilitating the instantaneous flow of data, electronic media extract fact after fact from their original contexts and transmit them seriatim, changing a holistic fabric into disjointed quanta that bombard the recipient as separate impulses of energy. Describing the inception of these media, Postman says:

> Theirs was a "language" that denied interconnectedness, proceeded without context, argued the irrelevance of history, explained nothing, and offered fascination in place of complexity and coherence. Theirs was a duet of image and instancy. . . .
>
> This ensemble of electronic techniques called into being a new world—a peek-a-boo world, where now this event, now that, pops into view for a moment, then vanishes again. It is a world without much coherence or sense; a world that does not ask us, indeed, does not permit us to do anything; a world that is, like the child's game of peek-a-boo, entirely self-contained. But like peek-a-boo, it is also endlessly entertaining.[13]

Preferring short-term stimulus to long-term reflection, a synchronous audience takes delight in this titillation of its senses and revels in trivia that masquerade as meaning. As a result, the reporting of reality is itself trivialized. According to journalist Robert MacNeil, the aim of television news has been "to keep everything brief, not to strain the attention of anyone but instead to provide constant stimulation through variety, novelty, action, and movement. You are required . . . to pay attention to no concept, no character, and no problem for more than a few seconds at a time."[14] News programming like this presumes viewers with a short attention span who fitfully graze and are easily bored—a presumption that may well be based on reality. As Lesley Stahl observes: "My colleagues in prime time tell me they have what they call minute-by-minute tracking and if they're doing a story on a foreign leader, for instance, the audience goes away and then they click back to see if the next story is more interesting."[15]

To fill what would otherwise be a vacuum, television news needs stories; and to keep its audience watching, it needs entertaining ones. As a medium based on pictures, it gravitates toward stories that are primarily visual and sensory, rather than cerebral and intellectual. Channels aggressively compete with one another in offering fleeting stimulation, vying for our attention by emphasizing sensationalism in the choice and treatment of subjects, presenting—in the words of veteran Detroit TV newsman Jim Herrington—"a menu of crime, sex, and animal stories."[16] Conditioned to such stories, an audience soon comes to expect sensationalistic news, sensationalistic sports, and even sensationalistic weather. Stories fast become boring and yield their air-time to others, not because they have ceased to be important, but merely because they have ceased to be interesting. A perverse but relentless egalitarianism soon reduces all facts, important and unimportant, to the same level, magnifying the trivial and trivializing the significant. In an electronic marketplace crowded with stalls of informational merchandise, vendors cry "Buy mine! Buy mine!" striving to outshout one another in a rising crescendo of hype that ultimately desensitizes the hearer to all but the loudest voices.

In a fast-moving world, it is perspective, more than anything else, that a person and a society needs—the perspective that lets one distinguish the significant from the trivial, the enduring from the transient, the true from the false. Such perspective is at the very heart of what it means to be truly informed, and being truly informed is at the very heart of democracy. As Thomas Jefferson long ago warned: "If a nation expects to be ignorant and free, in a state of civilization, it expects what never was and never will be."[17]

Yet in the time-compressed world of electronic media, sound bites are readily substituted for discourse. In fact, the sound bites themselves have been getting shorter.[18] According to a study by Harvard University researcher Kiku Adatto, the average block of uninterrupted speech by presidential candidates on the evening news in 1968 was 42.3 seconds long. Twenty years later, it had shrunk to only 9.8 seconds.[19] To counter this trend in 1992, CBS News announced it would give presidential candidates 30 seconds of uninterrupted coverage, but soon retreated. Said ABC's Peter Jennings: "It's sort of arbitrary to give every candidate 30 seconds. . . Candidates now don't talk in 30-second sound bites. They talk in 12–second sound bites, 9-second sound bites."[20] Jennings' remarks among other things reveal how sound-bite journalism affects candidates: if they want to get on TV, they have to avoid complexity. Simplistic statements, however, and simplistic thinking can be dangerous to a nation's life.

Superficiality notwithstanding, television's aura of immediacy lends it great authority. A nowist society places a premium on instantaneous communication. As a result, the information systems at our disposal tell us what we need to know far faster than we could learn for ourselves. That efficiency, in turn, leads us to respect their authority and accuracy more so than other sources of knowledge, more than even our own personal experience. Former president Richard Nixon put it best. Watergate, he said, hadn't hurt him until the Senate hearings were televised. "The American people don't believe anything's real until they see it on television," he observed.[21]

The realism of a visual image, its fidelity to lifelike appearance (as opposed to the abstract quality of the printed word), gives to a pictorial medium a persuasive power that other media lack. The vitality of a colorful televised image may actually transcend its artificiality or combine with it to produce in the viewer a condensed emotional impact greater than that which the event itself, being more diffuse, could ever produce. Hence, televised close-ups of football action deliver more to a viewer at home than the real game does to a fan high up in the stands. The visual impact of television makes it more convincing than any other medium, indeed, more convincing than reality itself.

Yet as television more and more becomes our source for knowing reality, more and more of our personal autonomy is paradoxically surrendered. Though TV news can keep us up to date on current events, most of the time our very notion of reality is being shaped by other images—contrived images that represent a deliberate sorting, rearrangement, and distortion of what is real or a portrayal of things that have never happened. Taken as truth, these images—from talk shows and commercials to movies and soap operas—become the raw material out of which we construct our attitudes and beliefs. As critic Jerry Mander explains:

> When you are watching TV, you are not daydreaming or reading, or looking out the window at the world. You have opened your mind, and someone else's daydreams have entered. The images come from distant places you have never been, depict events you can never experience, and are sent by people you don't know and have never met. . . . Once their images are inside you, they imprint upon your memory. They become yours.[22]

Ideally, the information technology of a civilization grants its members access to vistas wider than the narrow range of their own limited experience, holding out to them knowledge beyond their own lives and times, replacing walls with windows. Ideally, what they see through those windows could help them and their civilization grow. But they must make certain that what they see through those windows is really there, especially if they are allowed to look only through distorted glass.

To truly know the weather, we may in fact have to turn our eyes from the window—stepping through our own front door to behold an open sky, to feel the fresh air with our very own skin.

THE MANIPULATION OF THE PAST

As we have seen, our need for information invokes the electronic power of now and leads us to rely on its help. But in helping us, the power of now isolates us in a present whose form and substance are artificially contrived. In effect, the power of now manufactures a synthetic version of the present, which we then consume.

The present, however, is not the only dimension of time influenced by the power of now, for nowism also has an impact on the past. As we noted early in chapter 1, a fixation on the present can blind us to the reality of the past. But the power of now also has the capacity to alter history. In so doing, it can exercise a profound influence on the future of democracy.

For decades, comedian Jack Benny insisted he was only thirty-nine years old. Along with the running joke about his stinginess, Benny's reluctance to confess his real age perennially delighted his audience, especially when the passing of time made the chronological truth more and more apparent.

Of course, Jack Benny was not the first show business personality—or the last—to hide his years. Face-lifts and altered birth dates have often been used to make aging stars seem more youthful. Other figures in public life, politicians included, have creatively edited their resumes to court greater public acceptance, deleting what they would rather have forgotten. Indeed, in politics, revelations about a candidate's past life have often proved more damaging than revelations about his or her platform.

The political manipulation of biographical reality has at times been motivated by malice. Twentieth-century Soviet history is replete with examples of writers and statesmen who were erased from history books only to be rehabilitated years later and returned to those self-same pages. Now you see 'em; now you don't: with a wave of a totalitarian wand, the dictator can magically depopulate or repopulate history. Nor is this a modern phenomenon only: Egyptian pharaohs and Roman emperors tried to erase the memory of hated predecessors by smashing their statues and deleting their names from inscriptions. In these instances, ancient and modern, the biographical past was adjusted to fit the propagandistic needs of the present.

It was the rulers of the past who first realized the power of media. By predetermining the intellectual nutrients the masses were fed, they could control their thought. Public art and oratory were the favorite devices by which ancient dictators achieved their desired results. Such dictatorships grew up in societies characterized by economic dependency and central-ized control.

In antiquity, censoring history was far less complicated than it is today. Until the classical Greeks came along, professional historians didn't even exist. Herodotus, the father of historical research, flourished in the fifth century B.C., after twenty-five centuries and more of Near Eastern kingship and war had already rolled by. Whatever annals had been previously kept were government controlled, whether written on scrolls or inscribed in stone. Such records were commissioned by the state and embodied the state view of truth. Thus, for example, when the superpower armies of the Egyptian and Hittite empires fought to a draw in Syria, each ruler returned home and ordered monuments built to celebrate his "victory." Unbiased accounts of events simply did not exist in antiquity or the Middle Ages, and the notion of an independent press was nonexistent.

With the invention of the printing press during the Renaissance, political leaders faced two new problems: privatization and distribution. Information was now being generated privately and distributed publicly. In the beginning, the politician's task of containing the truth was simplified by limited public literacy and the time it took to print early books. Eventually, however, leaders of both church and state recognized the need to reassert their control by more aggressive ideological measures, for knowledge was indeed power. If no one knew of an embarrassing event, it would be as though the event had never happened. Like the proverbial tree in the forest that falls with no one present to hear its crash, the crash of political truth could also be silenced.

Social changes since those days and modern technological progress would seem to thwart such manipulation. The current existence of millions of books in thousands of public libraries, the ease with which we can gain access to data through computers, and the availability of television as a medium of communication seem the perfect ingredients for insuring an educated and informed populace. Yet ironically, historical revisionism may be even easier today than ever before.

The vast multiplicity of materials that can be read—more with each passing day—has produced a flood of information in which the well-intentioned reader can drown unless he or she is thrown an intellectual life preserver. The true danger of such multiplicity lies in its leveling effect, one that makes the good seem equal to the bad, because the act of distinguishing truth from falsehood amidst such confusion is altogether too trying. In such situations there will always be those who offer to guide us free of charge, luring us with the seductions of simplicity and the comfort of lies.

Nor will it suffice that the necessary facts exist somewhere in a book or data bank. For literacy alone is insufficient to save a civilization. There must also exist the will to apply literacy in the active pursuit of truth, however complex or painful that truth may be.

Yet as pictorial media come to dominate more and more of the public marketplace, there will be less and less incentive, personal or communal, to search for the printed record in black and white. Television, especially commercial television, will present us chiefly with those facts that amuse and will color the rest to please us.[23] For television, the ideal medium of the synchronous society, thrives upon the moment. Its memory is short-term, not historical. Evolving technologies are, in fact, making it easier and easier to manipulate the records of the past. Indeed, the very existence of such technologies encourages such manipulation.

Using computer-generated images, editors can artfully delete or insert visual elements (human or non-human) in a previously taken picture. Thus, a photograph or film can be made to lie in a way the eye cannot detect, and the visual lie can be perpetuated forever. Through the electronic addition or subtraction of people and props, history can be made or unmade. A smoking gun can be electronically removed from an assassin's hand and placed in the hand of another, or a politician can stand and address a peace conference he never attended. For, with current technology, both time and reality are negotiable.

In the film *Forrest Gump*, actor Tom Hanks was deftly blended into archival newsreel footage three decades old so he could "visit" the White House. And John Kennedy and Lyndon Johnson could "speak" to him through the electronic manipulation of their lips and the addition of a dubbed sound track. Commenting on these techniques, George Murphy, supervisor of computer graphics at Industrial Light & Magic, warned: "In *Forrest Gump*, our manipulation of history was gentle and innocent. We didn't change political views or do anything malicious. What it does show, however, is the potential to do extreme things."[24]

Such things, however, *have* already been done. In a 1992 Senatorial campaign, a photograph of Congressman Rod Chandler shaking someone's hand was altered to make the candidate look like he was holding a sackful of money.[25] Similarly, a 1992 picture of candidate Bill Clinton holding Al Gore's hand aloft was altered by substituting Senator Edward Kennedy's hand for Gore's to make it appear that Kennedy was being favored for a White House appointment.[26] There are no rules preventing the use of such doctored photographs or any other kind of deception in political campaigns except for the embarrassment that may come after discovery and, incidentally, after the damage has been done. The very seamlessness of electronic technology will no doubt inspire other such efforts in the future.

Public records also are not immune to such manipulation. In fact, electronic records are more vulnerable than handwritten or printed ones. For electronic data have no permanence, as the missing minutes of the Watergate tapes show. As impulses of stored energy, they exist in a timeless realm of infinite mutability. Says Tom Blanton, head of the National Security Archives: "Electronics make it [the document] far more valuable than in paper form, easier to search, easier to retrieve, easier to archive, but also easier to destroy."[27] While in the past a book had to burned or at least removed from circulation by censors, the electronic book or document has merely to be erased or, if it is more convenient, altered. Indeed, if all references to it are expunged from the memory of a computerized catalogue, it has for all intents and purposes ceased to exist.

Following the defeat of fascism in World War II, George Orwell had foreseen a totalitarian future in which history would be manipulated in just this way. In *1984*, Orwell described the operations of the "Ministry of Truth":

What happened in the unseen labyrinth to which the pneumatic tubes led, he did not know in detail, but he did know in general terms. As soon as all the corrections which happened to be necessary in any particular number of the *Times* had been assembled and collated, that number would be reprinted, the original copy destroyed, and the corrected copy placed on the files in its stead. This process of continuous alteration was applied not only to newspapers, but to books, periodicals, pamphlets, posters, leaflets, films, sound tracks, cartoons, photographs—to every kind of literature or documentation which might conceivably hold any political or ideological significance. Day by day and almost minute by minute the past was brought up to date. In this way every prediction made by the Party could be shown by documentary evidence to have been correct; nor was any item of news, or any expression of opinion, which conflicted with the needs of the moment, ever allowed to remain on record. All history was a palimpsest, scraped clean and reinscribed exactly as often as was necessary.[28]

We are, in fact, surrounded by household technologies that condition us to such transmutation, albeit in benign form. In the old-fashioned typewriter, if a typographical error was made, the error had to be carefully erased or whited-out. More substantial corrections would require retyping the whole page. In the modern electronic typewriter, a correction tape effortlessly lifts off the ink from misspellings, allowing new letters to be quickly typed in. In today's word processor, correction is easier still. Unwanted letters, words, lines, and even paragraphs can be electronically purged at a button's touch, vanishing as though they had never existed at all. Alas, should the writer wish to reflect on an earlier draft, he cannot, unless he had the foresight to store it in the computer's memory. There is no looking back at a crossed-out line, no retrieving a crumpled sheet from the wastebasket. Under the influence of electronics, the past acquires unprecedented disposability.

In the same way, the old-fashioned home movies that once recorded family birthdays and vacations for years to come have been replaced by today's camcorder, which accomplishes the same thing on tape instead of film. But the tape is always erasable, always reusable. It captures what is seen only temporarily until something else is deemed more significant.

It is important to note that the word processor and camcorder do not simply facilitate change; they invite it. While such devices can be praised in the name of convenience, they also exemplify the values of the society they serve, a society that disowns the past because it places a higher premium on the present. The camcorder is by no means evil, nor is the word processor. Each simply reflects the values of our culture, the sensibilities of a synchronous society accustomed to transience and enamored of now. Under their subtle influence, however, we become inured to the notion of an expendable past.

Much like the Hollywood starlet who defended her definition of marital fidelity by saying she always stayed faithful to a husband until she loved someone else more, we remain faithful to the past until a more appealing one comes along. Americans can be fickle lovers, always thirty-nine, always susceptible to the flattery of the present, a flattery that seduces them to forget the passing years.

PATRIOTISM PERVERTED

The abiding loyalty that gives a marriage and a family strength gives strength as well to a nation, where it is known as patriotism. It is no accident that the very word "patriotism" implies a familylike bond, for it comes from *patria*, the Roman word for "fatherland." As an obedient son is to his father, the ancient Romans believed, so must a citizen be to his country.

Classic Roman patriotism was rooted in a pervasive sense of past time, bounded by remembrance of history, reverence for one's ancestors, and respect for ancestral tradition. It was this temporal foundation that gave stability to the structure of the Roman state.

Like love in a family, patriotism stretches over the borders of time, bridging the shores of past and future with the arch of the present. Yet, without firm footings in the past and future, the bridge cannot stand. The future symbolizes the ideals of a nation yet to be fulfilled; the past, the dreams envisioned by its founders; and the present connects the two.

But if patriotism is a transtemporal attitude, bridging future and past, how can it persist in the midst of a synchronous society that lives almost exclusively in the present? And if patriotism itself is essential to the strength of a nation, how will a nation endure that is deprived of such love by its estrangement from the past?

One answer is that it simply will not endure; another, that it will continue, sustained by a warped patriotism that is the distorted product of speed and synchronism.

On the one hand, it may seem that a society ignorant of its history would be empty of patriotism, but such a society's historical ignorance makes it all the more susceptible to psychopolitical manipulation. Lacking direction, it craves a leader, and such a leader can invent or alter history to suit his or her own purposes, either as a means of attaining power or as a means of perpetuating it. The short-term memory of the populace makes their political management all the easier because they cannot refer to even the relatively recent past as a standard against which to measure the value of the present. Thus, little need exists to erase the tape, as it is blank already.

The public will eschew complex issues almost by instinct, because complex issues require time to digest. Instead, they will prefer the illusion of the "quick fix," which, at the least, makes the problem seem to go away for now. And, as now is all that matters, now is quite enough.

The continuous public hunger for the pleasure of the moment will be served by business/government (it will be hard to tell the two apart), which will manufacture a variety of entertaining artificial diversions (sporting events, wars, innocuous social causes). Even suffering will be tolerated, as long as it is perceived as the suffering of anonymous others.

And so life will go on, holidays will continue to be celebrated (albeit in commercialized form), and the flag will continue to wave.

It was the Romans who first invented "bread and circuses," free hand-outs of food and free entertainment designed to keep the urban masses happy.[29] But these were the Imperial Romans who had lost touch with the sterner values of the earlier Republic. Theirs was the primitive archetype of today's synchronous society, for in Imperial Rome every existing medium of communication (architecture, sculpture, even coinage) was used to mold people together into a unified whole—a machine that could rule the world.[30] The well-oiled society of the Caesars, however, possessed the weaknesses as well as the strengths of the machine: though strong, it was impersonal; though efficient, it was soulless.

It was another dictator, Adolf Hitler, who used interconnected media to build the modern prototype of today's synchronous society. Borrowing Greco-Roman materials and motifs to adorn his new regime with antique dignity and glory, he employed the architectural imagination of Albert Speer and the cinematographic vision of Leni Riefenstahl to create an inspiring hymn to national and racial destiny. As Jewish books and bodies were incinerated, the myth of Aryan supremacy was celebrated in nationally broadcast speeches and in torch-lit parades seen and reseen as newsreels in theaters across Germany. Germany's ignominious defeat in World War I had made it desirable to repress the painful memory of the recent past and to substitute for it a Wagnerian fantasy of Teutonic grandeur.[31]

Of course, neither Julius Caesar nor Adolf Hitler had the power of television at his disposal. Nor, more significantly, did either have the advantage of an audience like today's—an audience more isolated than ever before in the present and more insulated than ever before from the past, a pliable audience habituated to passivity and receptive to electronic manipulation.[32]

ELECTRONIC DEMOCRACY

Some have proposed that television, rather than being the enemy of a thoughtful democracy, can be the source of its salvation.

In 1969, a year before the publication of *Future Shock*, Ross Perot, founder of Electronic Data Systems, proposed the creation of an "electronic town hall," a concept that he later advanced as a 1992 presidential candidate and that he has since endorsed through the political organization he leads, "United We Stand, America," now known as the Reform Party.[33]

The electronic town hall would use national television to inform the American electorate about key problems and alternative solutions. After seeing and hearing the presentation, viewers would be free to express their opinions on the course of action the nation should take. These opinions would be registered by viewers from their homes using touch-tone phones linked to central computers by toll-free numbers. The results of the plebiscite would then be relayed to members of Congress to advise them of their constituents' wishes.

Though this system would seemingly employ the power of electronics to enhance the effectiveness of democracy, it has been criticized on a number of counts. By means of a carefully choreographed presentation, it is argued, a demagogue could manipulate public opinion to elicit the very response he wished to receive. Though the viewing audience might be relatively small and scientifically unrepresentative of the electorate as a whole, its response would then be presented to Congress as a true and valid reflection of popular sentiment. In addition, critics have pointed out some technical flaws in the system. Electronic "ballots," for example, could be cast by unqualified individuals (such as children), and each household (or more precisely, each telephone number) could only cast one vote. Furthermore, viewers are most likely to be influenced by the thing they have heard or seen last, and could well respond emotionally rather than rationally[34] (another proof that "whoever controls the pictures wins the argument").[35] The system, moreover, does not readily lend itself to complex problems requiring multiple and/or sophisticated answers, but instead reduces a vote to a simple "yes" or "no." And, given the actual size of the electorate, the potential for meaningful citizen input by call-in questions and comments is virtually nil. Instead, it will be the leader(s), rather than the led, who will do most of the talking. These weaknesses, in fact, have already been observed in the operation of electronic town halls tried out experimentally on urban, regional, and even national levels. In addition, they were strikingly evident in 1993 in Perot's first nationally televised "referendum." Viewers were presented with only one side of an argument, were prompted with what amounted to subliminal captions, and were given little time to reflect before making their choice.[36]

Weaknesses like the ones described above, however, are the inherent weaknesses of representative democracy itself. In campaigns, politicians do most of the talking, the electorate rarely turns out in great droves, and voting is by "yes" or "no." Likewise, people often vote emotionally, based on the last things they've seen or heard, a feature of democracy that had even worried founding father James Madison over two centuries ago.[37]

What is dangerous about the electronic town hall is that it exploits and institutionalizes these weaknesses.

The original New England town hall meeting was an activity organically suited to a small and cohesive community, a group whose size enabled its members to both speak and listen to one another and share ideas before arriving at a collective decision. Such intimate, direct democracy is very different from the more populous representative system under which we live. The form of a democratic system is, in fact, determined and limited by the size of its citizenry. In a nation containing a quarter of a billion people, the current population of the United States, true communication between citizens and government, or between citizen and citizen, would require a vast two-way system of intercommunication that would be both extensive and intensive, one that would hypothetically permit all citizens to communicate with one another—posing, challenging, and discussing ideas—while at the same time communicating in similar fashion with their elected leaders. Such communication is technically feasible even now (all we have to do is talk to each other on one vast, nationwide "conference call"), but for everybody—all 250 million of us—to be heard would require an immense amount of time—too much, in fact, to permit a consensus to be reached, let alone acted upon. There is simply not enough time to hear everybody out. Nor would using the Internet help, for it would still be impossible to carry on a dialogue with so many people, let alone read all their words.[38] It is for this reason that the president's E-mail address at the White House (president@whitehouse.gov) had meaning only so long as few people knew it; today, the thousands of messages sent there each month only receive the same "form letter" response.

The fact is that the central problem of modern democracy is not its mechanics but its scale. What the electronic town-hall concept does is impose a technological solution on a nontechnological problem, creating the illusion that it can actually make things better when, in fact, it cannot. A national "town hall" can only simulate genuine communication; it cannot deliver it. Moreover, true to its technical origins, the electronic town hall promotes instantaneous responses and instant answers instead of encouraging time-intensive deliberation and debate. Yet, if speed itself is at the heart of so many of our problems, more speed cannot guarantee their cure.

By using television as its instrument, the electronic town hall ratifies the power of now and television's place in American political life. Ever since its inception, television has nourished democracy: unifying America's people by eliminating the barriers of geographical distance and regional difference; educating them by showing them economic, social, and environmental conditions here and abroad; and even transporting them to the sites of political conventions, press conferences, hearings, and debates.

Such factual broadcasting has the potential to inspire informed activism. But television also has the capacity to weaken democracy by conditioning its national audience to be passive. Herbert I. Schiller has written of television's "pacifying effect on critical consciousness."[39] Todd Gitlin has observed that "the habitual watcher seems literally *entranced*, hypnotized" and has argued that television-viewing "flattens consciousness."[40] In addition, a psychological research project conducted by Rutgers University using monitored respondents found a distinct "passive spill-over effect following television viewing" among viewers of all ages.[41]

Though such arguments and findings can be challenged,[42] the fact remains that we are all engaged in a grand experiment in political consciousness unprecedented in history, one whose effects are bound to have a critical bearing on the future of democracy.

As Schiller has observed: "The content and form of American communications . . . are devoted to manipulation. When successfully employed, as they invariably are, the result is individual passivity, a state of inertia that precludes action. This, indeed, is the condition for which the media and the system-at-large energetically strive, because passivity assures the maintenance of the *status quo*."[43]

Viewed from this perspective, television becomes the *soma* of Aldous Huxley's *Brave New World*, a publicly distributed synthetic drug, "euphoric, narcotic, pleasantly hallucinant."[44] Media critic Neil Postman rightly warns us that we should not fear the totalitarian force of Orwell's *1984* as much as the seductiveness of a video *soma* that bathes us in a mindless now.[45] Says Postman: "In the end, he [Huxley] was trying to tell us that what afflicted the people in *Brave New World* was not that they were laughing instead of thinking, but that they did not know what they were laughing about and why they had stopped thinking."[46]

More than transforming merely the structure of a democracy, the power of now and its instruments have the capacity to transform democracy's very substance, the consciousness and conscience of its people.[47]

TIME AND THE CRISIS OF DEMOCRACY

The Synchronous Mind

The synchronous society looks upon time the way a diner looks at a buffet. To the diner it is irrelevant how long it took to prepare and cook the many dishes before him; what matters is how appetizing they look. Hungry, he puts on his plate whatever suits his taste. In the same way, the synchronous society acknowledges only those aspects of past belief that serve to confirm its own current attitudes. The rest is ignored. The synchronous citizen likewise lives for today. Neither past nor future are his concern.

The widening use of drugs, the burgeoning of crime, the deepening national debt, the rampant spread of sexual disease, and even the expanding destruction of the natural environment are all rooted in our sense of time. In seeking to gratify our desires instantly and in denying the ultimate consequences of our choices, we simultaneously reject the place of the future in our lives. At the same time, we turn our faces away from the past and the moral guidance it could provide. For the demands of the present are too insistent; its voice, too loud.

Were the separate problems of our society the result of disparate causes, we could deal with them one at a time. But cutting off the separate heads of this social Hydra will not cause the beast to die, for each of the heads will grow back anew. Though the problems of our society are by no means simple to solve, their separate causes stem from a basic attitude: the denial that we live in a temporal continuum, that our actions must be conditioned by the acknowledgment of future and past. It is from this one central principle that our major social ills radiate. Yet these ills are more threatening than the mythical Hydra, for their menace lies not within some alien monster but within ourselves, within the nature of the synchronous mind.

Unlike the totalitarian society, the synchronous democratic society is not unified by ideology. All effective totalitarian states have galvanized popular sentiment through the use of temporal imagery. The masses are called upon to join the great cause to fulfill their historic mission and spiritual destiny. To the cry of "Bonzai!," beneath the banner of the Third Reich, mouthing the sayings of Chairman Mao, the faithful have marched forth on totalitarian crusades across the ages, inspired by the image of an unfinished past and the glorious picture of a future yet to be. But these anthems are not sung by the synchronous democratic society, for it has allowed its citizenship in time to lapse, bound as it is by allegiance only to the present.

Nor is a synchronous society the same as a conformist one, in which the individual cooperatively and silently complies with an unspoken social code and thereby gains acceptance. For in the synchronous society there is no set of rules, only flux. Instead of statesmen with steadfast principles, there are candidates continually adjusting their positions to match the latest focus groups and polls.[48] Instead of communal consensus from discussion and debate there is media-induced opinion. Instead of cultural norms there are fickle fads and trends. The citizens of a synchronous society resemble not birds flying in formation but leaves blowing in a shifting wind. The individual scurries to catch the crowd, not knowing that the crowd itself is without lasting direction.

The synchronous mind is a solipsistic mind: self-absorbed, it knows only its own modifications and states. To it this is a sufficient reality. But, paradoxically, it is not alone in its solipsism. The synchronous mind is simultaneously linked to other minds as well, subconsciously sharing in their modifications and psychological states, joined to them by a neurological web of electronic stimulation. But the synchronous mind does not fully realize it is so joined. Instead, it perceives itself as autonomous and free, acting out its own decisions. Yet all the time, like a fish borne on the invisible stream of an undersea current, its life inexorably drifts toward the net.

Meanwhile, materialism leads to the erosion of ideals, which in turn leads to a pervasive cynicism about government and a suspicion about the motives of all institutions.

Reveling narcissistically in the present, the synchronous democracy averts its eyes from the past. It knows neither the sins of the past nor its virtues and couldn't care less as long as its creature needs are met. Because of its aversion to history and its absence of historical memory, such a society is vulnerable to manipulation by its leaders. But should its needs be denied, it will turn viciously against its keeper, or against those to whom the keeper points.

To the citizens of a synchronous democracy, time is not autonomous but malleable. History is not constant and self-contained, a fixed standard against which the present can be measured, but mutable and open, a fluid mirror that reflects whatever face the masses wish to see. Mutability is, in fact, one of the highest values of such a society. Since all verities (including historical facts) are by definition constant (and therefore uninteresting), unchanging verities are readily surrendered. Instead, the synchronous democracy prefers to watch lie "morph" into truth and fact "morph" into fantasy, as long as the change is entertaining. With proper casting, skillful direction, and a big budget for production, even a war can become an entertainment event.[49]

Chronocentrism

Contained in the vocabulary of our thought is a class of words we can call "centrisms." The most common of these words are "*ego*centrism" and "*ethno*centrism." "Egocentrism" means seeing oneself as central in one's life, looking upon one's own feelings and needs as more important than those of others. "Ethnocentrism" means seeing one's own ethnic group as culturally central, regarding its values and priorities as more important than those of other groups.

But in addition to these commonly met "centrisms," there is another term—less obvious, but more crucial—that we must understand if we are to comprehend the inner character of a synchronous democracy. That term is "*chrono*centrism," the habit of seeing one's own *time* as central. To be sure, such an attitude seems natural enough to have. After all, since we live in the here and now and must function in the present, it seems thoroughly appropriate to regard our own time as having the greatest significance. In the same sense, it can be argued that egocentrism and ethnocentrism are natural attitudes as well. After all, why wouldn't we think of ourselves and those we identify with as more important than others?

Yet reflection reveals that egocentrism, by its very definition, obscures the innate worth of others, just as ethnocentrism obscures the worth of other groups. These forms of blindness limit our very perception of reality, for reality stretches beyond ourselves and those we call our own. No individual or group is so self-sufficient that it cannot gain by widening the perimeter of its understanding. To do less would be to diminish its very capacity to survive and grow.

In the same way, chronocentrism also impoverishes us. For, by limiting the temporal sources from which we could draw strength, it forces us to depend upon the restricted diet of the present for all our nourishment. To grow strong spiritually and intellectually we must take our sustenance from other dimensions as well—from the collective visions of the future, defined by hope, and from the collective experiences of the past, refined as wisdom.

Yet the synchronous society, because it lives for today, is inherently antagonistic to both future and past. As it spins, it sucks into its temporal vortex those elements that might otherwise have floated free. And the faster the synchronous society spins, the more voracious its appetite becomes. The exclusivity of the present leaves citizens without the means to recognize true progress. As their memory is short-term, they lack the long-term measuring rods by which to gauge the deficiencies and real achievements of the times in which they live. Indeed, a built-in cultural bias against the past serves to alienate people from these very standards, precisely because such standards are noncontemporary. Thus, society is gradually deprived of the very sources of its potential salvation.

As this chronic disease persists, it becomes harder and harder to cure, for as it progresses, it makes its victims more and more oblivious to the very existence of the remedies that could save them. As time goes on, some have claimed, we will be less able to deal with environmental pollution, not because the pollutants themselves will have grown more potent, but because our own ability to think will have been crippled by them. A similar scenario may well apply to the pollution of our sense of time—with equally destructive, long-term effects upon the cultural environment of the land we inhabit.

As the disease intensifies, its victims will become more and more susceptible to the quackery of those who pander to their hunger for quick relief. Slower and more painful treatments will be rejected in favor of patriotic placebos, easy scapegoats, and the comfort of "bread and circuses."

The satirist Juvenal coined this term in the first century A.D. to describe the degradation of Roman society. Once a proud and self-reliant civilization, the Romans had been transformed into a mere audience, eager only for government-sponsored handouts of free food and government-financed chariot races and gladiatorial shows. This transformation from activity to passivity had been wrought not merely by a century of totalitarian rule but by an increasing emphasis upon the present.

We may, of course, derive some chronological solace from the fact that it took the Roman Empire five centuries to fall. Chronocentrism obviously doesn't cause cultures—theirs or ours—to collapse instantly.

But the real issue before us is not the collapse of culture but its inner transformation, not the end of human civilization (or anything so grandiose) but a thing at once more banal and devastating: the steady and irrevocable erosion of its humane potential. Thus (to paraphrase a twentieth-century poet, T. S. Eliot), it is not a bang we must anticipate but a whimper, a whimper from men and women made hollow from seeing their dreams come true.[50] For, as Juvenal also said, should the gods want to destroy us, they have but to grant our wishes.

Nor is it any protection that we live in a democracy. For democracy has a natural affinity for chronocentric behavior. The very meaning of democracy is that government should reflect the wishes of the people, and, through elections, government is made responsive to their will (or even whim). Totalitarian regimes, for their part, offer greater constancy, but at the high price of individual liberty and human rights.

At its finest, democracy tempers its fickleness by recalling the principles of its founding and the traditions of its history, measuring the moment against the time-tested standards of hallowed ideals. Yet, should a people be ignorant of its own past and of the need to act in keeping with that knowledge, it will lead the most shallow of political lives.

The inherent weakness of democracy—to act by whim instead of with wisdom—is exacerbated by all the forces of commercialism and communications that celebrate now at the expense of the past. Presentness creates an insatiable demand for more presentness, inspiring the development of new products and services that, in turn, reinforce a chronocentric view of reality. While some entrepreneurs may look beyond the present in order to make a profit from future trends, there are few financial incentives to study the past. Thus the economics of time conspire against the fulfillment of democracy's promise.

Catching the Third Wave

In his book *The Third Wave*, Alvin Toffler described how "a powerful tide [was] surging across. . . the world"—a tide of revolutionary social change.[51] The First Wave of global change had been set into motion by the Agricultural Revolution; the Second, by the Industrial Revolution. "We are the children of the next transformation," Toffler wrote, "the Third Wave."[52]

> Humanity faces a quantum leap forward. It faces the deepest social upheaval and creative restructuring of all time. Without

clearly recognizing it, we are engaged in building a remarkable new civilization from the ground up. . . .

This new civilization, as it challenges the old, will topple bureaucracies, reduce the role of the nation-state, and give rise to semi-autonomous economies in a post-imperialist world. It requires governments that are simpler, more effective, yet more democratic than any we know today. . . .

It could. . . turn out to be the first truly humane civilization in recorded history.[53]

Continuing this optimistic forecast in *Creating a New Civilization*, Alvin and Heidi Toffler proposed that American democracy can revive itself by embracing the spirit of a "'Third Wave'" information-age society."[54]

The Tofflers' argument, however, is seriously flawed. Revolutionary waves—agricultural, industrial, informational—reflect radical changes in technology, but not necessarily in government. As history clearly demonstrates, a whole variety of political systems are compatible with any given wave. Ancient Greek democracy was contemporary with Persian kingship during the agricultural "First Wave." Twentieth-century American democracy was contemporary with German fascism during the Industrial "Second Wave." Democracy thus existed in both periods, as did other political systems as well.

Certainly, technological and economic changes *affect* government, but they do not define it. The coming of an "information-age society" does not necessarily presage democracy's salvation. Media—"things in the middle"—are just that and nothing more. The content they carry will forever depend upon us. The same amoral signal that carries a political debate can transmit a tyrant's speech.

Chapter 7

The Transformation of
International Relations

THE INFLUENCE OF the power of now extends far beyond the borders of the United States. With increasing tempo, the same forces of commerce, transportation, and communication that have fused our country together are integrating parts of the globe once remote from one another in space and time. This global interconnectedness is accompanied by high speed. Accelerated by the speed-of-light energy of electronics, the world now spins faster than ever before. As Marshall McLuhan prophesied over twenty-five years ago: "Electronic circuitry has overthrown the regime of time and space and pours upon us instantly and continuously the concerns of all other men. It has reconstructed dialogue on a global scale."[1] In the words of J. T. Fraser, we now live in a "time-compact global society," a society in which technology has triumphed over distance and shrunk the earth, transforming international relations.[2]

The international spread of nowism may at first seem paradoxical. Countries with longer histories than America's lack the newness that made American culture a fertile soil upon which nowism took root. But the two other sources of now's power, technology and the senses, have a universal appeal that permits them—and the power of now itself—to leap over national boundaries. Combined, they can also erode an older culture's sense of its past and thus make such a culture more susceptible to rapid change.

As will be shown in this chapter, an increasing velocity of global activity has engendered a powerful centrifugality capable of disintegrating old and inflexible political structures even as it tends toward an eventual homogenization of culture on a worldwide scale. Significantly, among the principles espoused by Mikhail Gorbachev—along with the well-known ones of *perestroika* ("reconstruction") and *glasnost* ("openness")—was the less well-known but volatile principle of *uskorenie* ("acceleration").[3]

Though the idea of a high-speed, electronic culture began in America, it has been eagerly adopted by countries all over the world. This importation of culture has done more than just make foreigners look and act "American." More notably, it has established a visible and invisible global infrastructure of accelerated expectations and behaviors. This infrastructure, in turn, has reinforced nowist tendencies already at work domestically by feeding them with new international sources of energy and giving them transnational sources of direction. The result is a high-speed, electronically integrated global culture, a synchronous society on a planetary scale.

THE ORIGINS OF GLOBALISM

Aeons ago, before human beings made their first impact on the world of nature, that world was physically unified—first, by its elemental chemical ingredients; second, by its waters and lands and the gaseous atmosphere that enveloped them; third, by the variegated spirit of life that covered its surface; fourth, by the force of gravity that held all things together; and last, by the cosmic embrace of space.

For hundreds of thousands of years hominids and, later, homo sapiens blended into that world, into its jungle, its savanna, and its forest. They survived by hiding and then emerging to claim part of the earth's bounty as their own. The first humans were outnumbered by the other living things of earth and awed by the raw power of nature itself and the savage strength and competitiveness of its creatures. But as their culture developed and civilization arose, human beings began to change the world around them. Those who had first adapted to the environment made the environment slowly adapt to them.

The effects of their actions were magnified by the migration and expansion of their numbers and the enlargement of their technological capabilities. But the effects were also magnified by the organization of the earth's human population into increasingly larger political units.

The earliest villages eventually came to be united into kingdoms and ultimately into great empires. Fertile river valleys (such as those of the Nile, the Tigris and Euphrates, the Indus, and the Yellow rivers) provided ideal conditions for both the growth of large populations and their geographical unification under strong, centralized governments.

The territorial ambitions of leaders or the desire for territorial security led many of these early states into wars of conquest that reached beyond the spatial limits that had previously defined their existence. In the broad and open alluvial plains of southern Iraq, a succession of larger and larger kingdoms arose (Sumerian, Akkadian, and Babylonian), each in turn swallowing and digesting the other, until they were in turn gobbled up by the ravenous Assyrians of the north and, afterwards, by the mighty Persians to the east. In the fourth century B.C., not sated by his father's conquest of Greece, Alexander the Great defeated the Persians, amassing the largest empire the world had ever seen—until the rise of Rome, whose territorial appetite eventually ingested most of Europe, North Africa, and the Near East.

These political developments can be compared to the growth of bacteria on a culture plate, ever expanding outwards until the whole surface of the gelatin is covered. An empire, however, is not an accretion of simple microorganisms but a single entity, both vast and complex. Its existence can only be maintained by internal systems—of movement and communication—that provide for its nourishment, guidance, and defense. Yet more than these systems, an enduring empire that incorporates separate peoples must also embody a central point of view, an organizational principle of shared beliefs. Fear and repression, however forceful they may be as agents of control, cannot match the unifying power of a common ideal.

Alexander the Great understood this. To unify his far-flung empire, he founded scores of Greek-styled cities across its breadth to disseminate Greek culture on foreign soil. Further, he racially integrated his army's high command and encouraged his troops to intermarry with native-born women. With similar intent, the forward-looking Romans used city building and colonization to extend their conception of life to the rest of the world.

Though the fall of the Roman Empire led to the resurgence of autonomous kingdoms in Europe, the age of transatlantic exploration and colonization that began a thousand years later transplanted the people and values of Europe to distant lands, at once dissolving and expanding the traditional cultural boundaries of their original homelands. In the eighteenth century, thirteen colonies, bonded by a common belief in human equality and unalienable rights, joined together to form a greater entity, the United States of America, that eventually expanded "from sea to shining sea."

With the coming of the twentieth century, humanity witnessed the rise of ideological imperialism, as fascism, communism, and capitalistic democracy contended again and again to determine which system would prevail over the minds and resources of the earth. The phenomenon of "world war," an invention of the twentieth century, showed that war itself had been redefined spatially so as to encompass the entire globe. Global warfare, in turn, led to global efforts to maintain peace through the creation of the

League of Nations after World War I and the United Nations after World War II.

The United Nations, besides seeking to resolve conflicts between nations, was intended "to employ international machinery for the promotion of the economic and social advancement of all peoples." Its purpose, therefore, was not purely political, but economic and social as well. This global goal, moreover, was to be achieved through the use of new international mechanisms, not simply national ones. The year the UN charter was signed, 1945, the International Monetary Fund and the International Bank for Reconstruction and Development were established to stabilize the world's monetary system and extend loans and technical assistance to developing nations. Initiated by the United States two years later, the Marshall Plan provided European countries with billions of dollars in economic aid. Later, in 1956 and 1960, the International Finance Corporation and the International Development Association were formed to encourage the flow of private capital between nations and to underwrite loans to poor countries at favorable terms. In addition, in 1957, six Western European nations—France, Germany, Italy, Belgium, the Netherlands, and Luxembourg—joined together as members of the European Economic Council to promote the establishment of a "Common Market" by removing artificial barriers to trade, such as burdensome customs regulations and duties.

These international developments arose in the aftermath of World War II and the Cold War that followed. By creating new organizational structures that bridged old territorial divisions, these developments increased the circulation of money and goods between disparate nations and accelerated economic activity both domestically and internationally. By closing the gap between material desire and fulfillment, such structures made the power of now internationally attainable.

THE FUSION OF COMMERCE

The Borderless Economy

The fusion of separate nations into economic unions continues to this very day to support the evolution of a borderless world economy in which the commercial hearts of nations beat as one.

Under the Maastricht Treaty, a "United States of Europe" is being formed, a "Europe without frontiers" in which 350 million people will be able to trade freely "without so much as a wave to their border guards."[4] The treaty institutes a new politico-economic status, that of European "citizen," free to live and work in any of the twelve member and seven allied states. In addition, a single currency, the Euro, is to be established as well as a central representative government with broad fiscal, economic, and environmental powers.

Paralleling the emergence of the European Community are similar events taking place on the other side of the Atlantic. The North American Free Trade Agreement (NAFTA) seeks to unite the economies of the United States, Canada, and Mexico, effectively linking 370 million people representing 31 percent of the world's wealth. In addition, leaders of thirty-four Western Hemisphere nations have agreed in principle to create a free trade zone stretching from Argentina to Alaska.

Nor are international trade agreements simply continental. They can also reach across oceans. The General Agreement on Tariffs and Trade (GATT) aims to liberalize commercial transactions among over one hundred member nations that generate more than 85 percent of the world's trade. And, with different intent, oil-producing countries on three continents protect their mutual interests through OPEC.

The power of international trade can be gauged by the volume of currency exchanged daily on the world market—over $1 trillion a day, more than triple what it was in 1986. World trade itself is today twenty times what it was in 1950, while foreign direct investment stands at over $2 trillion worldwide.[5] The configuration of commerce is not only changing globally; it is changing at an increasing rate, with the world's gross product in the last ten years rising at a rate double that of the previous ten. Such growth is paralleled by the frenetic activity of stock and commodity markets circuiting the globe.

According to former U.S. Secretary of Labor Robert R. Reich, "the very idea of an American economy is becoming meaningless, as are the notions of an American corporation, American capital, American products, and American technology."[6] In his book *The Work of Nations*, Reich says that in the world that is coming "there will be no national technologies, no national corporations, no national industries."[7] Confirming this view, President Bill Clinton has observed that "we live in a globalized world in which the line between domestic and foreign policy is increasingly blurred."[8]

Walter B. Wriston, former chairman and CEO of Citicorp and Citibank, adds:

> The world is changing not because computer operators have replaced clerk typists, but because the human struggle to survive and prosper now depends on a new source of wealth; it is information applied to work to create value. Information technology has created an entirely new economy, an information economy, as different from the industrial economy as the industrial was from the agricultural. And when the source of the wealth of nations changes, the politics of nations changes as well. . . .
>
> Today the proliferation of information technology ranging from the telephone and fax machine to fiber optic cables has

flooded the world with data and information moving at the
speed of light to all corners of the world. . . . This explosion of
information and the speed at which it can be transmitted has
created a situation which is different in kind and not just in
degree from any former time. This change affects not only the
creation of wealth but also military power, the political structure
of the world and thus international relations. . . .

The world can no longer be understood as a collection of national economies. The electronic infrastructure that now ties the
world together, as well as great advances in the efficiency of
conventional transportation, are creating a single global economy.[9]

Entrepreneur Stephen D. Harlan argues that today's businessman must
become a "global thinker."

Thinking globally, both offensively and defensively, is an absolute business requirement of today and the future. . . . Being
global is not just *where* you do business, but *how* you do business. . . . It is the shift from having one national image in the
market to becoming "Stateless." . . . Being global means having
the ability to act as if boundaries are low (or, don't even exist).
This kind of structure eliminates isolationism and promotes
sharing.

Within a successful global company, top managers are not
seen as "Controllers." They are seen as "Connectors." They do
not "Pull the Strings" that make things happen. They connect all
the key parts. They coordinate. They interpret. They amplify.
They facilitate.

You cannot be truly global without being networked. Back in
the 15th century, for example, that meant having the fastest
ships. But today, as we approach the 21st century, this means
having the most on-target data bases, and the most effective
telecommunications.[10]

When business deals require personal contact, international travel is
speeded up by supersonic jet. From 1980 to 1990, U.S. arrivals from and
departures to foreign airports almost doubled, pointing to a substantial rise
in business as well as nonbusiness flights.[11] Throughout the 1990s, Asia and
the Pacific are expected to see air travel increase by double digits every
year.[12] As air carriers from different nations continue to form alliances and
merge, international flying becomes more and more seamless. For airline
executive John Dasburg, the international goal is for "the passenger [to] feel
as if he is on one airline."[13]

To reduce air traffic congestion and speed up travel, additional terminals and entire new airports are being built around the world, including a second terminal at Frankfurt that will serve 12 million additional passengers a year and a new airport under construction at Hong Kong that will be able to accommodate 87 million passengers annually, more than any other airport on the globe.[14] According to aviation author McKinley Conway, "the investment in new facilities will be greater than the combined total for all previous history."[15]

To further shrink travel time, increasing support is being given to expanding high-speed rail service, following the lead of Japan's "bullet" trains. By the year 2000, for example, construction in Europe will have multiplied high-speed rail lines ten times, from 1,800 to 18,000 miles, at a cost of over $76 billion, including the cost of standardizing voltages that now prevent locomotives from crossing many national borders. Meanwhile, trains can race between London and Paris in only three hours using the historic underwater "Chunnel."[16]

Where physical presence is not required for negotiations, international deal-making can be expedited by electronic telecommunications, with data and voice transmitted by fiber-optic, microwave, and satellite signals that continually travel without passport. The number of telephone calls between the United States and South America, for example, increased 500 percent between 1980 and 1990 and continues to grow. Meanwhile, hovering 22,300 miles above the earth, CNN's Galaxy 5 communications satellite can simultaneously transmit 15,000 global telephone conversations through each of its 24 transponders with only a three-second delay. Even this delay can be eliminated by taking the alternate route of international and transoceanic fiber-optic cable.[17]

"The trend is going to continue," international telecommunications specialist Joseph Markoski has observed. "There seems to be an insatiable demand or need to communicate and it just keeps getting stronger."[18]

Global Manufacturing

Only decades ago, international commerce was a two-way street with a solid white line separating the lanes. Domestically made exports went out as foreign made imports came in. As French wine and Swiss watches headed west to America, American steel and electronics headed east. Gradually, U.S. corporations extended their operations outward to countries where branch offices were set up. In turn, foreign corporations began to extend their operations to America.

In recent years, however, Americans have witnessed the "buying up" of America as foreign interests have acquired real estate and major domestic companies, including communications giants like RCA, CBS Records, MCA, Universal and Columbia Pictures, Bantam and Doubleday; manufacturers like Goodyear, Firestone, National Steel, Mack Truck, Borden, and Pillsbury; and retailers like A&P, Grand Union, and Bloomingdale's. During the first half of 1990 alone, $7.9 billion of American assets were bought by the British, $5.7 billion by the French, and $3.8 billion by the Japanese.[19] In addition, of the twenty-five largest banks in the world, ranked by 1996 assets, just two were American, Chase Manhattan in sixteenth place and Citicorp in twenty-fifth.[20]

More significant than the blatant takeover of American companies has been the subtle internal metamorphosis of companies worldwide through the creation of strategic alliances. As Robert R. Reich has noted:

> By the 1990s, most "trade" no longer occurred in arm's-length transactions between buyers in one nation and sellers in another, but between people within the same web who are likely to deal repeatedly with each other across borders. . . . In such global webs, products are international composites. What is traded between nations is less often finished products than specialized problem-solving (research, product design, fabrication), problem-identifying (marketing, advertising, customer consulting), and brokerage (financial, searching, contracting) services, as well as certain routine components and services, all of which are combined to create value.
>
> Such cross-border links now comprise most international trade among advanced economies. . . . In fact, in 1990 more than half of America's exports and imports, by value, were simply the transfers of such goods and related services *within* global corporations.[21]

Perhaps the most stunning evidence of this radical transformation of commerce is the automotive industry, where the hybridization of parts, assembly, and profit so blurred the picture of national product identity that the U.S. government compelled automakers, beginning in 1995, to put stickers on their cars showing their foreign content and its origin. As automotive writer Marshall Shuon complained back in 1992:

> Pity the poor consumer who wants an American car. Some full-size Chevies and Mercurys are built in Canada. Some of Ford's popular Escorts are made in Mexico. The Dodge Stealth is made in Japan. Pontiac's LeMans comes from Korea, and nearly every new automobile carries parts from all over the world.
>
> Not only that, but the designs and engineering and economics are also a case of mix and match.

General Motors owns all of Lotus, half of Saab and almost 40 percent of Isuzu. Ford owns Jaguar and about a quarter of Mazda—although its new Mercury Villager van is a joint venture with Nissan. And Chrysler, which owns all of Lamborghini and 15 percent of Maserati, holds an 11 percent stake in Mitsubishi.

It's hard to tell who is what anymore.[22]

The access of American manufacturers to cheap labor around the world, through foreign invitation and international accord, intensifies the meltdown of once-separate economies into a melded global pool in which traditional distinctions of space dissolve. Globalism, thus, has not only redefined the nature of business but has also radically altered the nature of manufactured goods. As the centrifuge of global commerce accelerates, its products become homogenized.

Global Retailing

Global economics are also changing the world's retail landscape.

McDonald's top ten restaurants in sales, for example, are all outside the United States. Operating in 101 foreign countries, McDonald's serves Moscow (McDonald's largest restaurant anywhere), Paris, Rome, and Tahiti, with almost 1,000 sites in Japan. 1991 marked the first year the company opened more restaurants abroad than in the United States. Two new foreign locations are now opening for every new domestic one, with half the company's profits coming from the over 4,000 locations outside the United States.

To match the Chinese restaurants that have been a feature of urban and suburban America for well over a century, McDonald's, Pizza Hut, and Kentucky Fried Chicken have set up fast-food outlets in Beijing. McDonald's Beijing restaurant seats 700, and, by 1995, McDonald's had opened over 27 restaurants in China at a cost of $50 million. KFC's Beijing outlet, one of 28 in China, ranks as the biggest KFC in the world, serving 40,000 customers a week. Over the next few years, Kentucky Fried Chicken will be investing about $200 million in China.[23]

The Chinese market has also attracted U.S. manufacturers like Coca-Cola, which now has thirteen bottling plants there including a facility for producing coke syrup.

These days foreign brands are as ubiquitous as Mao's little red books were two decades ago. Turn on Chinese television and you are likely to see commercials for Coca-Cola, Tang orange drink, Contac cold capsules, and Head and Shoulders Shampoo. Atop Shanghai's No. 1 Department Store. . . is a neon-lit billboard for Pond's facial cream and Vaseline Intensive Care lotion.[24]

Other advertised products in China range from Benetton to Barbasol and Ritz Crackers to Raid. As for Coca-Cola, it's also available in 196 other countries around the world—Libya, Iraq, Cuba, and North Korea being among the few exceptions.

Meanwhile, Toys-R-Us is looking forward to $4.1 billion in revenues from the 406 stores it plans to open globally, stores featuring identical floor-plans from Singapore to Spain. Closer to home and south of the border, in Mexico, J.C. Penney is distributing a catalogue in Spanish while Sears is running its operations in Mexico using data transmission via satellite. Further south, Walmart is exploring markets in Argentina and Brazil.

Big Macs in Beijing and pizza in Pushkin Square denote more than Yankee capitalism venturing across new frontiers.[25] They mean more than the Americanization of Ah Ling and Ivan. By scattering the crumbs of American-style fast-foodism on foreign soil, they represent nothing less than a corporate attempt to grow a new crop of consumer, the international consumer. What happened in America long ago—the replacement of the old lunch wagon by the new hamburger franchise, the displacement of the old corner grocery by the national supermarket chain—is now taking place around the world, globally distributing a common consumer culture even as it accelerates the pace of everyday life.

The clear message such changes convey is spatial *and* temporal: whatever is here is simultaneously there. For American tourists in China, for American tourists anywhere, the foreign country visited becomes merely a quaint setting for what they know is simultaneously present back home thousands of miles away. For with the interfusion of commercial enterprises and products on a global scale, material culture becomes universal, and arbitrary time zones lose significance.

THE WEB OF COMMUNICATION

The Empire of Now

In order for the present to exert its influence, it need do nothing, for all life exists in the here and now. But in order for the present to exert so overpowering an influence that it blinds people to past and future, it must intrude itself into every aspect of their lives, crowding out of their consciousness other dimensions of time. All elements of personal experience must simultaneously resonate to the same pitch. For the power of now to have this effect nationally and even globally, people everywhere must be attuned to the same temporal reality. An exclusive sense of the present must be implicit in their lives. Exceptions, whether they be actualities or perceptions, will only serve to undermine the view that the present is all, thus diminishing now's power and its mastery over communal life.

One of the impediments to simultaneity is distance, for the farther people are apart, they less likely it is that their experiences will be the same. The homes they live in will be different. The food they eat will be different. The clothes they wear, the money they use, the songs they sing—all will be different. "Foreign" languages owe their very foreignness to the spatial separation between lands and peoples. Indeed, even within the same language, differences called dialects reflect the same principle. The artificial borders we are familiar with—whether of regions or nations—merely affirm in a formal way the realities of relative location. And, as distances increase, so do differences. Hence time and space stand at odds, subverting the present's potentially universal reign.

Humanity's technological accomplishments, however, have bridged such gaps. In effect, achievements in transportation and communication have negated the separatist influences of geography. Today, rapid transportation and instantaneous communication make possible the realization of a global society, one in which all physical barriers that could impede the free interchange of goods and experiences are transcended. As the material content of people's lives becomes more and more similar, as the ideas to which they are regularly exposed become more and more alike, and as they are increasingly brought together under circumstances of mutual benefit, they will inevitably cease to think of themselves as apart and will instead come to think of themselves as one. As Walter Truett Anderson has written: "We live in the age of the fading boundary, the twilight of a mind-set that structured reality with sharp lines."[26]

In such an integrated environment where distance becomes an irrelevancy, the power of now is exponentially raised, for in such a situation space loosens its grip upon time. A new global syncretism can then come into being, one in which cultural distinctions, linguistic peculiarities, and political divisions fade away as the energies and aspirations of different peoples are synergistically fused.

As we have already seen, such syncretism is fostered by the expanding interconnectedness of commerce around the world. The electronic storage, analysis, and transmission of information have linked once separate economies into collaborative networks. The growth of continent-wide companies, the rise of transnational corporations and strategic alliances, the establishment of free trade across previously protectionist borders, and the round-the-clock global interlooping of stock exchanges and financial institutions are not independent economic phenomena but interrelated by-products of electronic technologies that have changed the way the world does business. Collectively, such institutions have affected how we define commerce and, by altering our thinking, have made it more likely that similar commercial developments will take place in the future and be regarded as desirable and normal.

Cultures can actively resist such economic symbiosis, however, especially if they see it as a threat to their ideology. The stern senators of the
Roman Republic opposed Hellenization for much the same reasons that,
two thousand years later, Japanese samurai opposed Westernization: the
fear that their own value system would be subverted by foreign ideas. Some
cultures, on the other hand, may naively believe they can accept economic
benefits without paying an ideological price. Material temptations, however, are inevitably accompanied by ideological seductions. Objects are not
merely things to be used but very often imply a certain style of life,
including a sense of life's purpose and the pace at which life should be lived.
It is for this reason that Club Med resorts forbid the use of currency and
island retreats like Mackinac Island, Michigan, and Fire Island, New York,
ban automobiles. Yet, what is true of a resort or retreat can also be true of a
country. A nation transformed commercially and technologically can be
transformed spiritually as well, especially if it is under the influence of a
powerful, worldwide system based upon speed, consumption, and profit.
To protect its peace of mind and way of life, an embargo of sorts may be
necessary. But in a borderless economy, embargoes are almost impossible
to enforce.

International Media

Material goods do not even have to travel physically in order for their
influence to be felt. Their images are potent substitutes for their presence
and for the life-style they represent. For images are far easier to distribute
and far quicker to deliver than physical objects, especially if such images
are electronic. Wherever we are, motion pictures and television can bring
us the world.

For decades, motion pictures have projected an image of America—for
better or worse—around the globe, an image potent enough to stir the
currents of revolution. In the words of one former Asian leader: "The
motion picture industry has provided a window on the world, and the
colonized nations have looked through that window and have seen the
things of which they have been deprived. It is perhaps not generally
realized that a refrigerator can be a revolutionary symbol—to a people who
have no refrigerators."[27] An influential ambassador of ideology, the movie
has been described by Jack Valenti, president of the Motion Picture Association of America, as "America's most wanted export."[28]

The distribution of that export, however, was severely limited as long as
movies were reels of film. Televised, they can instantly span the globe as
signals traveling at the speed of light. By 1993, in fact, 40 percent of the
revenue earned by the U.S. movie, TV, and home video industry came from
international markets ($8 billion out of a total of $18 billion).[29] While over
93 million households in America own at least one TV set,[30] there are over

a billion sets in use worldwide, a number that will soon double. Spanish schoolchildren spend more time watching TV than their passive American counterparts, and the French actually spend more time watching TV than working.[31]

Television cuts across borders like nothing else, with an audience and impact unmatched by radio, its nearest rival. Says media scholar Everette E. Dennis: "The nation-state is less and less able to control what goes in and out of it. It really makes customs and other nuances. . . irrelevant."[32] Assessing television's global influence, British political scientist Timothy Ash observes: "While it used to take decades or centuries for one culture to seep into another, television today spreads lasting images in a matter of seconds."[33] Television, as Ash notes, is not just an entertainment medium. It can affect the course of history by showing one part of the world how the other lives. When asked what caused communism to collapse in Eastern Europe, for example, Polish leader Lech Walesa had only to point to a TV set and say, "It all came from there."[34] Today, color TVs are found in at least 82 percent of Polish households.[35]

Adept at covering breaking political news on a global scale, Atlanta-based CNN is simultaneously watched in as many as 62 million homes in America, 50 million in Western Europe, and 30 million in the rest of the world.[36] By capturing the suppression of revolution in China, mass starvation in Africa, or genocide in what was once Yugoslavia, television news networks like CNN can provoke the conscience of an entire world. Indeed, even the transmission of pop hits on MTV has social impact because of its capacity to unify and sway the sensibilities of a global generation of young people.[37] Watched by an estimated 90 million viewers, MTV is available on every continent except Antarctica. For the even younger, "Sesame Street" is available in 180 countries.

The subversive potential of television has not been lost on leaders of repressive national regimes. For a time in China, "hundreds of thousands of satellite dishes. . . [were] sprouting. . . like bamboo shoots after a spring rain." Said one senior Chinese journalist: "The Government has already lost control over information. The leaders may not know it yet, but these days they simply can't control what people know." However, in an effort to crack down on "spiritual pollution" from the West, Prime Minister Li Peng in 1993 banned ordinary Chinese citizens from buying or using satellite dishes. At the time, the Chinese had some half million dishes serving about 15 million subscribers through cable hook-ups in apartment buildings, mostly tuned to English-language programming from Hong-Kong-based Star TV that relayed BBC, CNN, and MTV.

Western programming was also marked for extinction in the Islamic fundamentalist state of Iran, where popular militias burst into homes in Teheran to smash private receivers. "These programs, prepared by international imperialism," stated a government official, "are part of an extensive plot to wipe out our religious and sacred values." The shows most watched, especially by younger Iranians, had included re-runs of serials like "Dynasty" and "Baywatch" and talk shows like "Donahue" and "Oprah," cited as being immoral because of their open treatment of sexuality and sexual themes.[38]

The conspicuousness of satellite dishes in both China and Iran and the dangers of punishment make it unlikely that people will risk detection in the future. Further challenging the power of now, Iranian authorities intensified thought-control by delaying news broadcasts until the ideological impact of each item could be assessed.

Like the binary code of the computer, the pictures of television constitute an international language of deceptive simplicity and explosive power. As the actions of the Chinese and Iranian governments demonstrate, this language can transform not only the way we communicate but the very ideas we believe in.

The Negative Impact of Electronics

But there is also a dark side to the power of now and the instruments that dispense it.

An interconnected world is both stronger and at the same time more vulnerable than one characterized by geographical isolation and national autonomy. On this new and tighter game board, the stakes for winning are infinitely higher and the cost of losing infinitely more catastrophic. No better proof of this principle exists than the international dependence upon certain commodities (petroleum, uranium, cocaine) and the need to control their critical source and supply. A smaller world, a less insulated world, can also be a more dangerous world, for in the politics of proximity the match lies close to the fuse.

Electronic systems of communication, moreover, do not merely transmit events; they accelerate them by cutting down the time it takes for news to travel and by heightening the urgency with which tactical and strategic decisions must be made. Electronics jump-starts the engine of history, connecting the terminal of action to the terminal of diplomatic or military reaction with an electrifying jolt of direct current. In the past, it might have taken days or weeks for the outcome of a distant battle to reach a nation's capital; today, opposing leaders can watch a missile attack "live" on CNN. Thus, the leisurely chess moves of an earlier era are now made under the pressure of a ticking clock. The very speed with which destructive force can be delivered invites swift but irrevocable action.

The medium of television poses particular problems. Because it serves up a persuasive simulation of reality, television can be manipulated to support dubious policies. Provided politicians and generals artfully manage the news, an avoidable war can be converted into a thrilling and patriotic miniseries. In addition, writes Tom Rosenstiel about CNN, "the effect [of its international coverage] was to give voice to political leaders who otherwise lacked global standing. . . especially fading despots and sponsors of terrorism. . . Foreign leaders who needed a soapbox quickly recognized CNN's potential."[39]

Furthermore, television's capacity to communicate suffering on a global scale may actually do more harm than good. "There's so much that happens in the world every single day that even with the most sensitive people, there is a saturation point," notes veteran correspondent Jim Wooten.[40] "Does each succeeding struggle enlarge our understanding of the essential tie of humanity?" asks writer Anna Quindlen. "Or does it merely make us numb?"[41]

GLOBALISM'S PRICE

Technology's ability to erase borders can be seen as unifying the world, but the dissolution of borders can have negative consequences. Tearing down ancestral walls can release ancestral hatreds as ethnic groups rise up to declare age-old claims to territory. At the same time, others calling themselves ethnic "have-nots" may commit acts of atrocity against those they regard as ethnically favored "haves," or with equal violence may seek to redress the economic inequities they charge history has for too long visited upon their land. Still others may vent their frustration at their own statelessness by reaching far across national boundaries in heinous acts of premeditated international terrorism, making no distinction between soldier and civilian, guilty or innocent. For in a borderless world such distinctions fade to insignificance. Indeed, the power of now incites such acts by encouraging the gratification of all impulses even as it deauthoritizes the restraining influences of long-respected moral limits. Thus, in the short run at least, a borderless world becomes a far more perilous place than ever before. Some groups, indeed, may fiercely resist the inclusive power of now by building and defending fortresses of fundamentalist belief to guard the past with violent fervor.

The tendency toward globalism, which has produced international commerce and world war, has also spawned crime on an international scale. The Sicilian Mafia, the Chinese Triad, and the Colombian drug cartels all parallel in their rise the twentieth-century formation of legitimate commercial and diplomatic organizations, as do the international efforts like Interpol that have arisen to combat them.

Globalism has also affected the natural world. Regardless of our nationality or level of complicity, the punishments for the sins of capitalist greed and consumerist abandon have been, and are being, visited upon us all. The air knows no borders, nor does the food chain upon which we depend. Like it or not, we are all united as the common victims of global environmental crimes. Like urban drive-by shootings and terrorist bombs, the international dumping of toxic wastes testifies to a borderless world tyrannized by a power of now that has no conscience.[42]

In addition, the celebrated benefits of global communications can easily be overestimated. To begin with, we must recognize that global communication cannot in itself remake the world. However much a transmitted image or fact inspires or informs, it remains just an image or a fact, not a living social reality. It cannot feed the hungry or heal the sick. And those who are illiterate and oppressed will not be liberated by data alone.

Revolutions do occur, but what telecommunications and computer technology will almost certainly do in the long run is guarantee their benefits to those who are in the best position to enjoy them: those who have money and power and want even more money and power. The rest of humanity will likely gain only minimally and indirectly as impotent but grateful consumers.

Because governments are slower to act than businesses and have less aggressively used electronic technology for their day-to-day operations, we can expect business to act globally faster and more decisively than government. In fact, as Paul Kennedy has observed, the very nature of contemporary problems puts them beyond the reach of ordinary governments to solve.

> Various trends from global warming to twenty-four-hour-a-day trading are *transnational* by nature, crossing borders all over the globe, affecting distant societies, and reminding us that the earth, for all its divisions, is a single unit. They are largely out of the control of the authorities of the traditional nation-state, both in the direct sense that countries cannot prevent incoming atmospheric drift and in the indirect sense that if they banned such activities as biotech farming, robotics, and foreign-exchange dealing, that would not stop them operating elsewhere. Finally, these challenges cannot be met by military force, which is the normal way states have handled threats to their security. Carrier task forces and armored divisions have their uses, but they are unable to prevent the global demographic explosion, stop the greenhouse effect, halt foreign-exchange dealings, ban automated factories and biotech farming in foreign countries, and so on.[43]

Significantly, too, governments are legally defined by political borders, whereas corporations are primarily limited by ambition alone. As a result, thinking transnationally comes easier to business than to government. In the words of critic Herbert I. Schiller:

The corporate-driven economy, impelled to expand or suffer contraction—there is no middle ground—has pushed beyond its national boundaries. The adventurers are the companies that operate in scores of foreign locales. This transnationalism of enterprise has brought to the world scene a comprehensive, corporate, informational-cultural apparatus which fills more and more national living space wherever it operates. . . .

[Some], observing that the new information technologies routinely bypass national boundaries, conclude that the national state is no longer viable. What is not made clear is who or what is supposed to replace the national state. Though no one has suggested the transnational corporations should run the world (not even their executives), no other candidate has stepped forward. International organizations, to the extent that they are universalistic and allow each member-state a voice, are deemed unworkable by the dominant forces that now govern the main Western nations.[44]

More and more as a result, commercial expediency may come to dictate political decisions. From the days of the most ancient empires, imperialistic ambition shaped foreign policy. But in the future it may increasingly determine domestic policy as well, as a nation's agenda is set less by the ideals of its own people than by the pragmatic needs of transnational corporations and the parties and politicians they finance. Thus, a war may be fought to insure the profitable flow of oil from Kuwait, but will seldom be waged to halt a holocaust in a resource-poor land like Bosnia. A global economy, in short, may simply foster the internationalization of greed.

Such international policies have wide moral implications, for the more the globe is dominated by materialism and opportunism, the more world civilization will spiritually decline. Business, after all, pledges its highest allegiance to profit. But a culture that takes that as its highest principle will be poor indeed.

Corporations that measure long-term planning in years, and define "durable goods" as those that merely last for more than three, are strangers to values that are centuries old. As it undermines nationhood and replaces it with a global economy, the commercial power of now will of necessity obliterate tradition itself. Just as the Berlin Wall was toppled, so will the walls of all things past be thrown down—the good bulldozed with the bad. For to dissolve national borders and identities is to displace the treasured ethnic values and distinctions they ancestrally protected and contained.

Some would say, "Good riddance!" Ethnic differences, after all, have inspired centuries of hatred and civil war, as philosopher Immanuel Kant observed two centuries ago.[45] In today's world, ethnicity's energies have in fact created what Daniel Patrick Moynihan has termed an irrepressible and tumultuous "pandaemonium."[46]

Indeed, some would see in the end of ethnic separatism and in the emergence of global homogenization the basis for a new and creative reformulation of human culture. As Walter Truett Anderson has written:

> We are indeed seeing in our time the birth of a global supercul-
> ture that pours together bits and pieces of many different cul-
> tures. . . . We are learning the infinitely subversive lesson that we
> don't always have to simply believe this and not believe that.
> Amid the collapse of old ways of belief comes the discovery that
> we are capable of creating many layers of belief and unbelief, of
> living partly in and partly out of socially created realities.[47]

In essence, then, the public is invited to a mix-and-match fashion show of tradition, an eclectic medley of cultural styles from which they will be free to construct a rich psychic wardrobe drawn from a veritable bazaar of shimmering ethnic fabrics.

Such an image may seem subjectively charming, but it represents a total misreading of what traditions are. Traditions are like living trees rooted in time. They are not driftwood that can be plucked from a beach and made into art. Nor are they like tumbleweed, rootlessly mobile. For traditions to be vital they must have a native soil to grow in, a soil made deep and fertile by time's very duration. Transplantation of any sort incurs great risk.

If ethnicity causes strife, it does so because ethnicity tells people who they are and that they are different from others. If such differentiation becomes perversely destructive, it should be corrected by compelling people to acknowledge the common humanity and needs they share, not by encouraging the dissolution of their most enduring and vital source of identity.

Describing group identity in a postindustrial age, Harold R. Isaacs once wrote: "We spin out from a centrifuge, flying apart socially and politically, at the same time that enormous centripetal forces press us all into more and more of a single mass every year."[48] Civilization's test will be to surmount those forces, to resist now's capacity to crush what is unique.

Some, however, like former Citicorp chairman Walter B. Wriston, are exhilarated by globalism's democratic promise. In his book. *The Twilight of Sovereignty*, Wriston describes information technology as a liberating force with the capacity to revolutionize politics on a global scale.

> In many parts of the world, all news contrary to the official line
> used to be tightly controlled. Information about other political
> systems was hard to come by. Today information about these
> alternatives is bouncing off satellites into hand-held transistor

radios in remote jungles and moving across movie and television screens all over the world. The information technology,
which carries the news of freedom, is rapidly creating a situation
that might be described as the twilight of sovereignty, since the
absolute power of the state to act alone both internally against
its own citizens and externally against other nations' affairs is
rapidly being attenuated. . . . We have learned that freedom is a
virus for which there is no antidote, and that virus is spread on
a global electronic network to people in the far corners of the
world who previously had no hope or knowledge of a better way
of life. This process is in train and cannot be reversed, since the
technology on which it is based will not go away.[49]

To be sure, the power of an idea should never be underestimated,
especially when the means exist to disseminate that idea widely. And few
ideas are more potent than the idea of freedom. But freedom, however
precious, is merely a condition. Like an empty bottle, it can be filled with
whatever contents people wish.

For that very reason, the "better way of life" Wriston celebrates begs
definition. Will a free existence be one predicated chiefly on the gratification
of the senses at any price, even at the expense of others' freedom? Will the
liberation of one group inevitably lead to its repression of another?

And will this thing called freedom provide ample room for a life of the
spirit and of the mind? More specifically, will it encourage those very modes
of behavior that paradoxically require sacrifice and self-discipline, behaviors without which no culture, however free, can deservedly call itself
civilized?

A global economy, after all, is just an economy, nothing more. In and of
itself it does not guarantee freedom, only financial collaboration.

Who, we must ask, will determine the content of those messages so freely
broadcast? Information does not spontaneously broadcast itself, especially
when the means of transmission are sophisticated and expensive. Who,
then, will the broadcasters be, and what will be their motives? And how
will these motives influence the message they send?

The historic tendency of power-structures (whether government or
business) to use mass media to serve their own vested interests will surely
continue however much the media themselves may change. And if governments and businesses globally collaborate in defining the truth as materialistic, how will another truth be heard?

Each medium, in addition, has a natural affinity for a certain kind of
message. Like an invisible sieve, television filters out complexity even as it
allows oversimplification to flow through. Democracy, even global democracy, cannot for long subsist on such a strained diet. For information, in
order to nourish a nation, must come to it whole.

Ironically, the very need to transmit a world of data may generate a psychology of quantification, a reliance upon facts rather than meaning. Like money, numbers are an ideal international language—one, moreover, devoid of emotion and free of ethnic accent. And, in an increasingly global society, the pooling of information may become the perfect ethnic "cleanser," removing the patina of humane tradition and replacing it with a shiny inhumane veneer. Meanwhile, moral reflection may become rarer in a system that demands more and more decisions in less and less time.

Transnational television will be ready to fill the emotional void, providing equal quantities of tranquilizing trivia and voyeuristic excitement, even as commercials perpetuate materialism around the world. The "Age of Communications" will have become, in Russell Kirk's words, an "Age of Conditioned Responses."[50]

Certainly, such a scenario need not come to pass. Some might say that the democratic potential of the Internet will save us globally, subverting totalitarianism even as it bonds us together as individuals. But it would be naive to regard information technology itself as our savior.[51] All the changes we witnessed nationally in chapters 2, 3, 4, 5, and 6—the transformation of individual, family, society, and state—will not end, but instead will be magnified on an international scale because of the electronic integration of the world's cultures.

Freedom may well be "a virus for which there is no cure." But in a speeded-up global environment, the power of now has the potential to become a planetary epidemic.[52]

Should such an epidemic spread, it will have been anticipated some twenty years ago by playwright Paddy Chayefsky in his script for the motion picture *Network*. In one scene, Mr. Arthur Jensen, the head of the Communications Corporation of America, berates TV anchorman Howard Beale for his audacity in challenging on-air the rightness of a corporate takeover:

> You have meddled with the primal forces of Nature, Mr. Beale, and I won't have it. Is that clear? You think you've merely stopped a business deal. That is not the case. The Arabs have taken billions of dollars out of this country and now they must put it back. It is ebb and flow, tidal gravity. It is ecological balance.
>
> You are an old man who thinks in terms of nations and peoples. There are no nations. There are no peoples. There are no Russians. There are no Arabs. There are no Third Worlds. There is no West. There is only one holistic system of systems, one vast and immane, interwoven, interacting, multivaried, multinational dominion of dollars: petrodollars, electrodollars, multidollars, reichmarks, reis, rubles, pounds, and shekels. It is

the international system of currency which determines the totality of life on this planet. That is the natural order of things today.
That is the atomic and subatomic and galactic structure of things
today. And you have meddled with the primal forces of nature.
And you will atone. (Am I getting through to you, Mr. Beale?)

You get up on your little 21 inch screen and howl about
America and democracy. There is no America. There is no democracy. There is only IBM, and ITT, and AT&T, and Du Pont,
Dow, Union Carbide, and Exxon. Those are the nations of the
world today. . . .

We no longer live in a world of nations and ideologies, Mr.
Beale. The world is a college of corporations inexorably determined by the immutable bylaws of destiny. The world is a
business, Mr. Beale. It has been ever since man crawled out of
the slime. And our children will live, Mr. Beale, to see that perfect
world in which there's no war, or famine, oppression or brutality.
One vast and ecumenical holding company for whom all men
will work to serve a common profit and in which all men will
hold a share of stock—all necessities provided, all anxieties
tranquillized, all boredom amused.[53]

Chapter 8

The Transformation of
the Environment

EVEN AS TECHNOLOGICAL speed is shrinking the globe by melting borders and fusing nationalities, it is estranging people from the earth that is their common home. Under the progressive influence of the power of now, nature and—more significantly—humanity's attitude toward nature are being transformed.

The alienation of humanity from nature may be likened to the breakdown of a marriage. In ages past, human beings and nature lived together in a relationship marked by struggle but based on compatibility. Yet, as time has gone on, a state of seemingly irreconcilable differences has arisen between the two partners, differences that have led to increasing separation and the prospect of ecological divorce. Partners, human and natural, who once lived together in harmony are now torn apart by disparate purposes, standing as cosmic courtroom adversaries in a legal battle to determine not the custody of their children, but the future of their children's world.

As is the case with many a failed marriage, the potential causes of failure may have been present at the very inception of the relationship; it just took time for the failure to become evident. If that is true in this case, where did the original flaws lie that have led to this "cosmic divorce," and what caused such flaws to grow?

As we have already seen in our discussion of the family, the speed of our lives is one of the prime factors responsible for the breakdown of marriage. It remains for us to now measure the extent to which that same speed may be contributing to the dissolution of the organic bond between ourselves and our natural environment. To understand the underlying causes of such cosmic divorce, we will first need to examine humanity's own nature and development.

NATURE AND HUMAN NATURE

From Instinct to Intelligence

Just as animate life arose from the inanimate, so did reason emerge from impulse. The ladder of evolution is comprised of a series of transcendant steps: from inanimate to animate, and from instinct to intelligence. In ascending this cosmic ladder, human beings rose above the lower strata of consciousness to a higher plane that allowed them to survey their achievement.

Humankind's natural environment, obedient to physical law and organic instinct, was self-contained and self-sustaining. The human animal existed for countless generations, drawing its sustenance, securing its survival, and propagating its kind as an integral part of this larger organism.

Nevertheless, advanced intelligence led it to rungs by which it rose above static existence. By the power of invention, human beings made their lives safer and less difficult, thereby increasing both their life span and their numbers. Their mastery of fire frightened away predators who did not understand the tamed energy that blazed in the night; while their mastery of stone, edged and wedded to shafts of carved wood, won for them the flesh and hides of elusive prey.

Later, by planting crop-bearing seeds and by taming fecund herds, man manipulated the organic world for his own convenience. By this era, named the Neolithic, he had designed the rudiments of an architecture, his first step toward constructing an artificial world.

With the invention of civilization, humanity continued the evolutionary process of moving from a prefabricated world to an environment of its own contrivance. In its works of construction, humanity's combined powers of conceptualization and ambition carried it beyond the building instincts of less powerful creatures.

In addition, using the tool of verbalization and later of writing, the human race devised laws distinct from those of the natural world, so different in fact that multiple codes of behavior eventually existed within its species, unlike the uniform codes that characterized other forms of life.

Still dependent upon nature for its nourishment, still subject to nature's awesome power of destruction, mankind persisted in the elaboration of its own artificial, tangent universe.

The Price of Civilization

The tale of this transition, from nature to civilization, is preserved in two of humanity's earliest recorded legends, the Babylonian epic of Gilgamesh[1] and the Hebrew account of creation.

According to the Babylonian legend, the gods created a long-haired humanlike creature called Enkidu, who dwelt naked among the wild beasts he regarded as his brethren. Later, to lure Enkidu from this world of innocence, a king sent him a prostitute. After being seduced by the prostitute, Enkidu began to wear clothing and to consume the food and strong drink of civilized men. The animals, who had once been his companions, now shunned him, while Enkidu, for his part, helped shepherds and herdsmen by driving off the lions and wolves that had formerly been his friends.

It was not sexuality itself that undid Enkidu, that estranged him from the natural world he had called his own. After all, other creatures—not only men—engaged in intercourse. Rather, it was the guileful commercialization of a natural act that corrupted him. Yet in exchange for the naïveté he lost, he gained wider knowledge. As the prostitute declared: "You are wise now, Enkidu, and have become like a god."

The connection between the acquisition of worldly wisdom and the loss of natural innocence was later to become a theme in the Hebrew book of Genesis. Having tasted of the forbidden Tree of Knowledge, the first humans—Adam and Eve—became conscious for the first time of their animal nakedness and covered their genitalia with fig leaves. In God's eyes, not only their disobedience but their very enlightenment made them unfit tenants of Eden's garden. Henceforth, like Enkidu, they were banished from a pristine world in which they had lived in unselfconscious harmony with nonhuman creatures. Like Enkidu also, they would henceforth have to earn their living by the sweat of their brow.

In Genesis, the dangers of applying reason are further highlighted by the story of the tower of Babel, a moralizing tale in which God punishes mankind for its arrogance in trying to reach heaven through an act of architectural bravado.

Both the ancient Babylonians and the Hebrews understood that the civilization we possess was purchased at a high price, for to attain it we had to become expatriates from nature. The acquisition of higher intellect forevermore marked mankind as an exile. Only by obedience to the divine, the scriptures told him, could he find redemption.

The Legacy of Greece and Rome

Had Western civilization been governed by this Near Eastern and Biblical view, its eventual conflict with nature might have been forestalled. But Western civilization was also deeply influenced by the beliefs of two early

European peoples, the Greeks and Romans. It was their emphasis on the positive role of reason that led to the growth of science and technology. Reason's growth, in turn, gradually distanced humanity from its humble origins and increasingly deafened its ears to the primitive beat of nature. As civilization developed further, the pace of civilized life adopted a tempo that diverged more and more from that of its natural background. Out of synchronization with the basic processes of its environment, civilization eventually sought to impose on nature its own technological tempo.

The early Greeks, unlike the peoples of the Near East, had regarded intellectual potential positively and called it a divine gift. To them, reason was the faculty that distinguished human beings from lesser creatures. Intellectually proud, they scorned other, earlier cultures that did not acknowledge the primacy of individual thought. Reason, they said, was the gift of the goddess Athena, who herself was born directly from the brain of Zeus, king of the gods.

This positive attitude toward reason is evident in one of the most popular of Greek myths, the story of the battle of the Lapiths and the Centaurs. According to this story, a Greek tribe called the Lapiths invited their neighbors, the Centaurs, to the wedding of the Lapith king. The Centaurs were strange creatures, half-human (from the waist up) and half-horse (from the waist down). Intoxicated from drinking wine at the wedding feast, the Centaurs attacked the Lapith bride and bridesmaids and attempted to gallop off with them, much to the consternation of the Lapith men. In the ensuing battle, the Centaurs were driven off and the Lapiths were triumphant.

So significant was this victory to the Greeks that it inspired the sculptural decoration of two of their most revered shrines: the temple of Zeus at Olympia (home of the Olympic games) and the Parthenon, the greatest of Athena's temples, at Athens.

From our own perspective, it is hard to understand why the equivalent of a barroom brawl would merit depiction on what amounts to the stained-glass window of a church. The justification, however, becomes clear when we discover the underlying meaning the Greeks saw in the story.

The Lapiths, who defended the norms of civilization against the onslaught of the brutish Centaurs, were fully human. In their defense of law and order, of ceremony and custom, they symbolized the triumph of reason over instinct, of rational restraint over sensuous impulse. The animalistic Centaurs, however, were only half human. Drunk with wine, they lost all rational control and transformed a wedding into a rape.

Reason was thus the shining hallmark that distinguished man from the animals. Though reason alienated man from lesser creatures, it endowed him with higher abilities. While the natural world operated in response to impulse and instinct, man crafted a supranatural code of behavior that he enshrined in custom and law.

The power of reason, moreover, allowed humankind to see into the very workings of nature, to discover its inner laws and its own inner order. Thus, men whom the Greeks called philosophers, "lovers of wisdom," sought the essence of nature's own design and insight into the very processes by which ideas are conceived.

Instead of exploring the inner world through philosophy, the ancient Romans were to transfigure the outer world by conquest and construction. They believed it was incumbent upon them not to discover a secret order hidden in nature but to impose their own humanly designed order upon a chaotic and malleable world. For divine Jupiter had granted them "an empire without end."[2]

Just as the Romans conquered space militarily, so did they subdue it through engineering and architecture, traversing terrain with roads, bridges, and aqueducts and erecting colossal theaters, amphitheaters, spas, and entire cities. In a five-century-long orgy of self-glorification, the emperors of Rome consumed huge quantities of the earth's human and nonhuman resources on a global scale even as they ruled that world with Roman law. In the course of that endeavor, the Romans used materialism as a political tool, gratifying the senses of the masses as a means of insuring the allegiance of the people to imperial authority. Under the Roman Empire, reason became the facilitator of individual pleasure and the guarantor of social well-being.

During the Middle Ages that followed, reason became the handmaiden of theology; during the Renaissance, a guiding principle of art. But reason's greatest role lay ahead as the philosophical inspiration for European culture in the eighteenth-century Age of Enlightenment, and as the engine of science and industrialism in the nineteenth and twentieth centuries that followed.[3] As a result, a new and very secular culture—a technological society[4]—would emerge in modern times, a culture in which nowism could freely grow. The technological capacity of Western civilization and its materialistic success and ambition were to make it preeminent in the world.

Crazy Rhythm

As long as mankind's economy had been primitive, it remained steeped in the regular cycles and rhythms of the natural world and consciously dependent upon nature for its gifts. But to the extent that complex economies obliterated the natural world or obscured its importance, to that extent mankind became separate from it.

Clear structural analogies exist between the social world humanity created and the natural one from which it emerged. As the ancient Greek philosopher Protagoras once said, "Man is the measure of all things."

Comparable to the skeletal system of the human body were society's works of architecture and engineering. The body's muscular system became the power of labor, both human and mechanical. The circulatory system became transportation; the digestive and respiratory systems, commerce and the disposal of waste. The body's hormonal system was expressed in the growth and vigor of the populace; its nervous system, in the functions of communications and government. Thus, the civilization that descended from Adam and Eve can be understood as a complex extension of and elaboration upon their organic nature.

Yet the more "human" the organism of society became—that is, the more it was characterized by rational rather than instinctive traits (custom and law, science and technology)—the more distinct it became from the rest of nature. In other words, the higher and higher the edifice of civilization rose, the farther and farther away it grew from the earth. More and more, mankind's actions became self-justifying without reference to the natural world. And the more independently humanity acted, the more confident it became of its exemption from any external, nonhuman law. Indeed, the synthetic basis and artificial cadence of civilization desensitized its members to their ultimate dependency upon nature for life itself.

Patience is a virtue born of a slow-paced society, especially an agrarian one attuned to the measured rhythm of sunrise, sunset, and season. An industrial society, however, operates at its own autonomous rate. The moving assembly line and the on-line computer are oblivious to earthly tempos and to the fullness of time in which the earth bestows its bounty. Instead, technological culture operates at an insistent speed independent of the way nature behaves. As a cultural consequence, we come to live our lives at a "crazy rhythm," an artificial one only tangentially related to the underlying rhythms of the natural world. To the degree that man-made and natural rhythms clash, to that degree do the conditions exist for a way of life marked by discord and dysrhythmia.

Here we touch upon a fundamental explanation for the misalignment between nature and man. All the pious pleas for us to think of ourselves as an organic part of nature, as a thread in nature's great but delicate tapestry, are misguided in that they fail to take account of the innate cause of our disaffection. As the result of evolution, certain creatures on earth acquired a faculty—reason—that inexorably led them to design a parallel universe obedient to humanly devised rules and concepts, a universe necessarily dependent upon nature for its raw materials but driven by its own inner principles and its very own artificial sense of time. Thus, man became a creature apart. In turn, the most aggressive members of his species imposed their cultural will upon other groups—and upon nature itself. God's Genesis mandate, that humanity should "have dominion over the fish of the sea, and over the fowl of the air, and over the cattle, and over all the earth, and over every creeping thing that creepeth upon the earth"[5] was thereby perversely fulfilled.

Yet all the time, man subconsciously sought to return to Eden, to a paradise he remembered he had once lost. But it was not the original Eden he sought but another, not behind him but ahead—a paradise he believed he could somehow reach by continuing the self-assertive footsteps of Adam and Eve.

NATURE AND THE POWER OF NOW

Synchronism: Natural and Artificial

As we saw in earlier chapters, one of the striking effects of advanced technology is the creation of a synchronous society. Such a society is electronically interconnected and instantaneously responsive to stimuli on a national and global scale.

In one respect, a synchronous society is analogous to the world of nature. The rising of the sun that spreads its light across the earth, the coming of the seasons that warm or chill, are cosmic events to which the planet and its living inhabitants respond in unison. Furthermore, the instinct of creatures to survive is necessarily keyed to the present rather than to the future or past. Thus, the power of now, rather than being a social invention, is in fact immanent in the fabric of nature.

Even so, the synchronism of nature is different from that of an electronic society. The simultaneous behavior induced by sunrise or season is local not total. The roundness of the earth and its rotation on its axis cause sunlight to fall upon and then leave one planetary zone after another. Likewise, the orbital revolution of the earth around the sun causes seasonal change to progress from one hemisphere to another. In short, the earth's roundness, rotation, and revolution make its response to the sun sequential rather than instantaneous. Synchronism in nature is a spatially limited phenomenon, manifesting itself not with electronic immediacy but with gradual change.

Such planetary changes are, in fact, deeply imbedded in human physiology, from the circadian alternation of diurnal wakefulness and nocturnal sleep to the lunar phasing of the menstruation cycle to biorhythms far more subtle. Though we might prefer to think of ourselves as autonomous and in total control of our lives, our physiology teaches us otherwise—that our lives still tick in time with a clock not of our own making, an inborn natural clock that cannot be ignored.[6]

Technology, however, does not need to be synchronized with nature. A machine, for example, can start or stop without reference to the sun. Technology is obedient only to its own internal laws, not those of the world outside. Indeed, the more technologically advanced a culture becomes, the more it and its members are insulated from nature's ways. Technology adds to the impression—even the delusion—of our own autonomy, convincing us that we have outgrown the need for the earth's maternal nourishment and protection.

Yet when our technology contravenes the temporal laws of nature, the inevitable result for us is conflict—not only with some external thing called nature but with the nature that is part of our own innermost being. Jet lag is the physical and mental price paid by the traveler who races into the sun. High speed transportation can thus set us at odds with nature, as can instant global communication. The stockbroker in New York who wants to keep abreast of early trading on the Tokyo exchange will sacrifice a full night's sleep as must a U.S. president awakened at 3 A.M. by news of a coup halfway around the world.

Such disruptions to a more natural existence represent merely the most recent phase of a revolt against nature that began when the first caveman staved off the coming of the night with a camp fire. But even when they challenged nature with technology, early cultures still acknowledged the underlying continuity of time and humanity's place within its framework. Though an acute awareness of now was always a prerequisite for human survival, ancient cultures viewed the present as braced at one end by the past and at the other by the future. It was the desire to remember, on the one hand, and the impulse to prophesy on the other, that produced this perspective. Today's electronic culture, however, paradoxically returns its members to an even more primitive state by isolating them in the present. Even as it cuts humanity off from the age-old rhythms of nature, it erodes a cultural consciousness of both future and past. Under the hypnotic influence of high speed, man—like a cosmic expatriate—soon forgets the temporal mother tongue of his planetary homeland.

The Challenges of the Present

If the environmental issues that confront us require our urgent attention, the power of now would seem to be our ally, since it focuses us upon the present. But such a reasonable assessment is based upon a radical misconception of both our problems and their solution.

The problems of the present are in actuality rooted in attitudes deep beneath the current surface of our lives. To solve them, we must first recognize the primal forces that have brought us here. For without comprehending why we have gone wrong, we will never be truly able to find our way. So to solve the problems of the present, we must first look back to the past.

But in addition to looking back to the past, we must also be willing to face up to the future, to look squarely at the eventual consequences of our current acts. Looking to the future also means weighing realistic alternatives and their likely outcomes.

By keeping our eyes focused exclusively on the present, however, the power of now blocks out the past and future from our field of vision. Though it shows us where we are, it denies us the temporal perspective we need to act wisely. No amount of understanding can replace ecological commitment, but commitment without understanding will be pointless.

Yet the power of now does more than just prevent perspective. It actually collaborates in our misdeeds by encouraging short-term gain at the expense of both future and past. It entices us both to sacrifice what is irreplaceable and to ignore what we will replace it with. Energized by technological prowess and commercial greed, the power of now becomes an accomplice in the depletion and depredation of a devalued planet.[7]

Speed and the Natural Environment

Over the course of history, technological society developed an overwhelming attitude bent on material success, a commitment to its own "career," so overpowering that no amount of counseling today seems capable of mending its marriage with nature. The confessional list of civilization's marital sins is lengthy indeed: the poisoning of earth, sea, and sky; the despoilation of unmatched vistas; the insensate, wholesale extinction of species; and the contamination of our very own bodies and genes. But it is not my intention to recite the complete litany here. To that end, the pulp of whole forests has already been sacrificed. Suffice to say, man has taken a sacrament and made of it excrement.

The extent of civilization's impact on nature is a direct function of its velocity. Put simply, the faster humanity's life-style, the greater the damage it has done.

As a consequence of technology, human beings have replaced slower, more natural processes with faster ones of their own invention. Driving such inventions is the power of now that animates us with a desire to have things sooner rather than later. But to fuel the engines of our desire, we have had to draw upon the earth's resources. Where these resources are renewable, we have often drawn upon them at a rate greater than they can be replenished; where resources are nonrenewable, we have at times threatened their virtual exhaustion or polluted them with our mounting wastes.

An analysis that views our ecological problems as an aberrant trajectory of accumulated mistakes fails to probe to the very root of our problem. For humanity's ecological crisis is, in the final analysis, the inevitable product of human nature itself. In consciously changing from species to "*speed*cies," humanity has given new meaning to the term "human *race*,"[8] accelerating not only the extinction of other living things[9] but the exhaustion of nature's bounty.

The cause of our condition is two-fold: the biological capacity of the human race to multiply geometrically on a finite planet and its rational

ability to invent technologies to enhance its existence. Technology promotes population growth, in the short run at least, by helping to nourish,
heal, and protect the species; population growth, in turn, increases the
demand for technological support. Thus the two characteristics collaborate
and reinforce each other's potency.

Were the earth's population small, its needs would be far smaller and its
sins far less ruinous. But mankind has taken the Genesis mandate to "be
fruitful and multiply" far more seriously than it has the Ten Commandments.

In another year there will be almost 93 million more mouths to feed on
earth. In the last half century the earth's population doubled; in the next
fifty years it will double again even as its resources continue to shrink.
Moreover, nearly all this growth will take place in those regions of the
world—Latin America, Asia, and Africa—least capable economically of
absorbing the increase. Currently, the number of people living in absolute
poverty is estimated at nearly one billion. By the end of the decade, there
will be 100 million more.[10]

While the problems in poorer regions are urgent, and will become more
urgent as time goes on, even those parts of the world that are experiencing
slower growth—North America and Europe—will be unable to escape the
political, economic, and ecological repercussions of this demographic explosion.[11]

The development of an integrated global economy only serves to magnify globally the dimensions of ecological abuse by multiplying causes and
effects. The spread of technology and the worldwide dissemination of a
culture of materialistic consumption based upon resource exploitation
progressively accelerates environmental harm, especially when "have not"
nations eagerly try to imitate those that "have." The internationalization of
resource synergy sets the stage for massive ecological damage beyond the
territorial limits of any one nation, not only because the global transportation of hazardous materials (nuclear waste, petroleum) expands the circle
of risk, but also because the earth's vulnerable ecosystem is attacked on
multiple fronts.

It is debatable which force may have the greater impact on nature: a
fast-growing human population or speed-driven technology. Technology,
however, may be the more decisive factor. Microbes and insects, despite
their immense numbers, pose no planetary threat because they are incapable of invention. Indeed, the more primitive the level of human existence
(that is, the closer humans come to functioning in a purely biological mode),
the less ecological danger they pose. In fact, within a self-regulating organic
system, the population of any one species tends to be corrected to maintain
balance in nature. Given the multiplier effect of a powerful technology,
however, even a relatively small group can have an immense impact, even

to the extent of overriding those natural mechanisms that tend to promote equilibrium.

The impact of an asteroid with earth could theoretically terminate an entire species—a fate the dinosaur may have suffered aeons ago. But a human culture equipped with devastating technology can alter the current biological landscape of our planet in a similar way. On the societal plane, history teaches that a small but determined force armed with superior technology and the element of surprise can quickly defeat a far larger but unsuspecting and vulnerable adversary. (In the Spanish conquest of the mighty Aztec and Inca empires, for example, Cortes had but 700 men and Pizarro a mere 180.) On the battlefield of ecology, modern man can do damage at least as great.

Both the multiplication of the human organism and the technical multiplication of its strength are primitive expressions of the power of now. It is the sex drive, craving gratification, that is the chief impetus of propagation. It is the appetite for pleasure, hungering for satisfaction, that stimulates consumption. It is the repulsion at pain that inspires comforting invention. And it is the lust for power that incites domination. All these instincts insist their demands be met now. Transfigured into racist creeds, national anthems, and economic goals, they goad man on to great "glory."

REPLACING NATURE

For all that has been written about the wanton destruction of the natural environment, all too little has been said about the new man-made environment we are replacing it with.[12] For we are in the process of substituting a transient environment of plastic and electrons for an enduring one, furnishing our artificial stage-setting not merely with things but with things that signify a particular kind of time, reinforcing by our stagecraft the inevitability of the drama we subconsciously perform.

Time Made Visible

Our newfound sense of time is reflected in the substance of our man-made environment, for matter is time made visible.

Our faces and our bodies wordlessly confess to the passage of time. Could we leaf through the pages of an album carefully pressed with photographic images reaching from childhood to our later years, we could mark the transformation of our physical selves across time. Yet, so subtle are the changes, they escape our very notice as we live.

At a birthday party we are not simply the particular "year" we celebrate; we are, in fact, a summation of all the years we have ever lived. Thus, aging can be thought of as a cumulative process not unlike the recording of sound on disc or tape. When we play a record, the musical sound we hear at any particular moment is only one of many sounds. Yet the record itself holds all sounds, even the ones we no longer hear.

The cumulative embodiment of time in matter is true not only of human beings, of course, but of other living things as well. The towering tree records in its interior growth-rings the seasons of its life. Even inorganic matter, lifeless and mute, testifies by physical and chemical change to the passage of time: rusting iron and weathering stone are witnesses to their own earthly persistence. In addition, the natural forces that shape them resemble human energy, which, when invested in matter, alters its form. Thus, the time "put into" a piece of raw clay by the potter is ultimately immanent in the finished vase.

In ancient times, art forms intended for the elite often obliged the artist to invest great amounts of time. Jade, for example, one of the hardest of stones, was regarded as especially precious by the Maya and ancient Chinese. But because these cultures lacked hard-enough metal tools to sculpt jade, the stone had to be painstakingly shaped with toothless wire "saws" and abrasives. Years could be spent carving and polishing a single piece. Chinese red-and-black lacquer ware demanded a similar investment of time. Two to three hundred individual layers of lacquer had to be applied and separately allowed to dry. Afterwards, the upper layers were delicately carved away to reveal layers of contrasting color beneath. Even the creation of "ordinary" artifacts implied an investment of time in antiquity that is almost incomprehensible by modern standards. In ancient cultures all the objects used for everyday life were made by hand with only the simplest tools.

Taken together, such artifacts constituted a man-made environment of time that surrounded those who lived in ancient days and wordlessly spoke to them about the pace at which life should be lived—a pace that was slow, steady, and sure. Today, by contrast, we surround ourselves with quick-made things, objects manufactured without even the touch of a human hand. Such an artificial environment has its own message to communicate, a message about a radically different pace of life, one that is rapid and essentially impersonal. It is astounding that we should not realize this, how the props we have surrounded ourselves with dictate the lines we speak and the very tempo at which we speak them.

Lost Horizons

Nowism is amazingly self-reinforcing: the less the past exists, the less of a reminder there exists to preserve it. Thus, the more parking lots, the less incentive for parks. What was once wistfully nostalgic soon becomes barely remembered. In effect, the elaboration of an artificial environment tends to obscure and displace the essential role of nature in our lives.

Ironically, it is easier to enumerate stellar abstractions than to comprehend our earthly reality. We can observe stars in the heavens billions of miles away, but can only see ahead from ground level a distance of thirty miles. How far we actually see is a function of the open space before us. Should we stand in the openness of the countryside, we will be able to see farther than if we stand in the heart of a city. If buildings block our path, if streets turn, our vision is reduced by the man-made obstacles of our urban setting. The measure of ourselves will be ourselves, rather than some natural standard not of our own making. Thus, in building tall, we paradoxically confine our perspective. Only from a building's heights, if smog permits, will we see what we have surrendered.

The more man's works dominate the earth, the more the external points of reference fade against which we can gauge our place on earth. Highway signs and road maps are merely artificial distractions that keep us from asking where we are spiritually headed. *Quo vadis?* "Whither thou goest?" No wonder astronauts, by orbiting earth, have been able to see it—and themselves—for the first time.

In the landscape paintings of the ancient Chinese, tiny human figures can be discerned—sometimes on horseback, sometimes on foot—minute against the immense background of the natural world. Beneath lofty, towering mountains, beside the plummeting cascade of waterfalls, they appear, seemingly so small when compared to the grandeur of nature. Yet if man seems so small in such paintings, his relative size does not signify his insignificance. For to be even a small part of a great and wondrous whole, the ancient Chinese believed, is to be endowed with meaning.

To the texture of their landscapes the painters sometimes added mist. Not everything in life need be knowable, they seem to say. It is enough to see the mist and accept its reality.

But our society does not readily tolerate the unknowable, for the unknowable is hard to communicate. Instead, we insist upon what can be quantified, what can be factually transmitted. To meet our need, we even synthetically construct an artificial horizon, and with that horizon built, confidently move on. For ours is a mobile society. Its geographical transience is merely a spatial expression of the temporal transience that underlies our lives.

It is not a common direction that marks a society as synchronous, but persistent motion. Motion is a characteristic to be measured not in purpose but in process. It matters not that we lack a goal; it only matters that we are going.

Losing Time

The way a society views nature—and, indeed, the way it sees reality—is evident in the way it tells time.

The earliest measures of time came from the observation of change in the larger world of nature outside of man. The sequence of seasons, the positions of planets and stars, the phases of the moon, and the rising and setting of the sun constituted humanity's most ancient clock.

As civilizations arose, these natural changes were enshrined in calendars and stimulated the development of technologies to observe, record, and predict such cosmic events. The earliest astronomers were also the earliest timekeepers; and, by their skill in identifying seasonal cycles, they aided farmers in insuring human survival. Time was also the link between dependent humans and the powerful gods of nature, and the earliest astronomers were also the earliest priests.

Later, ancient civilizations conceived of natural devices that could measure out a single day's time for the purposes of work. The sundial employed the moving rays of the sun but—alas—could only function when the sky was clear. To compensate for its limitations, other inventions were created that used the response of natural elements to earth's gravity: the dripping water of the waterclock and the sinking sands of the hourglass. Yet all of these devices—sundial, waterclock, and hourglass—were still adaptations of processes already present in nature. As such, they testified to humanity's intimate dependence on the natural world.

The development of the mechanical clock during the Renaissance represented a radical departure from the timekeeping of earlier days.[13] Though the earliest mechanical clocks depended upon the effect of gravity upon weights, the essential parts of which they were composed were totally artificial. Whereas sun, water, and sand were already present in the world, gears and escapements existed nowhere until they were manufactured.

In addition, the mechanical clock was capable of measuring time with greater precision than earlier devices and was capable also of dividing up that time into smaller units than had ever before been possible to reckon. Though time had always existed, it was the mechanical clock that created the minute and the second. In so doing, it redefined the structure of work and the pace of human society.

The mechanical clock can also be understood as a reflection of change, as an expression in physical terms of a transformation that was taking place in human thinking, one in which man came to think of himself as more separate from nature, more autonomous, by virtue of the enhanced powers he had acquired through technology. In the face of that clock we can see the flowering of scientific inquiry and the coming of the Industrial Age.

Yet in that same circular face and in those moving hands we can also see the heritage of the past, a past in which human lives for aeons were measured out against seasonal cycles, cycles in which things always returned to where they had always been. Whatever the position of its hands, the old-fashioned clock reminds us with its numerals where time has been and where it is yet to go. It places the present moment within a larger context, subtly whispering to us of moments past and moments yet to be. Evenly spaced around a circular horizon, the numbers stand like dancers with hands joined, guarding the centerpoint whose radii point to their traditional places.

The digital clock, however, tells only of now, an isolated now disconnected from anything past or future, a numeric now that lives and evaporates as the next now is born. The digital clock allows us to focus on the present as never before, devoid of the distractions of "was" or "will be," until even the illusive present becomes a forgotten blank as luminous numbers nimbly transform themselves into other shapes.

The digital clock has banished all perspective, and as such it is the proper symbol of our age. Instead it promises precision, but precision will never be enough. Not as long as we wish to remain human, for being human means valuing a minute mended with compassion more than a second heartlessly split. Peace of mind can only come when life feels whole, when we can see ourselves—and those we love—secure within a natural framework of time that binds all things together and makes them one.

THE END OF MAN

The Road to Thebes

If the path humanity chose has proven destructive—destructive at least of nature and perhaps even of humanity itself—how can we explain this choice? If it were the result of mistakes and random miscalculations, that would be one thing. But if it is the natural expression of humanity's essential character, that is another.

Man was born of nature. Why then would nature produce an offspring in whose very character would lie the source of its own destruction?

Oedipus, so Greek legend tells us, was fated to kill his father. After hearing the prophecy, he fled to the city of Thebes, as far as he could go from home. But on the road to Thebes he got into an angry fight with an old man and slew him. Further down the road he was challenged by a monster called the Sphinx. "Answer my riddle," said the Sphinx, "or I will kill you. What walks at dawn on four; at noon, on two; and at dusk, on three?"

Brilliant Oedipus answered: "Man. For as a baby he crawls on all fours; in maturity he walks upright on two feet; and in old age hobbles on two legs and a cane!" And so Oedipus' life was spared. But, unknown to him, the old man he had slain on the road in a fit of rage was his very own father. In running from his destiny, Oedipus had unwittingly fulfilled it.

In the story, Oedipus is a metaphor for man, who is himself a riddle: a hurrying creature both intellectual and violent, as certain of his destination as he is ignorant of its consequences—man, whose very character is his destiny, whose natural parent (nature) is his ironic victim.

It is startling to think that earth's consummate progeny—mankind—is hostile to its parent's existence. If reason is the natural product of evolution, and if reason contributes to nature's destruction, then either reason must be a deadly mutation or nature itself must be suicidal.

In *Design with Nature,* landscape architect Ian McHarg commented on the first proposition:

> It is salutary to suggest that the path and direction of evolution may not be identical to human ideas of destiny; that man, while the current, dominant species, may not be an enduring climax; that brain may not be the culmination of biological evolution or it might in contrast be an aberration, a spinal tumor, and finally, although no man will hear it, the algae may laugh last.[14]

Even darker was the judgment of anthropologist Loren Eiseley:

> It is with the coming of man that a vast hole seems to open in nature, a vast black whirlpool spinning faster and faster, consuming flesh, stones, soil, minerals, sucking down the lightning, wrenching power from the atom, until the ancient sounds of nature are drowned in the cacophony of something which is no longer nature, something instead which is loose and knocking at the world's heart, something demonic and no longer planned—escaped, it may be—spewed out of nature, contending in a final giant's game against its master.[15]

Others, like naturalist Edward O. Wilson, do not willingly share Eiseley's pessimism. Yet even Wilson was concerned by what he saw as a genetic predisposition in man for short-range thinking, for placing now before tomorrow.

> It is possible that intelligence in the wrong kind of species was foreordained to be a fatal combination for the biosphere. . . , that people are programmed by their genetic heritage to be so selfish that a sense of global responsibility will come too late. Individuals place themselves first, family second, tribe third and the rest of the world a distant fourth. Their genes also predispose them to plan ahead for one or two generations at most.[16]

In effect, Wilson argued, unless humanity changes its now-centered behavior, it may precipitate its own suicide, taking countless other species with it to their deaths.

Long ago, Mayan astronomers declared that the earth had already passed through a number of successive "creations," each of which had been followed by cosmic destruction and later rebirth. This ancient belief is curiously echoed in the "Big Bang" theory of creation espoused today by leading astrophysicists. According to this theory, the universe began with a cosmic explosion that hurled energy and matter outwards from its center. The theory's corollary is the "Big Crunch," the idea that eventually—like an outstretched rubber band that snaps back—the matter and energy of the universe will cataclysmically contract, setting off by their compression another explosion from which a new universe will be born.

In human terms, the current expansion of human consciousness may someday reverse its course and end in a destruction of all knowledge. By the same token, our present-centered and wanton mistreatment of the natural world may not reflect errors on our part as much as the outworking of our own inner nature in keeping with a larger pattern of cosmic oscillation by which life on our planet will someday come to an end.

Some, however, see grounds for cosmic optimism. Named for the ancient Greek goddess of earth, the "Gaia" hypothesis of scientist James Lovelock proposes that our planet is a self-correcting, living entity, continually adjusting its components to restore balance.[17] Yet even this theory does not guarantee our own species' survival, only the long-term survival of the planet as a whole.

Early this century, theologian Pierre Teilhard de Chardin prophesied the end of the world as we know it—not, however, as something to be mourned but as the culminating event of human evolution. The union of minds in a global society, he wrote, would trigger a transcendant experience unifying man and God.[18] Expanding on this theme and linking it to the electronics revolution now taking place, author Peter Russell postulated the birth of a "global brain" through which humanity would be able to achieve and maintain a new level of spiritual consciousness.[19] In a similar vein, biochemist Gregory Stock has foreseen the emergence of a global superorganism he calls "Metaman" ("beyond, and transcending humans"), an organism—part human, part nonhuman—that even now draws upon planetary energy sources and acts through a telecommunicational "nervous system" guided by human intelligence and the power of computers. "Humankind," says Stock, "far from being at the brink of cataclysm is moving toward a bright future."[20]

Ultimately, each of us will choose the scenario we prefer, the one that best fits our personality. Indeed, it may be argued that every culture designs its own eschatology—its own communal vision of how things will end—based on how it sees the present. A technologically centered culture will see its salvation in a computer just as an earlier one saw it in a man on a cross.

Whatever we believe, however, it would be fatal to put too much faith in technology. Machines may make us faster, but they do not of themselves make us more compassionate, more responsible, or more wise. Indeed, by accelerating our actions, they may even precipitate our end.

An Electronic Destiny

For a long time thinkers have speculated that our animalistic side—the beast in the human Centaur—would draw us on into Armageddon; that, endowed with a penchant for inventing marvels of technological power, we would be led to exercise them out of blind fury and thus bring about our own destruction.

There is, to be sure, no assurance that we will ever be free of the terrors of the beast within us, of its propensity to rise and seize control of the hand that holds the switch. But it is the other side of our nature that we should fear just as much: the part that is logical, that is rational—man the creator and the inventor—for that part of ourselves is as natural as our other half and just as deadly.

Having perfected technology, we have unleashed the primal power of now, a power whose appetite is voracious and all-consuming, swallowing a sense of both what has been and what is yet to be. And, more than having unleashed it, we have, with circuitry and signal, fused it to our very being.

It is natural to assume we are nature's consummate design, in need of only minor modification. Yet we stand not at the top of Jacob's ladder but only on its highest visible rung, for above us the ladder rises through the clouds, we know not how high.

Though we seem to stand, we move. As though drawn on by Bernoullian law into a stream coursing at the speed of light, we may inevitably be heading for an evolutionary rendezvous with an electronic destiny. We will leave three-dimensional nature behind because it was only our most recent incarnation. We will shed our skin as the snake sheds its own, or we will be the moth becoming emergent butterfly—electronic butterfly—drawn into the flame, while the universe, like a cosmic bug-zapper, marks our passage with a momentary hiss emanating from a bluish glow deep in the dark night of space.

The Sirens of the *Odyssey* did not sing one song and one song alone to lure mariners to their deaths; they individualized the words to the heart of the hearer, seducing him with an articulation of his own deepest desire. The primal universe beckons to us, beyond reason, beyond passion, beyond the solidity of inanimate matter and the pulsing warmth of flesh, beyond substance itself, calling out to us from the darkness, calling us in.

It calls us home, for it is a going back home that it offers us, a cosmic return, not as ashes to ashes, nor as dust to dust, but as atom to atom, back to the very origins of creation, back before nature as we know it, back before the land was separated from the sea, before the firmaments parted, before light first came out of the darkness. For in the beginning was the Word, the *logos*, the immanent reason that is the heart of the universe, and it is this *logos* that calls us back now, knowing not past or future, but only now, a now that is eternal.

The Centaurs of old resulted from a mating of man and horse. The new Centaurs will represent not a wedding of beast and man but of man and atom, a mating of electrons that already whirl waiting, silent beneath our skin.

If such an end as this awaits us, the cosmic divorce we earlier foresaw will have been averted. Instead, an extraordinary reconciliation will have taken place. For civilization, by virtue of its advanced technology, will have been ineluctably drawn into an electronic stream as primal as the cosmos itself, a swiftly moving stream in which humanity's essence will once again become one with nature's.

Chapter 9

The Three Keys to Resisting Now's Power

THE INDIVIDUAL, the family, society, democracy, international relations, and the environment—all are being transformed by the power of now. Not only is the power of now altering their nature, it is changing the very meaning these words have in our minds. Thus, under its influence, both reality and our understanding of reality are being reshaped.

The transformations wrought by the power of now have positive and negative effects, which are summarized below.

Positive Effects of the Power of Now	Negative Effects of the Power of Now
1. By focusing us on the present, the power of now frees us from dwelling on the errors of the past.	1. By focusing us on the present, the power of now deprives us of the enriching experiences and lessons of the past.
2. By focusing us on the present, the power of now prevents anxiety about the future.	2. By focusing us on the present, the power of now blinds us to the consequences of our choices.

3. By liberating us from error and anxiety, the power of now frees us to live for the present.

3. By obscuring both experience and consequences, the power of now denies us the chronological perspective necessary for wise decisions.

4. By suppressing both the past and the future, the power of now enables us to recognize the preciousness and potentiality of the individual moments in our lives.

4. By obscuring both the past and the future, the power of now deprives us of a sense of continuity that could otherwise stabilize and strengthen our lives.

5. By stimulating and gratifying our senses, the power of now increases the sensual pleasures of existence.

5. By stimulating and gratifying our senses, the power of now distracts us from developing our capacity for rational reflection and critical judgment.

6. Because of the high-speed technology upon which it depends, the power of now adds instancy and excitement to our lives.

6. Because of the high-speed technology upon which it depends, the power of now adds stress and overstimulation to our lives.

7. By assigning the highest priority to speed, the power of now enhances the value of those activities that exemplify speed (electronic entertainment, computerization, electronic information transfer, automation, the rapid consumption of material goods, the development of systems of belief that promise instant answers and solutions.)

7. By assigning the highest priority to speed, the power of now undermines the value of those experiences that exemplify or require time to develop (psychological maturation, the building of meaningful human relationships, the doing of careful and responsible work, the appreciation and creation of the arts, and the search for the answers to life's greatest problems and mysteries).

8. The power of now enriches life by emphasizing the importance of satisfying our material needs.

8. The power of now impoverishes life by deemphasizing the importance of meeting our spiritual needs.

9. By heightening our sensory awareness, the power of now encourages the creation of an artificial environment that can efficiently deliver a continually changing supply of gratifications.

9. By making us insensible to what is durable and permanent, the power of now surrounds us with an environment of temporary and transient things that leave us unfulfilled.

10. The power of now gives us what we want when we want it, from fast food and ATM cash to emergency medical assistance, thereby promoting the happiness, health, and safety of the individual.

10. The power of now obscures the need for us to cultivate those skills and virtues—patience, commitment, self-denial, and even self-sacrifice—without which no civilization can long endure.

11. By accelerating the speed of everyday life, the power of now energizes the processes of social transformation and change.

11. By accelerating the speed of everyday life, the power of now contributes to the disintegration of social institutions, including the family.

12. The power of now permits us to know each other better by electronically connecting us with people of like interests, thereby building friendships and communities.

12. By interposing technology between human relationships, the power of now displaces flesh-and-blood relationships with synthetic ones.

13. By distancing us from the ways of the past, the power of now increases the likelihood of creating a truer, more prejudice-free democracy.

13. By erasing history and eroding traditions, the power of now undermines the foundations of national and ethnic identity.

14. By means of electronic communications, the power of now can unify the disparate peoples of the world and contribute to global harmony and productivity.

14. By forcing nations together and accelerating the speed of global events, the power of now has created a world that is far more volatile and explosive than ever before.

15. By instantly showing us parts of the world we would not otherwise see without the aid of electronic technology, the power of now increases our knowledge of nature.

15. By setting a technologically driven pace that is inimical to the rhythms and organic needs of the environment, the power of now diminishes our understanding of and respect for nature.

Despite the many benefits it conveys, the negative effects of the power of now outweigh its positive ones. The explanation for this lies in the power of now's exclusivity. Nowism offers us the present as never before, but the price it demands is that we surrender our grasp of the past and future and the continuity and stability they can provide. This is the hidden cost of the power of now.

To look back to the past for guidance, however, and ahead to the future for direction, does not mean to abandon the present. We can still answer its call and meet its needs. Indeed, we can do so even more effectively if we can see the moment within a larger context of meaning and purpose. But because of its temporal exclusivity, the power of now blinds us to the importance of such perspective. Besides, immediacy's appeal is so persuasive; nowism's influence, so immense.

How then can we resist its negative influence so as to insure a humane future for our children and ourselves?

Recalling the sources of now's power—technology, history, and the senses—can help us to find our way. To resist the dangers inherent in the power of now we must simultaneously do three things: restrain our technology, retain our history, and regain our senses. Only then will we be able to reclaim our lives.

First, we must reassert control over technology. We must first define the kind of life we want—personally and communally—and then ask what technologies will or will not truly serve those ends. Furthermore, we must have the courage to act both individually and socially to reject those technologies that take more than they give.

Second, we must aggressively take steps to insure the preservation of the past and the dissemination of its wisdom and beauty.

Third, we must look beyond the artificiality and impermanence we have created to recapture a sense of what is natural, enduring, and true. To do so is not to renounce the moment, but to rediscover it and its potentiality. We must come to see that "slow" is not necessarily bad, nor "fast" necessarily good.

As much as we can, we must seek to balance the short term with the long, the immediate with the durable, the transient with the permanent, the sensory with the contemplative. If we do so, the power of now will cease to be a threat, for in it resides opportunity—the only opportunity we will ever have—to realize the present.

Our success, then, will depend on three things: restraining our technology, retaining our history, and regaining our senses. Let us now examine each of these approaches in turn.

RESTRAINING OUR TECHNOLOGY

In a fast-moving game like basketball, time-outs are built into the rules of the game. The coach sits attentively at the sidelines watching the game's ebb and flow. If he is skilled, he can sense those critical moments that demand that the team step out of the action's stream. "Time out" is a time to review, to evaluate, to plan new strategies appropriate to the difficulties or successes of the moment.

Yet in our own lives we seldom call such time-outs. Rather than being a coach with an outsider's perspective, we are the player rushing back and forth from one end of the court to the other with little time to catch our breath, let alone reflect on a larger plan. Instead, we rejoice in separate baskets made or blocked.

Even in sports that move at a slower pace there are time zones for reflection: in football, the huddle; in baseball, the conference on the mound.

Time Out for the Spirit

Thousands of years ago—long before basketball, football, or baseball— the ancient Hebrews committed themselves to a concept called the sabbath, a day set aside after six days of work, a day of prayer and physical rest. The Bible also tells us the sabbath was created to commemorate God's own rest taken after the six days of creation.[1]

Underlying the concept of the sabbath is the idea of human beings stepping outside the stream of work and entering into a zone of rest, the act of moving from one modality of time to another.

The time mode of work is linear and sequential. Particular activities are directed toward a goal that constitutes a point in time. Individual efforts progress by purpose, aimed in a single direction. Time itself is thereby directionally shaped.

Within the atmosphere of the sabbath, however, time is transformed. Time ceases to be the longitudinal product of linking one effort to another in a chosen direction. Instead, it becomes the spherical whole within which all separate elements of life are embraced.

The sabbath both joins and separates: it mends into wholeness the parts of our humanness torn by the centrifugal demands of work while separating that new-found wholeness from external forces that would destroy it.

The all-inclusive nature of the sabbath is illustrated by the nature of those it was meant to govern—not only the Hebrews themselves, but the sojourners within their gates and even their livestock. The whole community would thus constitute a sanctified space in which a new and special kind of time would exist.

As part of the Ten Commandments, man is instructed to "remember the sabbath day and keep it holy."[2] This act of sanctifying time parallels God's own action on the seventh day when he "blessed the sabbath day and hallowed it." Indeed, of all days in the Jewish ritual calendar, none is more sacred in tradition than the sabbath, not even the Day of Atonement, Yom Kippur.

The Ten Commandments also instruct man that he "shall labor six days." Thus, restored to spiritual wholeness, man is to reenter with vigor the world of linear time.

Temporal Communities

In the world of today, both time and space have been desanctified. Those who would attempt to preserve and honor the sabbath sojourn in an alien land where the reasons to earn money and the reasons to spend it pull with increasing centrifugal force upon individual lives. To resist these forces is immensely difficult for an individual or a family.

In uncommon places in our country, however, religious communities exist where against great odds age-old spiritual values are still honored. Such is the case, for example, among the Hassidic Jews of New York and the Amish of Pennsylvania. In such deliberately anachronistic communities the personal search for wholeness is less difficult, for a community signifies a special entity where time and space coexist organically, nurturing and protecting each other against the ravages of change.

But how ironic that such a sanctuary should be needed, a refuge designed to defend individuals against the psychic assaults of their own culture. And how ironic that a society should be so structured that its inhuman speed warps or kills those it should sustain. No wonder so many have turned to chemical agents to slow down their lives or speed them up to keep pace with the whirling world they anxiously cling to.

Few of us, however, would willingly trade in our car for an Amish buggy or today's fashions for Hassidic felt—nor could we readily do so, for we are, in fact, conditioned by and imprisoned by the temporal environment we have grown up in, as are indeed the Jews of Williamsburg and the Pennsylvania Dutch of Lancaster County. Yet do we really need to become expatriates from our culture in order to find a fuller existence? Need we journey so "far from the madding crowd" to live in peace?

The Etymology of an Idea

As we have seen, three things make us vulnerable to the power of now: our own nervous system, the newness of our nation, and the progress of technology. By understanding the ways these factors influence our responses and choices we can gain more control over our lives. But of these three factors, only one is directly subject to our will. We cannot change our nervous system; we cannot change our national history; but we can change the technology we use and the direction we let it follow.

Technology itself is an intriguing word. We normally think of it as a force: we speak of advances in "technology" or discuss how "technology" will affect our lives. But this meaning of the word is a recent one.

According to the *Oxford English Dictionary*, the word "technology" was first used in the year 1615. It then meant "a discourse or treatise on art or the arts; the scientific study of the practical or industrial arts." That is, "technology" referred to a field of study, like other words that have the same "ology" suffix. So "geology" (from the Greek *ge*, "earth," and *logos*, "study") is the study of the earth, and "biology" (from the Greek *bios*, "life") is the study of life. Thus, "technology" originally meant the study of *techne*, the ancient Greek word for an art, a craft, or a skill.

For over two centuries, that is the meaning "technology" retained. But during those two centuries the world was changing.

It was only in 1859, when the Industrial Age was in full swing, that "technology" acquired its modern meaning: "the practical arts collectively." In short, technology changed from being thought of as a field of study, as something humanity can act upon, to a collective entity that acts upon man.

To be sure, changes in semantics often reflect changes in society: as machines and factories began to make more and more of an impact on everyday life, people began to see industry and invention in a new light. Consequently, old words acquired new social meaning.

Despite this semantic development, however, technology had acquired no life or mind, no matter how powerful its instruments and effects had become. It was still incumbent upon human beings, as creatures endowed with reason, to determine the purposes their machines would serve.

Defining Ourselves

Yet, before human beings can make the right technical decisions, they must first make the right human ones. They must first ponder what they want themselves to be and how much of their lives they want dominated by things.

It was the Stoic philosophers who long ago argued that we are never freed by the things we own but are instead possessed by them, that he is most free who is possessed by the fewest possessions. This is not an argument for poverty, but rather an attempt to define the true meaning of wealth. It leads us to ask: how much do we really need to be happy? and what is it that we truly require? For by simplifying our lives, we may paradoxically enrich them.

No doubt such an approach to the future may be dismissed as too "philosophical," too unsuited to the materialistic world we live in, too incompatible with the quick-fix solutions our society seems to prefer. But that is precisely why it is the right approach to take, for rarely does a disease find its proper cure attractive.

Nor is such a "philosophical" approach meant for everyone. Even now, the mass of humanity on this planet needs not more philosophy but more food and clothing; not better principles, but better housing, sanitation, and health care. And even after these basic and undeniable needs are met, many will be made truly and lastingly happy by the possessions the Stoics were quick to scorn.

The real question is: should that be our highest definition of happiness? Should such things be the be-all and end-all of life, with leisure and ease the highest purpose of man, or should we aspire to something more? Indeed, should fleeting happiness itself be our aim or something else—as yet undefined—that may ask of us more than it gives?

A Humane Agenda

Beyond understanding ourselves better, what attitudes must we adopt within the context of modern technology to build a more humane world?

First, we must reject two illusions: that what is new is automatically better than what is old, and that what is fast is necessarily better than what is slow.[3] Next, we must be wary of the subtle but cumulative price we pay for every element of artificiality we install in our lives. Last, we must be mindful to conserve those parts of our world not yet invaded by technology, for—beyond its innate beauty and inner harmony—nature offers clear testimony to each generation that there can be an alternative to the seemingly inevitable world we have created, that there is an alternative to the suffocating exclusivity of artificial existence. Indeed, just realizing that speed can have negative consequences gives us immeasurable control over the course of our lives by rousing us from passivity.

RETAINING OUR HISTORY

In 1972, NASA launched the first two spacecraft ever to leave our solar system. Called Pioneer 10 and 11, they carried the first messages from our planet ever intended for extraterrestrial beings. Inscribed on gold-anodized aluminum plates were engravings of a male and female earthling along with a cosmic "road map" to help aliens locate our planet. In 1979, Voyager 1 and 2 traveled on a similar journey with pictures of life on earth and recordings of music and human speech. These Pioneer and Voyager messages were the first cosmic letters postmarked "Earth."

In their continuing search for extraterrestrial intelligence, scientists have also listened for messages from outer space. Huge radiotelescopic antennas have scanned the heavens in efforts to detect such signals.

Should such a transmission ever be intercepted or should one of our spacecraft ever land on another world, the message it bears will have crossed immense reaches of space and time. Just as the lights we see in the night sky may represent stars that no longer exist, stars that emitted their last light thousands of years ago before dying, so the cosmic message we may ultimately receive may represent the words of a civilization long dead. Indeed, our own Pioneers and Voyagers may not make landfall, if ever they do, until thousands of years have passed on Earth.

To reach a safe harbor, these spacecraft will need to survive many perils in dark space: collisions with meteors and asteroids, extreme temperatures and hostile atmospheres, and the very vastness of space where near-misses can carom a missile into infinity.

Alien Wisdom

The amazing fact is that such spacecraft have already landed. More amazingly still, they have landed here on Earth.

Their capsules crushed almost beyond recognition, their alien crews long since dead, they have impacted on the surface of our planet. The messages they bore still survive, etched in mysterious symbols on charred and broken plaques. The word of these time-travelers is waiting to be deciphered, its import weighed. Indeed, on the success of this crucial enterprise may hang the fate of our own civilization.

These spacecraft are not, however, from another planet or galaxy, however distant their point of origin may appear, however long ago they were launched into the vastness of time. Battered by their journey through the millennia, they are in fact an ancient testament from earthlings like ourselves, the cracked inscriptions and shattered artifacts of lost worlds and vanished civilizations from our own human past.

The obstacles these objects had to endure to reach our time were as formidable as any encountered in outer space. The natural processes of our planet are unremitting in their effort to obliterate the works of humankind, to level by weathering what was once raised on high, to reduce by oxidation what was once strong. The human spirit, the most precious part of our being, is, paradoxically, the least stable element of our existence. Evanescent, it vanishes at death unless recorded in matter that is itself fragile.

And where nature leaves off in its pursuit of disintegration and dissolution, humankind stands ready with its potent will to destroy. The lust for god and gold, the flame of religious fervor and the torch of conquest, have condemned books to the bonfire, statues to the melting pot, and history to oblivion. The human hunger for power has been as consuming in its destructive energy as nature's own reductive force.

To this add destruction from neglect, the passive process by which the past is not wantonly brutalized but wantonly forgotten, its delicate substance left to evaporate on the winds of time. Here marches the new barbarism, the kind that comes not to burn libraries but to ignore them, not to enslave a culture but to be itself enslaved to numbing comfort.

Thoughts need not be ancient to be rejected in this way. For the accelerative thrust of our society prematurely ages anything past, turning insights centuries or even only decades old into rejected anachronisms. What was past ceases to prologue. Instead, it becomes curbside trash.

The Electronic Curtain

A half century ago at Westminster College in Fulton, Missouri, Sir Winston Churchill warned that an "iron curtain" had descended across the continent of Europe, a line of control behind which lay the capitals of ancient states. Today, across America and across the world, another curtain is descending, an electronic curtain, less apparent and more pervasive than the curtain of Churchill's day. It is a curtain not geographical but temporal, one that isolates us from all other times but now.

The Power of Then

To raise that curtain in our personal existence we must struggle to keep ancestral memories, ethnic traditions, and religious rituals alive, so that by regaining a sense of context our families and communities will be able to withstand the leveling force of now.

To raise that same curtain publicly we must redirect education, insisting that "back to the basics" always includes a solid foundation of history and a solid core of traditional works, works respected not simply because they are old but because they embody "momentous questions of permanent relevance,"[4] questions that can lead us to measure our own values against those of an earlier day. Such works can help us to see that our own struggle for meaning is not an isolated one, but part of a larger continuum, and can sensitize us, through a study of alternatives and consequences, to choose our own path with greater wisdom.

To See Clearly

Over forty years ago, when I was a boy, I sat fishing by the edge of a small lake near my home. A bright summer sun shone on the waters of the lake. As I sat there, an older fisherman approached holding something in his hand. "Here, son. Why don't you try these?" he said, offering me a curious pair of glasses. "Try 'em on and you'll really see something," he said proudly.

As I put them on, the glare on the water suddenly disappeared and I could see big fish gliding slowly beneath the surface. The polaroid lenses (a newly invented marvel then) had banished the glare of the sun and allowed me to see the very fish I sought, hidden until then by the sunlight.

Literature, especially from another time, can be like these glasses of my boyhood, filtering out the bright light of current trends, permitting us to see beneath the glaring surface that many call reality. Looking into old books can disclose unexpected truths about our world, granting a depth of vision we can find nowhere else.

REGAINING OUR SENSES

There are unseen worlds, worlds that lie beyond the natural powers of human sight. Some are realities too small for us to perceive even though they are near; others are too far away to be discerned despite their immense size. Yet aids exist, should we choose to use them, to extend the range of our sense: the microscope for the unseen world within, the telescope for the world without.

But other unseen worlds exist as well, worlds before our eyes that escape our conscious notice. These are the worlds too near to really see or too large to fully comprehend.

Near my workplace is a street, a very undistinguished street that I have driven down countless times. Several months ago I needed to stop at a government office on that street but, finding no parking places, drove to the very end of the block and walked back. Though it seemed a tedious thing to do, the errand was necessary and I had no choice.

Walking from my car to the office, I made some startling discoveries— things on that street I had never seen before though I had driven down its length hundreds of times before: wildflowers and curious stones and even an entire house with marvelous carved wood detail. I even happened upon a little side street whose existence I had never known. All that I saw was new to me, yet it had always been there.

How much we can lose by going so fast! How little we truly see! The very world we inhabit is one our senses construct, a world shaped by the pace at which we travel through life. In a very real way, time *creates* space. If I walk down a street slowly, a house appears; if I drive down the street quickly, no house exists. It is time that fabricates the world we naively call reality.

How many other things, like the magical wildflowers and stones, are in or out of our lives because of the tempo by which we live? How many parallel worlds exist that we are alien to, worlds unseen but coexisting with our own?

Three decades ago I left Florida behind and headed north to New York by car. The warmth of spring had already come to the land I left behind, lifting it from the barrenness of drab winter to the lush promise of summer. I headed north through Georgia and the Carolinas, and, as I did, the world changed around me, turning from spring green to winter brown. Time turned backward the further north I drove until, in New York, I stopped in icy cold.

Then, as I rested, slowly, almost imperceptibly, the change began once again, only now winter surrendered to spring. Spring came now as it had always come before—in melting mud and blossoming dogwood—but came as I had never seen it before, for now I studied its presence slowly emerge, sensitive to its coming.

Grasping spring's meaning for the first time, I realized at that very moment how many springs I had never truly known, how many I had let slip through my fingers as I had gone about the business of daily living. It had been so big, so close, I had been oblivious to its existence.

Not only are there sights, but sounds too that we do not perceive, not sounds pitched too high or low for our ears to detect, but sounds unheard because of our hurried pursuits. The noises of mechanical transportation overwhelm the quieter sounds that come from the remaining natural environment around us. And our accelerated pace of life leaves us deaf to spoken words that vibrate with human need. It is simply too "time-consuming" to listen.

As habit and culture reinforce the structure of the artificial world we have built, we become less and less able to see and hear the things we must if our world is to be humane. Despite the revolution in electronic communication we have witnessed in this century, the earth's population grows more alien to itself, society more fragmented, and the individual more self-absorbed.

Years ago, I lived at the edge of a college campus, a single tenant in a concrete-block row of one-bedroom apartments. The hot summer night was humid and still, except for the relentless hum of air-conditioning units. Then, suddenly, the power went out. With all lights off and the air-conditioner dead, there was nothing to do but go outside. I did so and sat down in an aluminum folding chair outside my apartment door, facing the pitch-black parking lot.

At the beginning of summer a new tenant had moved into the apartment adjoining mine and for whatever reason (I cannot remember why) I had taken a dislike to him. Because the power was out, he, too, now did the inevitable, coming out of his apartment and sitting in his aluminum folding chair.

It was then that both of us discovered something almost simultaneously: we could see the stars in the night sky. More than just being seen, they had become a bright and insistent presence in the darkness that surrounded us. As we looked at them together, we began to speak, to talk together.

Twenty minutes later the street lights and parking lot lamps shot back on, as did the lights in our separate apartments. It was like a glaring symbol announcing to the reasonable and civilized that it was time to go back in. The stars had now all but disappeared, obscured by the atmospheric reflection of fluorescent light. Once again the compressors hummed. Never again would the two of us share our lives.

Since that night I have pondered how much our technology blinds us to, however much else it may reveal. We will never know the stars as did the

Babylonians or the builders of Stonehenge, never feel their power, their mystery. It is so because of all that we know now, all that our science has taught us and explained. Having tasted of the apple, we can no longer remain innocent tenants of Eden.

To be sure, it was not a Paradise even then, for the unknown can terrify as well as awe. But the fact remains: we will never see the world as once it was seen. And as perception changes, so does the reality.

Having "understood" the world, having acquired powers that were once the province only of the ancient gods, we have become less human in exchange, emptier in spirit for all our knowledge. For as our perceptions have altered our sense of reality, so in turn have we ourselves been altered too.

A Sensory Strategy

It is too much to expect that we can reverse time and return to an earlier, simpler day. But that does not mean tranquillity is beyond our reach.

Attaining peace will require a behavioral strategy. We will need, first, to insulate ourselves from the sensory overstimulation which today's hyper-culture generates. And second, we will need to discover simple activities that can bestow peace on our lives. Our "battle plan" need not be grandiose, for the "battlefield" will have the scale of ordinary, everyday existence. Even so, victories secured in such a struggle will not be small.

If we cannot turn the clock back for our entire culture, persuading it to return to slower ways, we can, as individuals, slow the pace of our lives by deliberate choice. Rather than letting a shallow and arbitrary present tyrannize our lives, we can learn to explore the hidden riches of each moment. And if we share these skills with those we love, teaching them to our children, our personal victory will be a lasting one, reaching beyond the limits of our own being.

For the rewards of such patience can be great even if they emanate from things seemingly small—wildflowers rising rebellious through concrete steps, the frigid earth melting into May, and a million stars insistent above our heads in the summer night.

Mastering Time

In a society where there seems to be too little time to do what has to be done, the skill of time management has assumed great importance. The frequent subject of seminars and books, time-management's goal is efficiency: through proper planning and work habits, time that would otherwise be wasted can be saved and applied to tasks that would otherwise lie undone. Time, we are told, can be mastered.[5]

In actuality, however, we can no more "master" time than a mariner can "master" the sea, or an explorer "master" the wilderness. Time, the sea we must sail during our lifetime, the wilderness we must traverse during our lives, cannot be mastered. To think so is an act of presumption.

What we *can* do, however, is examine our lives so our journey has meaning. We need to decide what things are truly important and what things are not and then act upon our decision.

A Multiplicity of Nows

In reality, the power of now is an illusion sustained by a societal speed that precludes reflection. Now is not one but many. The consumerist now, the mass-marketed now, the televised now that reinforce each other are but one version of reality. There are others, but they can only be found by the individual human heart. Yet to find them, our minds and senses must be freed from the materialistic indoctrination of contemporary society.

We cannot "seize the moment" until we can see it. And we can only see it by liberating ourselves, breaking the bonds that compel us to look only at illusory images flickering on the solitary wall of our darkened cave.

In activist Robert Theobald's words: "We must learn to live *in the moment*, with a profound sense of both the past that has made us and the future we can create by our actions,"[6] not because the past was wiser or the future will be easier, but because the full meaning of the present can only be realized in their embrace.[7]

RECLAIMING OUR LIVES

As the speed of our lives increases, we come closer and closer to an invisible "sound barrier" that can destroy our craft. Already we can feel the fuselage shutter as it begins to enter a zone of air turbulence that can rend it apart. Already we feel the controls becoming resistant to our will.

The everyday stresses we experience warn us we are going too fast, that even now we are accelerating toward possible social and self-destruction. Yet the challenge of breaking the barrier lures us on.

When we land, the engineers who debrief us redesign our plane, and soon we are airborne again, questing anew for greater and greater speed. What lies beyond the barrier, what awaits us on the other side, we do not know. Nor do we wait to ask, so powerful is our compulsion to soar.

But unlike the science of aeronautics, the modifications in design we have made represent changes in ourselves. In order to maintain acceleration, we have adapted the very structure of human behavior to the demands of an artificial environment hostile to humane values. Thus, it is not the plane alone that is transformed, but its passengers as well. What lies "on the other side" is not simply more speed but another kind of us, a kind we are already becoming.

Hence, "warp speed": a velocity that warps both our behavior and our being, desensitizing us at the same time to the metamorphosis we undergo. It is a velocity generated by our own inner need and sustained by the powerful technology at our touch, a velocity sanctioned by a hyperculture in love with speed.

Is there anything that can stay such headlong flight? Is there any way to resist its power? Yes, but only if we steadfastly refuse to fly so fast.

And that is what many are doing: simplifying their lives by turning off the turbine of materialism; slowing their lives by switching off the generator of electronic stimuli; energizing their lives instead with the engine of spirit and mind.[8]

But even if some can slow their lives down, can society's own speed be reduced? Or is the force of cultural momentum so great that human will cannot deflect it.

It has been said that nothing succeeds like success and, equally, that nothing fails like failure. And the fast life, the life of a hyperculture moving at warp speed, *has* been failing—failing individuals, failing families, failing society, failing democracy, failing the world's nations, and failing the natural world. All that is needed is for enough people together to acknowledge that catastrophic failure, and make up their minds to change it.[9]

Will it happen? As Robert Theobald says: "Believing that it will happen is not necessary. Believing that it has to happen is enough."[10]

The odds may be against such success, but the odds haven't always been right. Linear thinking, after all, the kind that only sees straight ahead, fails to acknowledge the presence of other dynamic trajectories.[11]

But belief alone may not be enough.

If Not Now

Two thousand years ago, a teacher named Hillel tried to define our duty as human beings.

"If I am not for myself," he reflected, "who will be for me?" In saying this, he affirmed the necessity of selfishness, for who but ourselves can better know or defend our needs?

To the first question, however, he added a second: "But if I am only for myself, what am I?" In saying this, he enunciated the necessity of selflessness, for unless we respond to the needs of others, our own worth is diminished.

Having proclaimed the paradox of human existence—our simultaneous need to be both selfish and selfless—Hillel went on to pose yet a third question: "And if not now, when?"[12]

With this final decisive question he transformed what otherwise might have remained only an intellectual puzzle. In the face of life's urgency, he insisted, we must somehow act. For what the world needs most is not more philosophizing, but more deeds.

Hillel's words reveal that now is more than an electronic illusion, more than a source of elusive gratification. Now is also an ethical command, for it is the only dimension within which we can take action. It is the only opportunity we will ever have to redeem our lives.

From this perspective, stress—rather than being something to be universally shunned—becomes the necessary concomitant of a moral existence.[13] In wartime, collaborators tend to have more stress-free lives than members of the underground, but that is no reason to envy or admire them. Peacetime, in turn, may demand of us just as high a price if we are to build a world of decency.

To fulfill such a peacetime agenda we will need one another's help, for the societal forces that oppose such a reconstruction are immense. To protect ourselves and those we love from electronic and materialistic assault, we will need to construct "chronocosms"[14]—private domestic worlds that operate at a slower pace than the hyperculture outside, worlds within which we can heal the wounds of time and rediscover through intimacy a sense of purpose. Indeed, the real cure for our chronopathology[15] may lie not so much in individual efforts as in combined ones in which individuals are strengthened by their mutual commitment and love. As Paul Pearsall has cogently argued: "The centrifugal force is so powerful, you can't handle this alone. We'll have to fight this thing two by two."[16]

The Power of Now Revisited

Earlier in this book, the power of now was portrayed as our enemy, an enemy that has established a tyranny of the present over our lives.

But viewed from a different perspective, the present takes on a different personality. For the present is the only framework in which we can act. We can no more act in the future than we can in the past. Only in the present can we actively shape our lives.

Furthermore, it is only in the present that we can share our lives and love with others. However impassioned their words, the dead cannot hear our own. However impassioned our prayers, those yet unborn cannot answer.

Seen in this light, the power of now ceases to be our enemy, for in it resides opportunity—the only opportunity we will ever have to live.

Conclusion

Beyond Future Shock

THE CHANGES Alvin Toffler described in his book, *Future Shock*, were in 1970 largely external to the landscape of everyday life. Like alien meteors plummeting through the atmosphere of time, they impacted on the surface of our earth, sending shock waves across its surface as an unexpected future collided abruptly with the present. In his book, Toffler suggested strategies to help his readers and their world weather the meteor storm.[1]

But it was not to be just a storm. Instead of being a sudden aberration, it was the violent beginning of a new atmospheric environment in which we would all come to live. In this environment, the changes Toffler had described were transformed from external events into the subtle internal mechanisms of a new society. In the synchronous society that emerged, transience and impermanence came to be accepted as natural and normal.

In such a transformed environment, the essential strategies for survival must themselves be transformed, as old techniques of avoidance will no longer be effective against the current threat. It is one thing to escape a meteor that can be seen, another to evade radiation that is invisible.

Yet, it is not only the nature of the danger that is different but the nature of the damage we may suffer. Rather than guarding ourselves against the psychobiological assaults of sudden change, we must now protect ourselves from more insidious effects of an acceleration that warps our values and distorts our very perceptions. In short, the challenge is no longer neurological: it is ethical and moral. While our previous problem was one of adaptation (the ability to adjust to new circumstances), our problem today is one of retention (the ability to preserve the essentials for a humane culture). Ultimately, our problem may be one of reconstruction, as society struggles to recapture the once familiar shape of forgotten dreams.[2]

So has it been with the history of the natural environment, which humanity first adapted to, was later compelled to conserve, and ultimately may need to rebuild, if power and will permit.

Yet, like the hydrofluorocarbons that eat away at the ozone layer, the very instrumentalities that threaten us are the products of our own preferences: for pleasure instead of pain, for ease instead of effort, for self-absorption instead of self-sacrifice. To transcend the hyperculture we have invented, we will need to transcend some of our most basic instincts.

Because our society is synchronous, we will also need to transcend synchronicity itself, swimming against the tide of time to a shore that seems ever more distant. But it is only from such a shore that we will be able to look up into the night sky and see, beyond the blaze of meteors, the stars that can ultimately lead us home.

Notes

INTRODUCTION: THE TIME MACHINE

1. H. G. Wells, *The Time Machine* (1895), chap. 2.

CHAPTER 1: WARP SPEED

1. Alvin Toffler, *Future Shock* (New York: Random House, 1970).

2. Ibid., 2. More than a decade before *Future Shock* was published, others had already sensed the coming of radical changes that would present immense challenges to mankind. In 1955, physicist J. Robert Oppenheimer said: "In an important sense this world of ours is a new world, in which. . . the very notions of society and culture have changed and will not return to what they have been in the past. . . . One thing that is new is the prevalence of newness, the changing scale and scope of change itself, so that the world alters as we walk in it, so that the years of man's life measure not some small growth or rearrangement or moderation of what he learned in childhood, but a great upheaval. . . . What is new in the world is the massive character of the dissolution and corruption of authority, in belief, in ritual, and in temporal order. . . . We need to recognize the change and learn what resources we have" (from "Prospects in the Arts and Sciences," Columbia University Bicentennial lecture, reprinted in *This Is My Philosophy*, ed. Whit Burnett [New York: Harper, 1957], 104–113). Later, in 1960, anthropologist Loren Eiseley wrote: "The technological revolution . . . has brought a social environment altering so rapidly with technological change that personal adjustments to it are frequently not viable. The individual either becomes anxious or confused or, what is worse,

develops a superficial philosophy intended to carry him over the surface of life with the least possible expenditure of himself. Never before in history has it been literally possible to have been born in one age and to die in another. Many of us are now living in an age quite different from the one into which we were born. The experience is not confined to a ride in a buggy, followed in later years by a ride in a Cadillac. Of far greater significance are the social patterns and ethical adjustments which have followed fast upon the alterations in living habits introduced by machines" (*The Firmament of Time* [New York: Atheneum, 1960], 133f.).

3. Toffler, *Future Shock*, 11 and 2.

4. From the preamble to episodes of the television series, "Star Trek."

5. 55 percent, according to a 1994 survey conducted by the *Times Mirror* Center for the People and the Press.

6. According to the U.S. Bureau of the Census, 24.6 percent of all those working in 1984 used a computer at work.

7. According to the U.S. Bureau of the Census, 8.1 percent of American households had computers in 1984 compared to 15 percent in 1989. By 1993, 35 percent had computers, based on estimates by the Electronics Industries Association.

8. By mid-1995, home computers were outselling TVs and VCRs (according to Larry Mondry, executive vice president of merchandising for CompUSA).

9. According to figures from the Electronic Industries Association and the Computer and Business Equipment Manufacturers Association.

10. New copper and "flash memory" chips may double current computer speed in just nine years. "Biological" computing employing DNA reactions may in the future lead to even greater speed (see Gina Kolata, "A Vat of DNA May Become Fast Computer of the Future, *New York Times*, April 11, 1995, B5; *New York Times* citations, here and below, refer to the National Edition).

11. According to the Electronic Industries Association and the Computer and Business Equipment Manufacturers Association. The cellular phone was first marketed in 1983. In America today, there are almost 30 million cellular phone subscribers.

12. According to the Electronic Industries Association and the Computer and Business Equipment Manufacturers Association.

13. According to Motorola, the largest manufacturer of electronic pagers. At least 19 million Americans currently subscribe. Motorola predicts the number may reach 50 million by the year 2000.

14. According to Nielsen Media Research and *Broadcasting Cable Magazine*. As of mid-1996, some 400 million TV remote controls were in use in the United States, an average of four per household (according to the Consumer Electronics Manufacturers Association).

15. James Twitchell, *Carnival Culture: The Trashing of Taste in America* (New York: Columbia University Press, 1992).

16. According to A. C. Nielsen and *TV & Cable Fact Book*.

17. "These days, you are what you plug in" (bank executive Robert Goldman, quoted in *The New York Times*, December 10, 1995, F14). Says Avram Miller, Intel Corp. Vice President, "Face it—we're speed junkies" (quoted in *The Wall Street Journal*, December 27, 1995, 13).

18. Sculley, quoted in "Technology on Brink of Its Future," *Detroit News*, May 19, 1993, 3E.

19. John Malone, quoted in ibid.

20. Kenneth J. Gergen, *The Saturated Self: Dilemmas of Identity in Contemporary Life* (New York: Basic Books, 1992).

21. Manhattan architect James Trunzo, quoted by Nancy Gibbs, "How America Has Run Out of Time," *Time*, April 24, 1989, 59.

22. See Richard Saul Wurman, *Information Anxiety* (New York: Doubleday, 1989).

23. This condition may be alleviated someday by electronic "navigators," pre-programmed to search for and alert us to shows that match our personal interests.

24. Timothy R. Gaffney, *Chuck Yeager: First Man to Fly Faster than Sound* (Chicago: Children's Press, 1986), 54.

25. See Louis Harris, *Inside America* (New York: Random House, 1987), 9–10.

26. Survey conducted by Princeton Survey Research Associates, Inc. See *American Demographics*, September 1994, 14–15.

27. Tabulations are drawn from *The Reader's Guide to Periodical Literature* and *Books in Print*.

28. "The 1991 *McCall's* International Job Stress Survey," *McCall's*, March 1991, 71ff.

29. See especially the works of Hans Selye, *The Stress of Life* (New York: McGraw Hill, 1956) and *Stress without Distress* (New York: Lippincott, 1974).

30. John Butterfield, "Unload Stress for '94," *USA Weekend*, December 31, 1993–January 2, 1994, 5.

31. Brochure, American Institute of Stress, Yonkers, NY.

32. Monte Williams, "Are You About to Short Circuit?," *New York Daily News*, October 4, 1992, citing data from the *Archives of Internal Medicine* on causes of peptic ulcers.

33. *Manager's Magazine*, August 1992, 3.

34. Mitch Vinicor, "Stress Is Doing a Job on Workers," *New York Daily News*, May 8, 1991.

35. *Manager's Magazine*, August 1992, 3.

36. Northwestern National Life Insurance Company reports that stress-related disability cases it handled doubled between 1982 and 1990, from 6 percent to 13 percent.

37. Based on estimates from the American Institute of Stress.

38. Edward Iwata, "Workers as Time Bombs," *Orange County Register*, May 24, 1993.

39. Kathleen Allen, "Workplace Violence Increasing," *Tucson Citizen*, June 8, 1992, quoting Bruce Blythe, president of Atlanta-based Crisis Management, Inc.

40. See "The 1991 *McCall's* International Job Stress Survey," 78; Craig Brod, *Technostress: The Human Cost of the Computer Revolution* (Reading, MA: Addison-Wesley, 1984); and Jeremy Rifkin, *Time Wars: The Primary Conflict in Human History* (New York: Henry Holt, 1987).

41. Juliet B. Schor, *The Overworked American: The Unexpected Decline of Leisure* (New York: HarperCollins, 1993), 11.

42. "I know people who routinely get 50 to 100 E-mails per day and some receive as many as 500," reports David W. De Long, research fellow at Ernst & Young. On the burden of this overload and methods of coping, see Judith H. Dobrzynski in the *New York Times*, April 28, 1996, 2E.

43. Brod, quoted by Kathleen Osborne Clute in "Labor-Saving Wonders Pushing a Lot of Us to Work Longer, Harder," *Boston Globe*, November 11, 1991.

44. See Brod's book, *Technostress*.

45. Pamela R. Geddis, a producer of business reports and promotional materials, quoted by Kathleen Osborne Clute, "Labor-Saving Wonders Pushing a Lot of Us to Work Longer, Harder," *Boston Globe*, November 11, 1991.

46. Computer engineer, quoted by Ralph Keyes, *Timelock: How Life Got So Hectic and What You Can Do About It* (New York: HarperCollins, 1991), 94.

47. The artificial urgency of E-mail is intensified by new systems that inform the sender that the message was received and read. "They can measure how long it takes you to respond," says MIT research associate Michael Schrage, "so you feel like you have to respond immediately" (quoted in *The Wall Street Journal*, April 8, 1997, B1).

48. See Brod, *Technostress*, especially pp. xi, 17f., 92–95, and chap. 5, "An End to Romance."

49. Comments executive recruiter David Beirne, "There is no line between work and home. I put my pager next to my bed. . . . I have to." Reports human resources consultant Freada Klein, "A plane ride is no longer time to work quietly or read the trashy novel. It's time to be scheduled and invaded" (quoted in *the Wall Street Journal*, April 8, 1997, B1). According to Gil Gordon, a telecommuting consultant, "This mobile technology is the ultimate good-news, bad-news joke. The good news is you can work from anywhere. And the bad news is you can work from anywhere" (quoted in the *San Francisco Examiner*, September 1996).

50. See Schor's book, *The Overworked American*.

51. Murray Horowitz of National Public Radio, on the television documentary, "Running Out of Time" (coproduced by KCTS [Seattle] and Oregon Public Broadcasting, 1994).

52. In 1973, 23 percent of Americans rated home air-conditioning as a necessity; by 1996, 51 percent did. As for automobile air-conditioning, 13 percent rated it a necessity in 1973, 41 percent in 1996. The microwave oven, unheard of in 1973, was by 1996 rated a necessity by 32 percent of Americans (1973 data from The Roper Organization; 1996 data from a *Washington Post*/Henry J. Kaiser Foundation/Harvard University national survey).

53. On the way the desire for luxuries increases labor, see Gary Becker, "A Theory of the Allocation of Time," *Economic Journal* 75.299 (1965), 493–517, and Staffan B. Linder, *The Harried Leisure Class* (New York: Columbia University Press, 1971).

54. Schor, *The Overworked American*, chap. 5.

55. See his remarks in "How Americans Use Time" (interview with Edward Cornish), *The Futurist*, September-October 1991, 23ff., as well as articles by him published in *American Demographics* magazine. See also his book (in collaboration with Geoffrey Godbey), *Time for Life* (Pennsylvania State University Press, 1997).

56. See John Robinson, interview in *The Futurist*; "Time's Up," *American Demographics*, July 1989, 33–35; and "Quitting Time," *American Demographics*, May 1991, 34–36.

57. See John Robinson, "The Time Squeeze," *American Demographics*, February 1990, 32–33.

58. "Americans' Use of Time Project" and the results of the National Recreation and Park Association Survey, 1992, reported in *American Demographics*, April 1993, 26.

59. See Arlie Hochschild (with Anne Machung), *The Second Shift: Working Parents and the Revolution at Home* (New York: Viking, 1989).

60. "Multitasking," a term originally applied to advanced computers, is now being applied to people (see Scott McCartney, "The Multitasking Man: Type A Meets Technology," *Wall Street Journal*, April 19, 1995, B1).

61. Noted by Lee Burns, *Busy Bodies: Why Our Time-Obsessed Society Keeps Us Running in Place* (New York: Norton 1993). See the *Statistical Abstract of the United States*, 1993–94, No. 406.

62. The average length of vacations has been shrinking. People are taking shorter trips, with the average length of a vacation dropping from five days (1986) to four (in 1996), according to the Travel Industry Association of America.

63. John Robinson, "Your Money or Your Time," *American Demographics*, November 1991, 22–26.

64. Rifkin, *Time Wars*.

65. Substitute teacher and mother of two, quoted by Ralph Keyes, *Timelock*, 141.

66. Writer Letty Cottin Pogrebin, quoted by Keyes, *Timelock*, 130.

67. Legal secretary, quoted by Brod, *Technostress*, 25.

68. First grade teacher, interview with author.

69. Medical receptionist and nurse, interview with author.

70. Corporate lawyer, quoted by Keyes, *Timelock*, 4.

71. Adman, quoted by Keyes, *Timelock*, 11.

72. Lawyer, quoted by Keyes, *Timelock*, 4.

73. Survey reported in Robinson, "Your Money or Your Time," *American Demographics*, November 1991, 22–26.

74. Charles Chaplin, *Modern Times* (1936).

75. Source: Baseline II, Inc.; basic data, Nielsen Media Research. See Bart Andrews, *Lucy & Ricky & Fred & Ethel: The Story of "I Love Lucy"* (New York: Dutton, 1976), 1.

76. Broadcast September 15, 1952; script by Jess Oppenheimer, Madelyn Pugh, and Bob Carroll, Jr.

77. Jerry Mander, *In the Absence of the Sacred: The Failure of Technology and the Survival of the Indian Nations* (San Francisco: Sierra Club, 1991), 11.

CHAPTER 2: THE THREE SOURCES OF NOW'S POWER

1 For the myth of Daedalus and Icarus, see Ovid, *The Metamorphoses*, Book 8.

2. See Bruce Watson, "For a While the Luddites Had a Smashing Success," *Smithsonian* 24.1 (April 1993), 140–54 and bibliography.

3. Quoted by Watson, "For a While," 147.

4. *Ibid.*, 142f.

5. So-called neo-Luddites would include Jerry Mander (television) and Jeremy Rifkin (genetic engineering).

6. Sigfried Giedion, *Mechanization Takes Command: A Contribution to an Anonymous History* (New York: Oxford University Press, 1948), 714.

7. See the biblical book of Jeremiah, and Sidney B. Hoenig and Samuel H. Rosenberg, *A Guide to the Prophets* (New York: Yeshiva University, 1957), chap. 8.

8. See Plato's *Apology*.

9. For this term, see Patricia Galagan, "How to Avoid Datacide," *Training and Development Journal*, October 1986, 54–57.

10. "It's the kind of thing the Electrogenie does all the time. This too-fecund spirit of the ether says, 'You want data? I'll give you data up the wazoo. Do what you can with it'" (Nicholas von Hoffman, "Browsing in Virtual Bookstores," *Architectural Digest*, August 1997, 70ff.).

11. On these themes, see Toffler, *Future Shock* (New York: Random House, 1970), and Orrin E. Klapp, *Overload and Boredom: Essays on the Quality of Life in the Information Society* (Westport, CT: Greenwood, 1986).

12. MacLeish, "The Hamlet of A. MacLeish," *Collected Poems 1917–1982* (Boston: Houghton Mifflin, 1985). For similar sentiments, see T.S. Eliot's 1935 "Choruses from 'The Rock.'"

13. Notes Sven Birkerts: "Electricity and inwardness are fundamentally discordant. Electricity is, implicitly, of the moment—*now*. Depth, meaning . . . flourish only in that order of time . . . called "duration" ("The Electronic Hive: Refuse It," *Harper's*, May 1994, 18).

14. Sandburg, "The Sins of Kalamazoo," in *Complete Poems of Carl Sandburg* (New York: Harcourt Brace Jovanovich, 1970), 172–175.

15. Stevenson, speech, "The Atomic Future," Hartford, CT, September 1952, in *Major Campaign Speeches of Adlai Stevenson 1952* (New York: Random House, 1953), 134–139.

16. Jacques Ellul, *The Technological Society* (New York: Knopf 1964), 6 and 97.

17. Millay, Sonnet from *Huntsman, What Quarry?* (1939), in *Complete Lyrics of Edna St. Vincent Millay* (New York: Harper & Row, 1956), 697. Compare its sentiments and imagery to those of the first choral ode from Sophocles's *Antigone* ("Numberless are the world's wonders but none/More wonderful than man" [trans. Dudley Fitts and Robert Fitzgerald]).

18. Cohan, "Yankee Doodle Dandy."

19. Lazarus, "The New Colossus," (1886), inscribed inside the Statue of Liberty's pedestal.

20. Saint-Exupéry, "Letter to General X," reprinted in *A Sense of Life*, trans. Adrienne Foulke (New York: Funk & Wagnalls, 1965), 219f.

21. Mander, *In the Absence of the Sacred* (San Francisco: Sierra Club, 1991), 64.

22. Schiller, interview with author.

23. Packard, *The Hidden Persuaders* (New York: McKay, 1957).

24. Ibid., 37.

25. See Packard, chap. 2; also Dichter, *The Strategy of Desire* (Garden City, NY: Doubleday, 1960).

26. See Packard's discussion in chap. 2; also Cheskin, *Color for Profit* (New York: Liveright, 1950).

27. See Henry Assael, *Consumer Behavior and Marketing Action* (Boston: PWS-Kent, 1992), 129 and n. 5.

28. The sense of smell itself has also been enlisted to enhance productivity and influence buying decisions. "Volunteers performed puzzle-solving tasks 17 percent faster when exposed to a floral scent, according to a study conducted by the

Smell and Taste Treatment and Research Foundation of Chicago. The Good Housekeeping Institute found that proofreaders do much better when peppermint or lavender scents are piped into their atmosphere. A Japanese company discovered that lavender and jasmine soothed keypunch operators, while lemon increased production. Several companies now manufacture dispensers that emit scent into the atmosphere, covering thousands of square feet with fragrances designed to provide a particular motivating ambiance. Some retailers have picked up on this research and believe that the right scent can compel shoppers to buy. Stores are now paying as much as $50,000 to fragrance experts to develop scents that match their store's clientele, or what they think their customers want to smell as they linger at the clothing racks. Dr. Alan Hirsch. . . . has shown that people are more likely to buy Nike shoes and pay more for them when trying them on in floral-scented dressing rooms. The study states that this is the case even when the scent is too faint for people to notice." (Maxine Wilkie, "Scent of a Market," *American Demographics*, August 1995, 47)

29. See Gilbert D. Harrell, *Consumer Behavior* (San Diego: Harcourt Brace Jovanovich, 1986), 92f., and Assael, *Consumer Behavior and Marketing Action*, 133f.

30. See Sandra H. Hart and Steven W. McDaniel, "Subliminal Stimulation: Marketing Applications," in James U. McNeal and Steven W. McDaniel, eds., *Consumers' Behavior: Classical and Contemporary Dimensions* (Boston: Little, Brown, 1982), 165–75.

31. See Erik Larson, *The Naked Consumer: How Our Private Lives Become Public Commodities* (New York: Henry Holt, 1992).

32. For this term, see Larson, *The Naked Consumer*, 25f.

33. See Harrell, *Consumer Behavior*, 280–90.

34. See Larson, *The Naked Consumer*, chaps. 4 and 8.

35. Herbert I. Schiller, interview with author.

36. See two tragedies by Sophocles, *Oedipus the King* and *Antigone*.

CHAPTER 3: THE TRANSFORMATION OF THE INDIVIDUAL

1. Heraclitus, fragments 20 and 21.

2. Says Microsoft's Bill Gates, "Everything is in a state of flux, including the status quo" (quoted in *U.S. News & World Report*, January 13, 1997, 68).

3. Nielsen Media Research, cited in *The World Almanac and Book of Facts, 1998* (Mahwah, NJ: World Almanac Books, 1997), 259.

4. Nielsen Media Research, cited in *Information Please Almanac, 1998* (Boston: Information Please LLC, 1977), 746.

5. Nielsen Media Research, cited in *Information Please Almanac, 1998*, 747.

6. John P. Robinson, "I Love My TV," *The Demographics of Time Use* (Ithaca, NY: American Demographics, 1994), 14–15.

7. Ibid.

8. See interview with Robinson in *The Futurist*, September/October 1991, 25.

9. See Robert W. Kubey and Mihalyi Csikszentmihalyi, *Television and the Quality of Life: How Viewing Shapes Everyday Experience* (Hillsdale, NJ: Lawrence Erlbaum Associates, 1990), chap. 5 and p. 171.

10. Note the comments of Neil Postman, *Amusing Ourselves to Death: Public Discourse in the Age of Show Business* (New York: Viking Penguin, 1985), 136:

"Television is a speed-of-light medium, a present-centered medium. Its grammar, so to say, permits no access to the past. Everything presented in moving pictures is experienced as happening now, which is why we must be told *in language* that a videotape we are seeing was made months before."

11. According to a 1993 *TV Guide* report, the average American spends ten years of his or her life watching television, including two whole years watching commercials.

12. For data on the proportion of TV programming devoted to commercials and their frequency, see the annual *Television Commercial Monitoring Report* issued jointly by the American Association of Advertising Agencies and the Association of National Advertisers, Inc., New York.

13. On the use of variety to arrest our attention, see Jerry Mander, *Four Arguments for the Elimination of Television* (New York: Morrow, 1978), 300–310, and *In the Absence of the Sacred* (San Francisco: Sierra Club, 1991), 84–86.

14. See Postman, *Amusing Ourselves to Death*, esp. chap. 6.

15. *Advertising Age*, May 5, 1997, 42.

16. See Kubey and Csikszentmihalyi, *Television and the Quality of Life*, chap. 7 and p. 172.

17. See Clifford Stoll, *Silicon Snake Oil: Second Thoughts on the Information Highway* (New York: Doubleday, 1995).

18. See the interview with John P. Robinson in *The Futurist*, September/October 1991. Says Robinson (p. 26): "Socializing is one of the most enjoyable things that people do during the course of the day. Yet, people are spending less time on it. . . . Interpersonal get-togethers have declined between 15 percent and 25 percent over a 20–year period, though conversation in the home actually may be going up somewhat. Our data indicate that, while TV has pulled people back home more, they're probably watching the set rather than interacting as a family unit."

19. According to Kimberly Young, assistant professor of psychology at the University of Pittsburgh, 80 percent of the 500 heavy Internet users she studied exhibited a condition she called IAD, Internet Addiction Disorder. Psychological help is available to such people, but, paradoxically, it is available on-line (see Ariana E. Cha, "Caught in the Net," *Detroit Free Press*, May 20, 1997, 1f.).

20. In using the phrase "goes with the flow", I refer to the tendency to let one's life merge with the external flow of one's social environment. In this sense, my use of the term "flow" differs from that of Mihalyi Csikszentmihalyi, who uses it to refer to a fundamentally *internal* psychological state involving creative concentration. (See Kubey and Csikszentmihalyi, *Television and the Quality of Life*, 140ff.; and Mihalyi Csikszentmihalyi and Isabella Selega, *Optimal Experience: Psychological Studies of Flow in Consciousness* [New York: Cambridge University Press, 1988].

21. Computers themselves are transient as obsolescence usually occurs within three years.

22. In the first chapter of *The Magnificent Ambersons* (Bloomington, IN: Indiana University Press, 1989 [1918]), Booth Tarkington describes how this phenomenon took place in turn-of-the-century mid-America: "Dressmakers, shoemakers, hatmakers, and tailors, increasing in cunning and in power, found means to make new clothes old." This image of change was effectively conveyed in visual terms by Orson Welles at the beginning of his 1942 film adaptation of Tarkington's novel.

23. Quoted by Irene Daria, *The Fashion Cycle: A Behind-the-Scenes Look at a Year with Bill Blass, Liz Claiborne, Donna Karan, Arnold Scaasi, and Adrienne Vittadini* (New York: Simon & Schuster, 1990), 205.

24. See Michael Gross, "Fashion's Fickle Seasons," *New York*, August 21, 1989, 30–32.

25. Ibid., 30.

26. See Naomi Wolf, *The Beauty Myth: How Images of Beauty Are Used Against Women* (New York: Morrow, 1991), 17.

27. *Health*, July/August 1992, 12, citing data from CARE, New York.

28. *U.S. News & World Report*, February 3, 1992, 60.

29. S. C. Wooley and O. W. Wooley, "Obesity and Women: A Closer Look at the Facts," *Women's Studies International Quarterly* 2 (1979), 69–79; data reprinted in "33,000 Women Tell How They Really Feel about Their Bodies," *Glamour*, February 1984.

30. See Wolf, *The Beauty Myth*, 17.

31. Kearney-Cooke, quoted by Dan Shaw in "The Peacock Principle," *Detroit Free Press*, June 14, 1994, 9F, reprinted from the *New York Times*.

32. From 1984 to 1994, exercise-equipment sales more than doubled, from $1.1 billion to $2.5 billion (*American Forecaster Almanac, 1994 Business Edition*, American Demographics, Inc.).

33. In addition, hair loss supports a $1.5 billion industry (David Fischer, "The Bald Truth," *U.S. News & World Report*, August 4, 1997, 44ff.).

34. "The amphetamine user. . . is a gross caricature of many of the pathological, ultimately destructive features of the society that produced him": Lester Grinspoon and Peter Hedblom, *The Speed Culture: Amphetamine Use and Abuse in America* (Cambridge, MA: Harvard University Press, 1975), 291.

35. See Rebecca Howard, "When Youth Counts More Than Ability, They Get a Lift," *Los Angeles Daily News*; reprinted in *Detroit Free Press*, November 29, 1992, H1f.

36. Wolf, *The Beauty Myth*, 10.

37. See Susan Bordo, *Unbearable Weight: Feminism, Western Culture, and the Body* (Berkeley: University of California Press, 1993), 37.

38. Ibid.

39. See Elisabeth Rosenthal, "Cosmetic Surgeons Seek New Frontiers," *New York Times*, September 24, 1991, C1f.

40. "Medical and Nonmedical Uses of Anabolic Androgenic Steroids," *Journal of the American Medical Association* 264.22 (December 12, 1990), 2923–27.

41. Interviewed on "Perfect Specimen," "48 Hours," CBS, 1992.

42. See Frank Kuznik, "The Steroid Epidemic," *USA Weekend*, May 15–17, 1992, 4–7.

43. Ibid.

44. Ibid.

45. Kuznik, "The Steroid Epidemic."

46. Kathy Schick and Nicholas Toth, *Making Silent Stones Speak: Human Evolution and the Dawn of Technology* (New York: Simon & Schuster, 1993), 315. Note also the remarks of Smith Kline and French Laboratories' president for Research and Development, Stanley T. Crooke: "Changing the genome is a primary event. . . . Biotechnology is. . . a tool of incredible power. Its capacity to alter the future of

mankind is essentially infinite" (from "Knowledge and Power: Biotechnology," in *Vital Speeches of the Day*, September 15, 1988, 732).

47. Jeremy Rifkin, *Declaration of a Heretic* (Boston: Routledge & Kegan Paul, 1985), 44f.

48. Neil Postman, *Amusing Ourselves to Death*, 27f.

49. 1995 sales of Prozac exceeded $2 billion. Prozac is used worldwide by 24 million people in 107 countries. 75 percent of the users (18 million) are American (*U.S. News & World Report*, December 9, 1996, 17).

50. "One out of every five Americans takes aspirin every day"; see Charles C. Mann and Mark L. Plummer, *The Aspirin Wars: Money, Medicine, and 100 Years of Rampant Competition* (New York: Knopf, 1991). The authors note that the American analgesic market reached $2.668 billion in 1990 and could reach about $6 billion by 1995 (see p. 336).

51. See Jo Ann Tooley, "Keeping the Faith," *US News & World Report*, November 19, 1990, 16.

52. Thomas A. Stewart, "Turning Around the Lord's Business," *Fortune*, September 25, 1989, 116–24. See also Michael Bryan, *Chapter and Verse: A Skeptic Revisits Christianity* (New York: Random House, 1991).

53. See Quentin J. Schultze, *Televangelism and American Culture: The Business of Popular Religion* (Grand Rapids, MI: Baker, 1991); also Razelle Frankl, *Televangelism: The Marketing of Popular Culture* (Carbondale, IL: Southern Illinois Press, 1986) and Jeffrey K. Hadden and Anson Shupe, *Televangelism: Power and Politics on God's Frontier* (New York: Holt, 1988).

54. In 1995, the top visitor attraction in the United States was Minneapolis's Mall of America with 35 million visitors—more visitors than Disney World and the Grand Canyon combined.

55. Pioneered by psychologist Michael Hoyt at Kaiser Permanente Medical Center in Hayward, California. More than 80 percent of Hoyt's patients "found the one session very helpful." See Karen S. Peterson, "Psychotherapy on the Fast Track for a Quick-fix Society," *Detroit News*, November 9, 1994, 2A.

56. Used by New York-based therapist Bonnie Eaker and tried on a national basis by Summit Solutions Line. Ibid.

57. Wendy Kaminer, *I'm Dysfunctional, You're Dysfunctional: The Recovery Movement and Other Self-Help Fashions* (Reading, MA: Addison-Wesley, 1992), 165.

58. See Kathleen Murray, "When the Therapist Is a Computer," *New York Times*, National Edition, May 9, 1993, F25.

59. Among other things, the Internet allows users to adopt false age or sexual identities instantly and act out their new roles in conversations with other users.

60. See Ken Pimentel and Kevin Teixeira, *Virtual Reality: Through the Looking Glass* (New York: McGraw-Hill 1992), and Howard Rheingold, *Virtual Reality: The Revolutionary Technology of Computer-Generated Artificial Worlds & How It Promises to Transform Society* (New York: Simon & Schuster, 1992).

61. Quoted by Paul Katzeff in "Virtual Reality," *Boston Globe*, October 28, 1990. See also Phillip Robinson and Nancy Tamosaitis, *The Joy of Cybersex: An Underground Guide to Electronic Erotica* (New York: Brady Computer Books, 1992) and *More Joy of Cybersex* (New York: Brady Computer Books, 1994).

62. Liberman, interview with the author.

63. See Homer, *The Odyssey*, 4.351ff.

64. Robert Jay Lifton, *The Protean Self* (New York: Basic Books, 1993).

CHAPTER 4: THE TRANSFORMATION OF THE FAMILY

1. See in particular the erotic poetry of the ancient Egyptians, the ancient Greeks (especially Sappho), and the ancient Romans (especially Catullus).

2. "Carpe diem" (Horace, *Odes*, 1.11).

3. Note Allan Bloom, *Love and Friendship* (New York: Simon & Schuster, 1993), 81f.

4. For a discussion of how societal speed has accelerated modern courtship, see Staffan B. Linder, *The Harried Leisure Class* (New York: Columbia University Press, 1971), 83–89.

5. Source: Hallmark Cards, Inc., *1994 Date Book*.

6. See Sam Roberts, *Who We Are: A Portrait of America Based on the Latest U.S. Census* (New York: Random House, 1993), 42–49, and William J. Bennett, *The Index of Leading Cultural Indicators* (New York: Simon & Schuster, 1994), 55–60.

7. See Jan Larson, "Cohabitation Is Premarital Step," *American Demographics*, November 1991, 20.

8. Ibid.

9. Barbara Foley Wilson, "The Marry-Go-Round," *American Demographics*, October 1991, 52.

10. Amy Engeler, "Living Together: What Will It Mean to Your Marriage?" *Glamour*, January 1991, 150.

11. U.S. Bureau of the Census, *Marital Status and Living Arrangements*, March 1992 (1993). During the same period, the total population of the country grew by only 25 percent.

12. Shervert H. Frazier, "Psychotrends: Taking Stock of Tomorrow's Family and Sexuality," *Psychology Today*, January/February 1994, 64 (excerpted from Frazier, *Psychotrends: What Kind of People Are We Becoming* [New York: Simon & Schuster, 1994]).

13. *Open Marriage: A New Life Style for Couples* (New York: Avon, 1973). Note especially p. 95 ("Now for now").

14. Riche, "The Future of the Family," *American Demographics*, March 1991, 44.

15. Quoted by Michael Castleman in "Till Stress Us Do Part," *Atlanta Journal-Constitution*, July 24, 1991.

16. Quoted in ibid.

17. Cited by William R. Mattox, Jr., "America's Family Time Famine," *Children Today*, November/December 1990, 9.

18. Receipts and revenues, projected from data in the *Statistical Abstract of the United States*, Tables 610, 1322, and 1326.

19. According to the National Center for Health Statistics, cited by Bennett, *The Index of Leading Cultural Indicators*, p. 46. See also Shannon Brownlee and Matthew Miller, "The Lies Parents Tell about Work, Kids, Money, Day Care, and Ambition," *U.S. News & World Report*, May 12, 1997, 58ff.

20. U.S. Bureau of the Census, "Marital Status and Living Arrangements" (1994); see Steven A. Holmes, "Birthrate for Unwed Women Up 70% Since '83, Study Says," *New York Times*, National Edition, July 20, 1994, 1.

21. U.S. Department of Health and Human Services, *Vital Statistics of the United States, 1991,* Vol. 1, *Natality,* cited by Bennett, *Index of Leading Cultural Indicators,* p. 48.

22. According to the National Center for Health Statistics.

23. See David W. Murray, "Every Society Is Threatened by the Disappearance of Legitimate Marriage," *The Chronicle of Higher Education,* July 13, 1994, B5; reprinted from *Policy Review,* Spring 1994.

24. U.S. Bureau of the Census, cited by Bennett, *Index of Leading Cultural Indicators,* p. 50.

25. U.S. Bureau of the Census report, 1995.

26. See Bennett, *Index of Leading Cultural Indicators,* p. 68f.

27. See Brandon Centerwall, "Our Cultural Perplexities," *The Public Interest,* Spring 1993; cited by Bennett, *Index of Leading Cultural Indicators,* p. 103.

28. See Bennett, *Index of Leading Cultural Indicators,* p. 103.

29. See James McNeal, *Kids as Customers: A Handbook of Marketing to Children* (Ithaca, NY: American Demographics, 1992); Susan Antilla, " 'I Want' Now Gets." *New York Times,* April 4, 1993, Education Supplement, 17; and *Captive Kids: A Report on Commercial Pressures on Kids at School* (Yonkers, NY: Consumers Union Educational Services, 1995).

30. For statistics, see *U.S. News & World Report,* January 3, 1994, 12.

31. On the shallowness of this argument, see Mander, *In the Absence of the Sacred* (San Francisco: Sierra Club, 1991), 65.

32. Drugs such as Ritalin and Prozac are increasingly being used in childhood as chemical substitutes for parental patience and time-intensive guidance. On Prozac use for children, see Elyse Tanouye, "Antidepressant Makers Study Kids' Market," *Wall Street Journal,* April 4, 1997, B1f., and Arianna Huffington, "Peppermint Prozac," *U.S. News & World Report,* August 25, 1997, 28. Ritalin use rose 250 percent from 1990 to 1995 (see Gina Kolata, "Ritalin Use Is Lower than Thought," *New York Times,* December 17, 1996). Prozac is now being manufactured as a flavored liquid for children (see Tanouye, above).

33. David Elkind, *The Hurried Child: Growing Up Too Fast Too Soon* (Reading, MA: Addison-Wesley, 1981), xii-xiii.

34. Quoted by Susan R. Pollack, "Slowing Up Growing Up," *Detroit News,* May 13, 1994, 5C.

35. Joshua Meyrowitz, *No Sense of Place: The Impact of Electronic Media on Social Behavior* (New York: Oxford University Press, 1985).

36. Neil Postman, *The Disappearance of Childhood* (New York: Delacorte Press, 1982), 80.

37. See Ramon G. McLeod, "Teen Sex Starting Younger, Study Says," *Detroit Free Press,* June 7, 1994, 5A; reprinted from *San Francisco Chronicle.*

38. Cited by Bennett, *Index of Leading Cultural Indicators,* p. 72.

39. Journalist Richard Low describes what he calls the "programmed generation," a generation of children whose free time has been displaced by structured time by parents who try to pack too many experiences into their lives, in part from fear that they and their children will somehow "fall behind" (Richard Low, *Childhood's Future: Listening to the American Family: New Hope for the Next Generation* [Boston: Houghton Mifflin, 1990], chap. 7). See also Lucinda Franks, "Little Big People," *New York Times Magazine,* October 10, 1993, 31.

40. In 1965, 45,000 advanced placement tests were taken by high schoolers. By 1995, the number had soared to 843,000.

41. Recent surveys suggest about 60 percent of high school and college students cheat on exams (see William L. Kibler and Pamela Vannoy Kibler, "When Students Resort to Cheating," *Chronicle of Higher Education*, July 14, 1993, B1f.; "Your Cheatin' Heart," *Psychology Today*, November/December 1992, 9; and Ken Schroeder, "Give and Take, Part 2," *Education Digest*, February 1993, 73Af.). Note also Kevin Davis, "Student Cheating: A Defensive Essay," *English Journal*, October 1992, 72ff.

42. See Stephen Bertman, ed., *The Conflict of Generations in Ancient Greece and Rome* (Amsterdam: Grüner, 1976), and Lewis S. Feuer, *The Conflict of Generations: The Character and Significance of Student Movements* (New York: Basic Books, 1969).

43. Quoted by David Poponoe, "The Controversial Truth: Two-Parent Families Are Better," *New York Times*, National Edition, December 26, 1992, 13.

44. Judith Stacey, *Brave New Families: Stories of Domestic Upheaval in Late Twentieth Century America* (New York: Basic Books, 1993), 269.

45. Stephanie Coontz, *The Way We Never Were: Families and the Nostalgia Trap* (New York: Basic Books, 1992), 278.

46. Report prepared for the Carnegie Corporation of New York; see Susan Chira, "Study Confirms Worst Fears on U.S. Children," *New York Times*, National Edition, April 12, 1994, 1f.

47. According to a study by Norval Glenn and Kathryn Kramer, University of Texas, cited in Barbara Kantrowitz, "Breaking the Divorce Cycle," *Newsweek*, January 13, 1992, 48ff., and noted by Bennett, p. 59.

48. Alan Pifer and Lydia Bronte, eds., *Our Aging Society: Paradox and Promise* (New York: Norton, 1986), 4.

49. U.S. Bureau of the Census, and American Association of Retired Persons, cited in *Detroit News*, June 28, 1992, 10A.

50. Ibid.

51. See Michael Clements, "High Cost of Aging," *Detroit News*, June 28, 1992, 1Af.

52. Daniel Callahan, "Health Care in the Aging Society: A Moral Dilemma," in Pifer and Bronte, *Our Aging Society: Paradox and Promise*, 337. See also Callahan's *The Tyranny of Survival, and Other Pathologies of Civilized Life* (Lanham, MD: University Press of America, 1985).

53. The observations in this section were presented orally by the author at the 43d Annual Scientific Meeting of the Gerontological Society of America (Boston, 1990); see *Vital Speeches of the Day*, January 1, 1991, 185f.

CHAPTER 5: THE TRANSFORMATION OF SOCIETY

1. Recalling William Wordsworth's "The World Is Too Much with Us; Late and Soon" (1807).

2. See Richard T. Wright and Scott H. Decker, *Burglars on the Job: Streetlife and Residential Break-ins* (Boston: Northwestern University Press, 1994).

3. Gambling is another indicator of the power of now's lure. In 1996, for example, Americans spent $22 billion at casinos, twice as much as they had seven years before. Estimates place illegal gambling for 1996 at $90 billion.

4. See Peter Carlin, "The Jackpot in Television's Future," *New York Times Magazine*, February 28, 1993, 36–41.

5. The Home Shopping Channel and QVC each operate secondary channels, Home Shopping Channel 2 and (for upscale fashion) Q2/On Q.

6. Carlin, "The Jackpot in Television's Future," 39.

7. Ibid., 38.

8. Ibid., 41.

9. Cecilia Deck, "Shopping the Electronic Mall," *Detroit Free Press*, October 10, 1994, 10F.

10. To date, concerns over credit card security have inhibited large-scale on-line consumer buying.

11. Commercial endorsements also help colleges financially. As of 1996, Nike, for example, had exclusive athletic shoe agreements with ten universities.

12. Channel One was originated by Whittle Communications of Knoxville, TN, and later was sold in the wake of financial losses the corporation suffered.

13. For this concept, see Marshall McLuhan, *Understanding Media: The Extension of Man* (New York: New American Library, 1964).

14. Quoted by Hugh McCann, "Electronic Highway," *Detroit News*, April 5, 1993, 2F.

15. In his book *Powershift: Knowledge, Wealth, and Violence at the Edge of the 21st Century* (New York: Bantam, 1990), Alvin Toffler speaks of the "neuralization" of the economy (p. 120). Elsewhere (pp. 108–110 and 385) he uses the expression "neural network," but applies it in a specialized sense to electronic systems that learn from their own experience and adjust their actions accordingly.

16. Jeremy Rifkin, *Entropy: A New World View* (New York: Viking, 1980), 241, summarizing Prigogine's view. See also Ilya Prigogine, "Thermodynamics of Evolution," *Physics Today* 25 (November 1972) 23–28 and (December 1972), 38–44.

17. Herodotus, *History*, 8.98 (trans. George Rawlinson).

18. Significantly, "more than three-quarters of the Federal Government's growth from 1776 to 1876 was in the post office alone" (Alan Robbins, "E-Mail: Lean, Mean and Making Its Mark," in the *New York Times*, National Edition, May 11, 1997, F13). The expansion of communication went hand in hand with nation-building. Without such expansion, nation-building would have been impossible.

19. For the extent and growth of on-line computer services, see Peter H. Lewis, "America Online Says Users of Service Exceed 1 Million," *New York Times*, National Edition, August 17, 1994, C4.

20. These figures are extrapolated from the belief that an average of ten people use each of the 2–3 million computers hooked up to the Internet. Actual user figures may, in fact, be much lower, perhaps as low as 7–10.5 million users worldwide. What is not in doubt is the phenomenal growth rate of the Internet, which is certain to reach the 20–30 million figure in the very near future. (See Peter H. Lewis, "Doubts Are Raised on Actual Number of Internet's Users," *New York Times*, National Edition, August 10, 1994, 1f.)

21. James Tobin, "10–Millionth Cellular Phone Sale Rings In Future," *Detroit News*, December 7, 1992, 1A.

22. In 1996, 7.6 million Americans telecommuted to work (source: LINK Resources).

23. Echoing a phrase used by mobile businessman Perry Solomon, interviewed on "Fast Times," *48 Hours* (CBS, 1990)

24. An in-flight shopping service called Skymall (based in Phoenix, Arizona) permits passengers to shop by phone from their plane using a catalogue. Purchases can be picked up immediately upon landing or can be delivered in twenty-four hours.

25. Claude Fischer, author of the 1992 book, *America Calling: A Social History of the Telephone to 1940*, quoted by Dan Gilmore, "Voice Mail? Learn to Like It," *Detroit Free Press*, March 3, 1993, 1A.

26. Quoted by James Gleik, "The Telephone Transformed—Into Almost Everything," *New York Times* Magazine, May 16, 1993, 29.

27. Quoted by Joseph B. Verrengia, "TV or Not TV," *Detroit News*, November 14, 1992, 20D.

28. See Howard Rheingold, *The Virtual Community: Homesteading on the Electronic Frontier* (Reading, MA: Addison-Wesley, 1993). As one computer user writes: "The absence of a face, voice, accent, race, ethnic origin, social class, etc., strips us of our facades and allows us to communicate with another person without our own programmed bias and prejudice. We are free to find common ground and common feelings" (Marc Gunther, "Life Connections: Computers Turn Users into Communities of People Who Care," *Detroit Free Press*, January 3, 1994, 3B). As Gunther notes, such on-line connections have blossomed into face-to-face friendships and even marriages.

29. *Ibid.*, 13D. In 1993, a group of seventy-one nonprofit organizations, the Telecommunications Policy Roundtable, announced "a joint effort to urge policy makers to guarantee that the proposed national 'data highway' serves the public interest" (*Chronicle of Higher Education*, November 3, 1993, A23).

30. Quoted by Bill Powell, "Eyes on the Future," *U.S. News & World Report*, May 31, 1993, 41.

31. Quoted by Verrengia, 20D.

32. The phrase "data merchants" is used by Theodore Roszak, *The Cult of Information: The Folklore of Computers and the True Art of Thinking* (New York: Pantheon, 1986), chap. 2.

33. Fisher, "Technology Titans Sound Off on the Digital Future," *U.S. News & World Report*, May 3, 1993, 64.

34. Quoted by Bill Powell, "Eyes on the Future." *US News & World Report*, May 31, 1993, 41.

35. The counterargument is that a potential learner's curiosity will be stimulated by the interactivity and audiovisual format of computer-based technology. On the other hand, students may simultaneously lose touch with those books that are not on-line and become even more estranged from traditional literature than they already are. In this connection, see Sven Birkerts, *The Gutenberg Elegies: The Fate of Reading in an Electronic Age* (Boston: Faber & Faber, 1994).

36. Thoreau, *Walden*, chap. 1, "Economy."

37. Ibid.

38. Merton in his introduction to Jacques Ellul's *The Technological Society*, vi.

39. Thoreau, *Walden*, chap. 1, "Economy."

40. From the poem of the same name.

41. Plautus, *Boeotians*, fragment quoted by Aulus Gellius, 3.3.3, cited and trans. by Donald R. Dudley, *Urbs Roma* (New York: Phaidon, 1967), 99.

42. See Horace, *Satires* 2.6.

43. Seneca, *Letters*, 57 (translation by author).

44. Juvenal, *Satires*, 3, trans. Rolfe Humphries (*The Satires of Juvenal* [Bloomington: Indiana University Press, 1968], 42).

45. In 1869, an American neurologist named George Beard identified a type of nervous exhaustion he attributed to the stressful pace of late-nineteenth-century life. He called it "American Nervousness," or neurasthenia (see Tom Lutz, *American Nervousness, 1903* [Ithaca, NY: Cornell University Press, 1991], and Cynthia Crossen, "Losing It," *Wall Street Journal*, December 3, 1996, A1.)

46. Tarkington, *The Magnificent Ambersons* (Bloomington: Indiana University Press, 1989 [1918], chap. 19.

47. In 1990, 31 percent of American adults traveled by air. (Industry data supplied by SkyMall.)

48. Statistics from the American Automobile Manufacturers Association and the U.S. Bureau of the Census, *Statistical Brief*, "Americans and Their Automobiles" (1992).

49. Mander, *Four Arguments for the Elimination of Television* (New York: Morrow, 1978), 44.

50. Recalling Frost's poem, "The Road Not Taken."

51. Charles Kuralt, *A Life on the Road* (New York: Putnam, 1990), 192.

52. For the history of the credit card, see Nancy Shepherdson, "Credit Card America," *American Heritage*, November 1991, 125ff. There are currently more than a billion credit cards in circulation.

53. George Stalk, Jr., "Time—The Next Source of Competitive Advantage," *Harvard Business Review*, July/August 1988, 41.

54. Christopher Meyer, *Fast Cycle Time: How to Align Purpose, Strategy, and Structure for Speed* (New York: Free Press, 1993), 9. In a similar vein, business consultant Peter G.W. Keen argues that today success in business is more than ever before a race against time (see his *Competing in Time: Using Telecommunications for Competitive Advantage* [New York: Harper & Row, 1988], esp. chap. 1). Adds David Vice, vice chairman of Northern Telecom: "The nineties will be a decade in a hurry, a nanosecond culture. There'll be only two kinds of managers: the quick and the dead" (quoted on the book jacket of *The Quick and the Dead: Brian Mulroney, Big Business and the Seduction of Canada*, by Linda McQuaig [New York: Viking 1991] and cited by Tom Peters in *Liberation Management* [New York: Knopf, 1992]).

55. Peters, addressing the New England Booksellers Association Spring Seminar (Manchester Village, VT, April 22, 1990); see *Publishers Weekly*, May 25, 1990, 25.

56. See Kenneth R. Sheets, "Firms Now Lease Everything But Time," *U.S. News & World Report*, August 14, 1989, 45f.

57. William Bridges, "Tomorrow's 'Jobs' Defy Description," *Detroit News*, February 27, 1994, 5B.

58. I owe the time-machine metaphor to Craig Brod (interview with author).

59. Data from Technomics, Inc. McDonald's has become the world's largest holder of real estate and the largest job-training institution in America, training

more personnel than even the U.S. army. See Joseph Monninger, "Fast Food," *American Heritage*, April 1988, 68–75.

60. Drive-thru funeral parlors have appeared in Florida, Texas, and California (see Mede Nix, "A Window of Opportunity," *Dallas Times Herald*, March 25, 1991). A funeral parlor in Lancaster, Texas, features a tilting device to make it easier for drivers to see the casket.

61. Thanks to Simplex Knowledge Co., mourners can now attend a funeral on-line. Using the Internet, cybermourners can see the coffin, click on icons to send sympathy cards or flowers, and chat about the deceased with other bereaved digitati (see Deborah Solomon, "Mourning Becomes Electric," *Detroit Free Press*, October 27, 1996, 7E).

62. See Ari L. Goldman, "Religion Notes," *New York Times*, National Edition, February 12, 1994, Y7.

63. According to Ketchum Advertising, San Francisco, the agency that has promoted Orville Redenbacher popcorn since 1975, "snackers aged 25 to 34. . . prefer potato chips or pretzels to popcorn because the gratification found inside a microwave oven isn't instant enough" (quoted in *The New York Times* National edition, July 17, 1995, C8).

64. See Sandy Bauers, "Night Work Is on the Rise for a Nation That Never Sleeps," *Detroit Free Press*, January 4, 1993, F1. Jane E. Brody ("America's Falling Asleep," *New York Times* Magazine, April 24, 1994, 64ff.) points out that "some 100 million Americans are seriously sleep-deprived and a potential hazard to themselves and others. Some are compelled by their jobs to work when others sleep: a quarter of employed Americans work rotating shifts that discombobulate their biological clocks. Studies show that many night and shift workers regularly fall asleep operating hazardous machinery, driving trucks, overseeing nuclear power plants and piloting commercial jets."

65. See Edward J. Hay, *The Just-In-Time Breakthrough: Implementing the New Manufacturing Basics* (New York: John Wiley, 1988).

66. Ibid., vi.

67. See Christopher Meyer, *Fast Cycle Time: How to Align Purpose, Strategy, and Structure for Speed* (New York: Free Press, 1993).

68. Ibid., dust-jacket.

69. Institute is based at Memphis State University, Memphis, TN. I am grateful to its director, Dr. James C. Wetherbe, for his assistance.

70. See Taylor's *Principles of Scientific Management* (1911) and *Scientific Management* (ed. by C.B. Thompson; 1914), in *Scientific Management, Comprising Shop Management, the Principles of Scientific Management, & Testimony Before the Special House Committee* (Westport, CT: Greenwood, 1972). For a discussion of Taylor's approach to efficiency, see Jeremy Rifkin, *Time Wars* (New York: Holt, 1987).

71. Karen Nussbaum of the U.S. Department of Labor notes that some 26 million American workers currently have their efficiency monitored by management and that the number is growing. She relates how one clerical worker's video screen flashed: "You're not working as fast as the worker next to you!" (interviewed on *Running Out of Time,*) television documentary co-produced by KCTS [Seattle] and Oregon Public Broadcasting, 1994).

72. Information from author's interview with local Pizza Hut manager.

73. General Electric Co. Chairman Jack Welch notes that, as a result of deliberately emphasizing speed, "new GE products are now coming out with drumbeat rapidity. There is now a new product announcement at appliances every 90 days—unthinkable years ago" (James C. Hyatt [Dow Jones News Service], "Progress Is Easy as 1–2–3 Buzzwords," *Detroit Free Press*, March 2, 1994, 1E, quoting from Welch's 1994 annual report letter).

74. Quoted in "Tom Peters . . . and the Healthy Corporation," *Psychology Today*, March/April 1993, 58.

75. See James Tobin, "Consumed by Choices," *Detroit News*, November 18, 1992, 1A.

76. 1991, ibid.

77. Ibid.

78. Ibid.

79. The multiplicity of new brands is contributing to the elimination of many old-time favorites, now dubbed "ghost brands" because of their sinking popularity. Contributing to their demise are UPC scanners linked to supermarket computers that continually monitor how various brands are moving (see Stuart Elliott, "The Famous Brands on Death Row," *New York Times*, National Edition, November 7, 1993, 1Ff.). Another endangered species is books on bookstore shelves. Sales are monitored by computer. If a new book doesn't "take off" in ninety days or less, it may well be removed from the shelf to make room for another. New books and new authors are therefore given very little time to attract and build an audience unless they have been given substantial prepublication publicity by their publishers and/or by television shows.

80. For Diller's remarks, see Deirdre Carmody, "Slow Down on Technology, Diller Tells Magazine Chiefs," *New York Times*, National Edition, October 25, 1994, C18.

81. *New York Times*, November 10, 1996, F12.

82. "Tom Peters and the Healthy Corporation," 78.

83. In his book *The Third Wave* (New York: Morrow, 1980), Alvin Toffler says that industrial civilization is characterized by synchronization, i.e., clock-driven, mechanistic regimentation (pp. 51–53). In using the term "synchronous" here, however, I am describing society not as the product of industrialization but rather as the expression of electronic interconnectivity and instantaneous intercommunication. In its structure and operation, the synchronous society of today resembles not a factory as much as it does a neurological system.

84. Quote from Justice Louis Brandeis, dissenting opinion, *Olmstead v. United States*, 277 U.S. 438 (1928).

85. Karen Brandon, "There's No Hiding from Beeper Fever," *Detroit Free Press*, February 11, 1993, 3A.

86. See Erik Larson, *The Naked Consumer* (New York: Henry Holt, 1992), and David Lyon, *The Electronic Eye: The Rise of Surveillance* (Minneapolis: University of Minnesota Press, 1994).

87. For use of term, see Nathan Cobb, "The End of Privacy," *Detroit Free Press Magazine*, August 23, 1993, 6–12.

88. Ibid., 6.

89. Ira Glasser, executive director, American Civil Liberties Union, in a letter to the editor, *New York Times*, National Edition, January 24, 1993. The letter criticizes recent Supreme Court decisions.

90. See Neal Gabler, "The Brief Half-Life of Celebrity," *New York Times*, National Edition, October 16, 1994, 2.1f.

91. Antoine de Saint-Exupéry, *The Wisdom of the Sands*, trans. Stuart Gilbert (New York: Harcourt, 1950), especially 82.

92. In this connection, note the remarks of John Diebold, chairman of the Diebold Group, Inc., delivered to the House of Representatives Committee on Science and Technology, Washington, DC, September 10, 1985: "To an increasing extent, information technology is merging with developments in the field of neurobiology, opening the possibility of computers connected with human nervous systems" (reported in *Vital Speeches of the Day*, February 1, 1986, 244). Note also Jerry Mander, *In the Absence of the Sacred* (San Francisco: Sierra Club, 1991), 32: "Where evolution was once an interactive process between human beings and a natural, unmediated world, evolution is now an interaction between human beings and our own artifacts. We are essentially coevolving with ourselves in a weird kind of intraspecies incest. At each stage of the cycle the changes come faster and are more profound. The web of interactions among the machines becomes more complex and more invisible, while the total effect is more powerful and pervasive. We become ever more enclosed and ever less aware of that fact. Our environment is so much a product of our invention that it becomes a single worldwide machine. We live inside it, and are a piece of it."

93. See Lee Burns, *Busy Bodies: Why Our Time-Obsessed Society Keeps Us Running in Place* (New York: Norton, 1993).

94. Friedman and Rosenman, *Type A Behavior and Your Heart* (New York: Knopf, 1974), 1f.

95. Ibid., 14.

96. Robert V. Levine, "The Pace of Life," *American Scientist* (September-October 1990), 458, citing research conducted by psychologist Timothy Smith of the University of Utah.

97. Ibid. See also Robert V. Levine, Karen Lynch, Kuniyate Miyake, and Marty Lucia, "The Type A City: Coronary Heart Disease and the Pace of Life," *Journal of Behavioral Medicine* 12.6 (1989), 509–24.

98. Van Egeren, "A 'Success Trap' Theory of Type A Behavior: Historical Background," in Michael J. Strube, ed., *Type A Behavior* (Newbury Park, CA: Sage, 1992), 45–58. Apart from its perceptive discussion of the Type A personality and contemporary society, this article is very valuable for its concise description of the evolution of Western values (48–55).

CHAPTER 6: THE TRANSFORMATION OF DEMOCRACY

1. Tocqueville, *Democracy in America*, trans. Henry Reeve, rev. Francis Bowen, ed. Phillips Bradley (New York: Knopf, 1948 [1835–1840]; 2 vols.), chap. 10.

2. For this phrase I am indebted to Jeffrey B. Abramson, F. Christopher Arterton, and Gary R. Orren's book, *The Electronic Commonwealth: The Impact of New Media Technologies on Democratic Politics* (New York: Basic Books, 1988).

3. The most obvious hypothetical setting for such a crisis would be the aftermath of a thermonuclear war. But such helplessness has also been evident in instances of natural disaster, as when Hurricane Andrew struck Florida in 1992. In such cases, hypothetical or real, the economic and communicational infrastructure of society collapses and individuals and families must fend for themselves.

4. When asked to name their two top sources of information on national issues, 82 percent of Americans named television (Pew Research Center for the People and the Press, 1996, cited in *Wall Street Journal*, February 14, 1996, A16).

5. John P. Robinson, "Thanks for Reading This," *The Demographics of Time Use* (Ithaca, NY: American Demographics, 1994), 28–29.

6. See John W. Wright, ed., *The Universal Almanac, 1994* (Kansas City, MO: Andrews & McMeel, 1993), 222.

7. Quoted by David Barsamian, *Stenographers to Power: Media and Propaganda* (Monroe, ME: Common Courage Press, 1992), 136.

8. Sven Birkerts, *American Energies: Essays on Fiction* (New York: Morrow, 1992), 23f.

9. Quoted by Michael Kelly, in "Being Whatever It Takes to Win the Election," *New York Times*, National Edition, August 23, 1992, 4.1. Faxing, in particular, has significantly speeded up campaign activity and coverage by enabling opposing political camps to learn of and respond to each other's positions and charges far more rapidly than before.

10. Quoted in "The Media: Out of Control?" *New York Times Magazine*, June 26, 1994, 31.

11. Quoted by Geraldine Fabrikant in "For NBC, Hard Times and Miscues," *New York Times*, National Edition, December 13, 1992, 3.6.

12. Postman, *Amusing Ourselves to Death* (New York: Viking Penguin, 1985), 67.

13. Ibid., 77.

14. Robert MacNeil, "Is Television Shortening Our Attention Span?" *New York University Education Quarterly* 14.2 (Winter 1983), 2. Based on extensive interviews with media creators and executives, Rutgers University psychologist Robert W. Kubey has concluded that their belief in the shortness of the public's attention span is so pervasive that it has become a controlling principle of design (interview with the author, August 10, 1993). Currently, the most obvious evidence for this is television commercials, which are composed of a series of images that normally last for no more than three seconds. As Kubey notes, media products that presume a short attention span among viewers help to create the very thing they presume.

15. "The Media: Out of Control?," 29.

16. Quoted by Tim Kiska in "Herrington Is Mad as Hell about Show Biz in TV News," *Detroit News*, January 22, 1994, 4C.

17. Thomas Jefferson, letter to Charles Yancy (January 6, 1816), *The Harper Book of American Quotations* (New York: Harper & Row, 1988), 208.

18. See Marc Gunther, "CBS Drops the Small Talk So Candidates Spell Out Ideas," *Detroit Free Press*, July 7, 1992, 1Af., and Richard L. Berke, "Mixed Results for CBS Rule on Sound Bite," *New York Times*, National Edition, July 11, 1992, Y7. Additional data: "The Hotline" (American Political Network).

19. See Marc Gunther, 11A.

20. Quoted by Richard L. Berke, Y7.

21. Quoted by Roger Stone, "Nixon on Clinton," *New York Times*, National Edition, April 28, 1994, A15.

22. Mander, *Four Arguments for the Elimination of Television* (New York: Morrow, 1978), 240.

23. See Postman, *Amusing Ourselves to Death*.

24. Quoted by Jack Thomas (*Boston Globe*) in "How's Tricks?," *Detroit News*, August 5, 1994, 3D. For early attempts at such visual manipulation, see David King, *The Commissar Vanishes: The Falsification of Photographs and Art in Stalin's Russia* (New York: Henry Holt, 1997).

25. See *New York Times*, National Edition, November 1, 1992, E3.

26. See *Detroit News*, October 25, 1992, 13A.

27. Quoted by Karen De Witt, "Battle to Save U. S. Files from the Delete Button," *New York Times*, National Edition, April 11, 1993, 13. In a 1993 decision, however, the U.S. Court of Appeals for the District of Columbia ruled that electronic messages and memoranda by federal officials must be protected by the same standards that apply to communications on paper (see Neil A. Lewis, "Government Told to Save Messages Sent by Computer," *New York Times*, National Edition, August 14, 1993, 1).

28. *Nineteen Eighty-Four* (New York: NAL-Dutton, 1950 [1949]), 1.4.

29. Juvenal, *Satires*, 10.78–81.

30. See Stephen Bertman, *Art and the Romans: Roman Art as a Dynamic Expression of Roman Character* (Lawrence, KS: Coronado Press, 1976).

31. On the propagandistic use of mass media in Nazi Germany, see Helmut Lehmann-Haupt, *Art under a Dictatorship* (New York: Oxford University Press, 1954), chap. 2; Berthold Hinz, *Art in the Third Reich* (New York: Pantheon, 1979); and Igor Golomstock, *Totalitarian Art* (New York: HarperCollins, 1990). See also the autobiographies of Albert Speer and Leni Riefenstahl.

32. See Kubey and Csikszentmihalyi, *Television and the Quality of Life* (Hillsdale, NJ: Lawrence Erlbaum Associates, 1990), 172; Todd Gitlin, "Sixteen Notes on Television and the Movement," in George White and Charles Newman, eds., *Literature in Revolution* (New York: Holt, Rinehart, & Winston, 1972), 351; Herbert I. Schiller, *The Mind Managers* (Boston: Beacon Press, 1973), 30; and Jerry Mander, *Four Arguments for the Elimination of Television*.

33. See Michael Kelly, "Perot's Vision: Consensus by Computer," *New York Times*, National Edition, June 6, 1992, 1.8; and Jeffrey Abramson, Letter to the Editor, *New York Times*, National Edition, June 21, 1992, 16E.

34. On possible controls (such as a cooling-off period or a second vote before actual implementation), see Clark McCauley, Omar Rood, and Tom Johnson, "The New Democracy," The World Future Society *Bulletin*, November/December 1977.

35. Walter Goodman, "And Now, Heeeeeeeere's Referendum," *New York Times*, National Edition, June 21, 1992, H25.

36. Viewers using postcard ballots supplied by *TV Guide* could, however, have taken more time to deliberate. To my knowledge, no detailed results of the referendum were ever made public by Perot or his organization.

37. See *The Federalist Papers*, No. 49, on the danger of popular passion in the making of political decisions. Grave reservations of a similar type had been expressed over 2,000 years earlier by the Greek philosopher Plato (*Republic*, Book 8).

38. Such a system, however, can aid democracy by giving citizens access to governmental information. Through programming on C-Span, the medium of television gives citizens unprecedented live access to the goings-on of government. Through the Library of Congress's on-line system known as "Thomas" (named for Thomas Jefferson), citizens can access pending legislation and reports from Congressional committees.

39. Schiller, *The Mind Managers* (Boston: Beacon Press, 1973), 30.

40. Gitlin, "Sixteen Notes on Television and the Movement," in George White and Charles Newman, eds., *Literature in Revolution* (New York: Holt, Rinehart, Winston 1972), 351.

41. Kubey and Csikszentmihalyi, *Television and the Quality of Life*, 172.

42. Notably by Douglas Davis, *The Five Myths of Television: Or, Why the Medium Is Not the Message* (New York: Simon & Schuster, 1993).

43. Schiller, *The Mind Managers*, 29.

44. *Brave New World*, chap. 3.

45. Regarding seductiveness, see "Would You Give Up TV for a Million Bucks?" *TV Guide*, October 10, 1992, 10–17, esp. 11, on results of a survey: "Almost half (46%) of all American viewers say they would refuse to give up television for anything under a million dollars. One in four (25%) would refuse to stop watching TV even for $1 million."

46. Postman, *Amusing Ourselves to Death*, 163.

47. The leaders of a democracy also suffer the effects of the power of now. Leadership does not grant them immunity. In trying to formulate policies and reach decisions, those in high office are also affected by immense pressures on their time. Noting that Abraham Lincoln had time to open his own mail and William McKinley time to answer his own phone, Richard D. Lamm, former governor of Colorado, observes: "Being in office today is like drinking out of a fire hydrant. You look at the multiplicity of issues and public interest groups and the cacophony of things that demand public policy decisions and you wonder how anybody makes the right decision. . . . It's clearly dysfunctional, and it may be more than that. . . . It may sink a society. . . . It's hard for me to see how you can keep a democracy under conditions that we now have" (interview with the author, August 30, 1993).

48. See Elizabeth Kolbert, "Test Marketing a President: How Focus Groups Pervade Campaign Politics," *New York Times Magazine*, August 30, 1992, 18f.

49. In this connection, note the Persian Gulf War and its coverage by the media. In particular, see George Gerbner, Herbert I. Schiller, and Hamid Molwana, *Triumph of the Image: The Media's War in the Persian Gulf—A Global Perspective* (Boulder, CO: Westview Press, 1992); Philip M. Taylor, *War and the Media: Propaganda and Persuasion in the Gulf War* (Manchester, England: Manchester University Press, 1992); Hedrick Smith, ed., *The Media and the Gulf War* (Washington, DC: Seven Locks Press, 1992); Bradley S. Greenberg and Walter Gantz, *Desert Storm and the Mass Media* (Cresskill, NJ: Hampton Press, 1993); and Susan Jeffords and Lauren Rabinovitz, *Seeing through the Media: The Persian Gulf War* (New Brunswick, NJ: Rutgers University Press, 1994).

50. Recalling Eliot's poem, "The Hollow Men," in T. S. Eliot, *The Collected Poems and Plays, 1908–1950* (New York: Harcourt Brace, 1958), 96.

51. Alvin Toffler, *The Third Wave* (New York: Bantam, 1981), 1.

52. Ibid., 9.

53. Ibid., 10f.

54. Toffler and Toffler, *Creating a New Civilization: The Politics of the Third Wave* (Atlanta: Turner Publishing, 1994, 1995), 11.

CHAPTER 7: THE TRANSFORMATION OF INTERNATIONAL RELATIONS

1. McLuhan, in Marshall McLuhan and Quentin Fiore, *The Medium Is the Message* (New York: Simon & Schuster, 1967, 1989), 16.

2. J. T. Fraser, *Time, the Familiar Stranger* (New York: Harper & Row, 1987), 310 ff.

3. See Ilya Zemstov, "Lexicon of Glasnost," *Crossroads* 27 (1989), 3–24.

4. Jim Rower, "The Nation-State on Trial," *The World in 1993* (newspaper supplement: "*The [Toronto] Globe and Mail* Report on Business/*The Economist* Publications," January 1993), 35.

5. For statistics, see Rower, "The Nation State on Trail."

6. Robert B. Reich, *The Work of Nations: Preparing Ourselves for 21st Century Capitalism* (New York: Knopf, 1991), 8.

7. Ibid., 3.

8. Clinton, Inaugural Address (January 20, 1993), *New York Times*, January 21, 1993, A15.

9. Walter B. Wriston, "Clintonomics: The Information Revolution and the New Global Market Economy," *Vital Speeches of the Day*, April 1, 1993, 376.

10. Stephen D. Harlan, "Becoming a Global Thinker," *Vital Speeches of the Day*, January 15, 1992, 204–208.

11. Source: U.S. Department of Transportation, *National Transportation Statistics Annual Report*, 1996.

12. See John Naisbitt, *Global Paradox: The Bigger the World Economy, the More Powerful Its Smallest Players* (New York: Morrow, 1994), 116.

13. Dasburg, president and CEO of Northwest Airlines, quoted by Agis Salpukas, "The Big Foreign Push to Buy into U.S. Airlines," *New York Times*, National Edition, October 11, 1992, 11F.

14. See Naisbitt, 117ff.

15. Conway, quoted by Naisbitt, 119.

16. See Ferdinand Protzman, "To Track Unity in Europe, Watch Its Fast Trains," *New York Times*,National Edition, October 25, 1992, 5F; and Jennifer Fisher, "Finally, London to Paris by Train," *U.S. News & World Report*, November 21, 1994, 95.

17. See Scott Norvell, "The Forgotten Fourth in Long Distance," *New York Times* National Edition, December 27, 1992, 6F; Anthony Ramirez, "Battle Is Fierce on the Phone Front," *New York Times*, National Edition, November 27, 1993, Y13; Hiawatha Bray, "Long, Long Distance," *Detroit Free Press*, December 17, 1993, 1C; and Sandra Sugawara (*Washington Post*), "Long Distance Firms Help Callers Keep in Touch in Any Language," *Detroit News*, May 8, 1994, 2A.

18. Quoted by Norvell, "Forgotten Fourth in Long Distance."

19. See Martin and Susan Tolchin, *Buying into America: How Foreign Money Is Changing the Face of Our Nation* (New York: Random House, 1988) and *Selling Our Security: The Erosion of America's Assets* (New York: Knopf, 1992).

20. Source: *The Wall Street Journal Almanac 1998* (New York: Random House, 1997), 215.

21. Reich, *The Work of Nations*, 113.

22. Marshall Shuon, "From Geo, a Second-Generation Prizm," *New York Times*, National Edition, November 29, 1992, 3Y.

23. See Eben Shapiro (*New York Times*), "McDonald's Flips for Foreign Markets," *Detroit Free Press*, April 18, 1992, 6Af.; Roddy Ray, "Global Golden Arches," *Detroit Free Press*, February 20, 1993, 11A; Howard Witt, "The Big Mac Revolution," *Chicago Tribune Magazine*, July 25, 1993, 10–20; and Susan V. Lawrence, with Mike Tharp, "Chinese Chicken: Dancing for Fast-Food Dollars" (on KFC in China), *U.S. News & World Report*, July 18, 1994, 46. McDonald's international menus feature local favorites: e.g., fried rice and seaweed in Japan.

24. James Sterngold, "The Awakening Chinese Consumer," *New York Times*, National Edition, October 11, 1992, 3.1.

25. For this phrase, see Victor Ripp's *Pizza in Pushkin Square: What Russians Think about Americans and the American Way of Life* (New York: Simon & Schuster, 1990). See also Howard Witt, "From Russia with Relish. . . or How the Big Mac Conquered Moscow," *Chicago Tribune Magazine*, July 25, 1993, 10ff.

26. Walter Truett Anderson, *Reality Isn't What It Used to Be: Theatrical Politics, Ready-to-Wear Religion, Global Myths, Primitive Chic, and Other Wonders of the Postmodern World* (New York: Harper & Row, 1990), 256.

27. Indonesia's Sukarno, quoted in Marshall McLuhan and Quentin Fiore, *The Medium Is the Massage*, 131, citing *Variety* article: "Ice Boxes Sabotage Colonialism."

28. Valenti, interviewed on WJR (Detroit), December 18, 1992.

29. See Bernard Weinraub, "Directors Fight for GATT's Final Cut and Print," *New York Times*, National Edition, December 12, 1993, 14Y.

30. According to Nielsen Media Research.

31. See John Lippman (*Los Angeles Times*), "Television Is Becoming a Channel for World Change," *Detroit News*, November 1, 1992, 8A.

32. Dennis, quoted by John Lippman, ibid.

33. Ash, quoted by John Lippman, ibid.

34. Walesa, quoted by Lippman, ibid.

35. See "Small Polish Broadcaster Wins TV License," *New York Times*, January 29, 1994, 1.37.

36. See Tom Rosenstiel, "The Myth of CNN; Why Ted Turner's Revolution Is Bad News," *The New Republic*, August 22, 1994, 27ff.

37. By 1995, for example, MTV was broadcasting by satellite in English and Mandarin Chinese to thirty Asian countries. See "MTV Multiplies Its Asian Outlets," *New York Times*, May 3, 1994, D22.

38. For statistics and quotations relating to China and Iran presented here, see Nicholas D. Kristof, "Via Satellite, Information Revolution Stirs China," *New York Times*, National Edition, April 11, 1993, 1f., and "Chinese Left in Dark by Ban on Satellite Dishes," *Detroit Free Press*, November 22, 1993, 1A, reprinted from *The New York Times*; also Chris Hedges, "Teheran Journal: From Satellite Dishes, Spice for TV," *New York Times*, National Edition, August 16, 1994, A4.

39. Rosenstiel, "The Myth of CNN."

40. Jim Wooten, quoted by Marc Gunther in "Full Scope of the Rwanda Tragedy Escapes TV Cameras," *Detroit Free Press*, August 14, 1994, 6G.

41. Anna Quindlen (*New York Times* News Service), "The Numbness Factor: Do the Starving Move Us, or Make Us Give Up?" *Detroit Free Press*, July 26, 1994, 9A.

42. See Center for Investigative Reporting and Bill Moyers, *Global Dumping Ground: The International Traffic in Hazardous Waste* (Cabin John, MD: Seven Locks Press, 1990).

43. Paul Kennedy, *Preparing for the 21st Century* (New York: Random House, 1993), 129.

44. Herbert I. Schiller, *Culture, Inc.: The Corporate Takeover of Public Expression* (New York: Oxford University Press, 1989), 4f.

45. Kant, *Zum Ewigen Frieden* (1775), cited by Kennedy, *Preparing for the 21st Century* (New York: Random House, 1993), 133 and footnote.

46. See Daniel Patrick Moynihan, *Pandaemonium: Ethnicity in International Politics* (New York: Oxford University Press, 1993).

47. Anderson, *Reality Isn't What It Used to Be*, 24.

48. Harold R. Isaacs, *Idols of the Tribe: Group Identity and Political Change* (New York: Harper & Row, 1975), 215.

49. Walter B. Wriston, *The Twilight of Sovereignty: How the Information Revolution Is Transforming Our World* (New York: Scribner's, 1992), xii–xiii.

50. Russell Kirk, "Will Eliot Endure?" *The World & I*, August 1993, 414.

51. Wriston does acknowledge that technology is no panacea: "Advanced technology does not produce wisdom; it does not change human nature; it does not make our problems go away. But it does and will speed us on our journey toward more human freedom" (*The Twilight of Sovereignty*, 176).

52. The stress that has come to characterize American life is increasingly becoming international. The word "stress" has entered a number of foreign languages—pronounced ess-TRESS in Spanish, STRESS-a in Russian, and su-tor-es-u in Japanese. (See Richard A. Shweder, "America's Latest Export: A Stressed-Out World," *New York Times*, National Edition, January 26, 1997, E5). Stress-related death from overwork (*karoshi*) is a feature of modern Japanese life.

53. Paddy Chayefsky, *Network* (Metro-Goldwyn-Mayer, 1976). In the film, Howard Beale was played by Peter Finch; Mr. Jensen, by Ned Beatty.

CHAPTER 8: THE TRANSFORMATION OF THE ENVIRONMENT

1. For a moving, contemporary translation, see Herbert Mason, *Gilgamesh: A Verse Narrative* (New York: New American Library, 1970).

2. Vergil, *The Aeneid*, 1. 279.

3. For a discussion of the development of modern science, its collaboration with materialism, and their joint influence on Western thought, see Bryan Appleyard, *Understanding the Present: Science and the Soul of Modern Man* (New York: Basic Books, 1993), and Donald Worster, *The Wealth of Nature: Environmental History and the Ecological Imagination* (New York: Oxford University Press, 1993).

4. See Jacques Ellul, *The Technological Society* (New York: Knopf, 1964).

5. Genesis, 1:26.

6. On this point, see George Leonard, *The Silent Pulse* (New York: Viking Penguin, 1992).

7. Convincing evidence of this devaluation can be found in the pages of our nation's newspapers. Stories about technology and business far outnumber stories about nature and the need for its preservation, in large part because—except for disasters—nature is not as "exciting."

8. Used with this slant by Dan Rather in "Fast Times," *48 Hours* (CBS documentary, 1990).

9. Extinctions are now estimated to be taking place at 25,000 times the natural rate. Some experts believe that at this rate by the year 2050 half of all the species that are still left on our planet may disappear. (See David E. Pitt, "Biological Treaty, with the Goal of Saving Species, Becomes Law," *New York Times*, National Edition, January 2, 1994, 4Y.)

10. See Edward O. Wilson, "Is Humanity Suicidal?," *New York Times Magazine*, May 30, 1993, 24ff.

11. Since the 1992 Earth Summit at Rio de Janeiro, there has been little international progress on the ecology front, except in the area of population control. Nevertheless, in the 21st century world population is expected to reach 11 billion from its present level of 6 billion (see *The New York Times*, National Edition, June 17, 1997, B14).

12. On the vanishing notion and reality of a wilderness see John Markoff, "The Lost Art of Getting Lost," *New York Times*, National Edition, September 18, 1994, 4.1, and Bill McKibben, *The End of Nature* (New York: Random House, 1989) and *The Age of Missing Information* (New York: Random House, 1992).

13. See Lewis Mumford, *Technics and Civilization* (New York: Harcourt Brace, 1934), chap. 1; Daniel J. Boorstin, *The Discoverers: A History of Man's Search to Know His World and Himself* (New York: Random House, 1983), Part 2; and Sebastian de Grazia, *Of Time, Work, and Leisure* (New York: Twentieth Century Fund, 1962), chap. 8.

14. Ian McHarg, *Design with Nature* (Garden City, NY: Doubleday, 1969), 44.

15. Loren Eiseley, *The Firmament of Time* (New York: Atheneum, 1962), 123f.

16. Wilson, "Is Humanity Suicidal,?" 26.

17. James Lovelock, *Gaia: A New Look at Life on Earth* (New York: Norton, 1988).

18. See Pierre Teilhard de Chardin, *Hymn of the Universe* (New York: Harper & Row, 1965).

19. Peter Russell, *The Global Brain: Speculations on the Evolutionary Leap to Planetary Consciousness* (Los Angeles: Jeremy P. Tarcher, 1983).

20. Gregory Stock, *Metaman: The Merging of Humans and Machines into a Global Superorganism* (New York: Simon & Schuster, 1993), xix.

CHAPTER 9: THE THREE KEYS TO RESISTING NOW'S POWER

1. On the distinction between sacred and profane time, see Eviatar Zerubavel, *Hidden Rhythms: Schedules and Calendars in Social Life* (Chicago: University of Chicago Press, 1981), chap. 4.

2. Exodus 20:8–11.

3. Two decades ago, confronting large-scale technology, E. F. Schumaker argued that "small is beautiful" (E. F. Schumaker, *Small Is Beautiful* [New York:

Harper & Row, 1973]). Today, asserts Jerry Mander (interview with the author), an equally valid maxim would be "*slow* is beautiful."

4. Moses Hadas, *Old Wine, New Bottles: A Humanist Teacher at Work* (New York: Pocket Books, 1963), 129.

5. For this notion, see especially Jean-Louis Servan-Schreiber, *The Art of Time*, trans. Franklin Philip (Reading, MA: Addison-Wesley, 1988).

6. Theobald, *The Rapids of Change: Social Entrepreneurship in Turbulent Times* (Indianapolis, IN: Knowledge Systems, 1987), 34.

7. In this connection it is worth reflecting on Russell Kirk's observation: "We can redeem the time only if we apprehend the timeless" ("Will Eliot Endure?," *The World and I*, August 1993, 417).

8. For a discussion and suggestions, see David Shi, *The Simple Life: Plain Living and High Thinking in American Culture* (New York: Oxford University Press, 1986); Duane Elgin, *Voluntary Simplicity: Toward a Way of Life That Is Outwardly Simple, Inwardly Rich* (New York: Morrow, 1981); and Joe Dominguez and Vicki Robin, *Your Money or Your Life: Transforming Your Relationship with Money and Achieving Financial Independence* (New York: Viking Penguin, 1992). For testimonials, see Adair Lara, *Slowing Down in a Speeded Up World* (Berkeley, CA: Conari Press, 1994).

9. In *The Structure of Scientific Revolutions* (2d ed. enl.; *International Encyclopedia of Unified Science*, 2.2; Chicago: University of Chicago Press 1970), Thomas S. Kuhn describes how a "paradigm shift" can occur when a community that has traditionally looked upon reality from one perspective suddenly sees it from another in a conversion-like experience (see especially Kuhn's chap. 12 and "Postscript").

10. Theobald, letter to the author, dated September 29, 1993.

11. See the interconnection of vision and intellectual conceptualization discussed in chap. 2.

12. Hillel, quoted in *The Ethics of the Fathers* (*Pirkei Avot*), 1.14. See *Sayings of the Fathers*, ed. and trans. by Joseph H. Hertz (New York: Behrman House, 1945), 25.

13. In this connection, note the comments of Hans Selye: "The goal [of man] is certainly not to avoid stress. Stress is part of life" (*The Stress of Life* [New York: McGraw-Hill, 1956], 299); "Stress, applied in moderation, is necessary for life" (ibid., 300); "Complete freedom from stress is death" (*Stress without Distress* [Philadelphia: Lippincott, 1974], 32); and, lastly, "It is only in the heat of stress that individuality can be perfectly molded" (*The Stress of Life*, 277).

14. Robert Grudin (*The Grace of Great Things: Creativity and Innovation* [New York: Ticknor & Fields, 1990], 83f.) uses this term in speaking of the isolation necessary for creativity. In *Time and the Art of Living* (New York: Ticknor & Fields, 1982), he also speaks of the psychological value of building protective "nests in time" (p. 90ff).

15. For this term I am indebted to Dr. Paul Pearsall (interview with the author).

16. Ibid.

CONCLUSION: BEYOND FUTURE SHOCK

1. See Toffler, *Future Shock* (New York: Random House, 1970), Part 4 (chap. 17–20). Also, Friedman and Rosenman, *Type A Behavior and Your Heart* [New York: Knopf, 1974], chap. 15–17. Though intended specifically for internally driven

Type A's, Friedman and Rosenman's advice also has value for others trying to
survive in a speeded-up world.

2. "If we are to build a stable cultural structure above that which threatens to
engulf us by changing our lives more rapidly than we can adjust our habits, it will
only be by flinging over the torrent a structure as taut and flexible as a spider's
web, a human society deeply self-conscious and undeceived by the waters that
race beneath it, a society more literate, more appreciative of human worth than any
society that has previously existed. That is the sole prescription, not for survival—
which is meaningless—but for a society worthy to survive. It should be, in the end,
a society more interested in the cultivation of noble minds than in change" (Eiseley, *The Firmament of Time* [New York: Atheneum, 1962], 147).

Recommended Reading

THE SCIENTIFIC UNDERSTANDING OF TIME

Appleyard, Brian. *Understanding the Present: Science and the Soul of Modern Man.* New York: Basic Books, 1993.

Aveni, Anthony. *Empires of Time: Calendars, Clocks, and Cultures.* New York: Basic Books, 1989.

Barrow, John D. *Theories of Everything: The Quest for Ultimate Explanation.* New York: Fawcett Columbine, 1991.

Boorstin, Daniel J. *The Discoverers: A History of Man's Search to Know His World and Himself.* Book One. (New York: Random House, 1983).

Bruce, Roger R., ed. *Dr. Harold E. Edgerton and the Wonders of Strobe Alley.* Cambridge, MA: Publishing Trust of George Eastman House/MIT Press, 1995.

Coveney, Peter, and Highfield, Roger. *The Arrow of Time.* New York: Ballantine Books, 1990.

Doob, Leonard. *Patterning of Time.* New Haven, CT: Yale University Press, 1971.

Epstein, Lewis Carroll. *Relativity Visualized.* San Francisco: Insight Press, 1981.

Fraser, J. T. *The Genesis and Evolution of Time: A Critique of Interpretation in Physics.* Amherst, MA: University of Massachusetts Press, 1982.

_____. *Time as Conflict: A Scientific and Humanistic Study.* Boston: Birkhauser, 1980.

_____, ed. *The Voices of Time: A Cooperative Survey of Man's Views of Time as Understood and Described by the Sciences and by the Humanities.* New York: Braziller, 1966.

_____, and Rowell, Lewis. *The Study of Time* Series, 8 vols. 1969–1996. Vols. 1–4, New York: Springer-Verlag; 5, Amherst, MA: University of Massachusetts Press; 6–8, Madison, CT: International Universities Press.

Hawking, Stephen. *A Brief History of Time*. New York: Bantam, 1988.

_____, ed. *Stephen Hawking's "A Brief History of Time": A Reader's Companion*. New York: Bantam, 1992.

Lieb, Irwin C. *Past, Present, and Future: A Philosophical Study of Time*. Champaign: University of Illinois Press, 1991.

Morris, Richard. *Time's Arrows: Scientific Attitudes toward Time*. New York: Simon & Schuster, 1984.

Priestley, J. B. *Man and Time*. New York: Crown, 1989 (1964).

Prigogine, Ilya. *From Being to Becoming: Time and Complexity in the Physical Sciences*. San Francisco: W. H. Freeman, 1980.

Rifkin, Jeremy. *Declaration of a Heretic:* Boston: Routledge & Kegan Paul, 1985.

_____. *Time Wars: The Primary Conflict in Human History*. New York: Holt, 1987.

_____, and Howard, Ted. *Entropy: A New World View*. New York: Viking, 1980.

Szamosi, Geza. *The Twin Dimensions: Inventing Time and Space*. New York: McGraw-Hill, 1986.

THE PERSONAL AND SOCIAL IMPLICATIONS OF TIME

Adam, Barbara; Giessler, Karlheinz; and Held, Martin, eds., *Die Nonstop-Gesellschaft und ihr Preis*. Stuttgart: Hizel/Wissenschaftliche Verlagsgesellschaft, 1997.

Allen, George. *The Importance of the Past: A Meditation on the Authority of Tradition*. Albany: State University of New York Press, 1985.

Ausubel, Jesse, "Rat Race Dynamics and Crazy Companies," *Technological Forecasting and Social Change*, 39 (1991): 11–22.

Bedini, Silvio A. "The Scent of Time." *Transactions of the American Philosophical Society* 5.3 (1963):5.

Burns, Lee. *Busy Bodies: Why Our Time-Obsessed Society Keeps Us Running in Place*. New York: Norton, 1993.

Castelli, Enrico. *Il tempo esaurito*. Rome: Bussola, 1949. Retitled *Le Temp harcelant*. Paris: Presses Universitaires de France, 1952.

Conner, Daryl R. *Managing at the Speed of Change: Guidelines for Resilience in Turbulent Times*. New York: Random House, 1993.

Coupland, Douglas, *Generation X: Tales for an Accelerated Culture*. New York: St. Martin's Press, 1991.

Csikszentmihalyi, Mihalyi. *Finding Flow: The Psychology of Engagement with Everyday Life*. New York: Basic Books, 1997.

Eiseley, Loren. *The Firmament of Time*. New York: Atheneum 1962.

Fraser, T. *Of Time, Passion, and Knowledge*. Princeton, NJ: Princeton University Press, 1975.

_____. *Time, the Familiar Stranger*. New York: Harper & Row, 1987.

_____. ed. *The Voices of Time*. New York: Braziller, 1966.

_____, and Rowell, Lewis. *The Study of Time* Series, 8 vols., 1969–1996. Vols. 1–4, New York: Springer-Verlag; 5, Amherst, MA: University of Massachusetts Press; 6–8, Madison, CT: International Universities Press.

Friedman, Meyer, and Rosenman, Ray H. *Type A Behavior and Your Heart*. New York: Knopf, 1974.

Gibbs, Nancy. "How America Has Run Out of Time." *Time*, April 24, 1989, 59ff.

Gonzalez, Alexander, and Zimbardo, Philip G. "Time in Perspective." *Psychology Today* 19 (March 1985): 21–26.

Grazia, Sebastian de. *Of Time, Work and Leisure*. New York: Twentieth Century Fund, 1962.

Grudin, Robert. *Time and the Art of Living*. New York: Ticknor & Fields, 1982.

Hall, Edward T. *The Silent Language*. Garden City, NY: Doubleday, 1954.

Harrigan, Anthony. "Ignoring the Past." *National Review*, January 11, 1985, 32–36.

———. "The Inner Life in a Fragmented World." *This World* 16:88–94.

———. "A Lost Civilization." *Modern Age*, Fall 1992, 3–12.

———. "The Poignancy of Human Existence." *Modern Age*, Winter 1986, 6–9.

Kane, Madeleine Begun. "When Executives Should Just Say No." *New York Times*, National Edition, April 14, 1991, 3.11.

Keyes, Ralph. *Time-Lock: How Life Got So Hectic and What You Can Do About It*. New York: HarperCollins, 1991.

Kundera, Milan. *Slowness*. New York: HarperCollins, 1996.

Lara, Adair. *Slowing Down in a Speeded Up World*. Berkeley, CA: Conari Press, 1994.

Lauer, Robert H. *Temporal Man: The Meaning and Uses of Social Time*. (New York: Praeger, 1981.

Levine, Robert. *A Geography of Time: The Temporal Misadventures of a Social Psychologist*. New York: Basic Books, 1997.

———. "The Pace of Life." *American Scientist*, September-October 1990, 451–459.

———. "The Pace of Life across Cultures." In *The Social Psychology of Time: New Perspectives*, edited by Joseph E. McGrath, 39–59. Newbury Park, CA: Sage Publications, 1988.

———. Lynch, Karen; Miyake, Kunitate; and Lucia, Marty. "The Type A City: Coronary Heart Disease and the Pace of Life." *Journal of Behavioral Medicine* 12.6 (1989): 509–24.

———. and Wolff, Ellen. "Social Time: The Heartbeat of Culture." *Psychology Today* 19 (March 1985): 28–35.

Lieb, Irwin C. *Past, Present, and Future: A Philosophical Study of Time*. Champaign: University of Illinois Press, 1991.

Lowenthal, David. *The Past Is a Foreign Country*. New York: Cambridge University Press, 1985.

MacLachlan, James. "What People Really Think of Fast Talkers." *Psychology Today* 13.6 (November 1979): 113–117.

Mattox, William R., Jr. "America's Family Time Famine." *Children Today*, November/December 1990, 9ff.

Meyer, Christopher. *Fast Cycle Time: How to Allign Purpose, Strategy, and Structure for Speed*. New York: Free Press, 1993.

Moore-Ede, Martin. *The Twenty-Four Hour Society: Understanding Human Limits in a World That Never Stops*. Reading, MA: Addison-Wesley, 1993.

"The 1991 *McCall's* International Job Stress Survey." *McCall's*, March 1991, 71ff.

O'Malley, Michael. *Keeping Watch: A History of American Time*. New York: Viking Penguin, 1991.

Peel, Kathy. *How to Simplify Your Life*. New York: New International Bible Society, 1994.

Price, Virginia Ann. *Type A Behavior Pattern: A Model for Research and Practice*. New York: Academic Press, 1982.

Priestley, J. B. *Man and Time*. New York: Crown, 1989 (1964). Chap. 7, "This Age."

Rifkin, Jeremy, *Time Wars: The Primary Conflict in Human History*. New York: Henry Holt, 1987.

Robinson, John P. "How Americans Use Time: An Interview with Sociologist John Robinson." *The Futurist*, September–October 1991, 23–27.

_____ . "The Time Squeeze." *American Demographics*, February 1990, 32–33.

_____ , and Godbey, Geoffrey. *Time for Life: The Surprising Ways Americans Use Their Time*. University Park, PA: Pennsylvania University Press, 1997.

Russell, Peter. *The White Hole in Time: Our Future Evolution and the Meaning of Now*. San Francisco: Harper, 1992.

Saltzman, Amy. *Downshifting: Reinventing Success on a Slower Track*. New York: HarperCollins, 1991.

Selye, Hans. *The Stress of Life*. New York: McGraw-Hill, 1956.

_____ . *Stress Without Distress*. Philadelphia: Lippincott, 1974.

Servan-Schreiber, Jean-Louis. *The Art of Time*. Translated by Franklin Philip. Reading, MA: Addison-Wesley, 1988.

Sisk, John P. "How Fast Should We Go?" *The Antioch Review* 44 (Spring 1986): 137–148.

St. James, Elaine. *Inner Simplicity*. New York: Hyperion, 1995.

_____ . *Living the Simple Life*. New York: Hyperion, 1996.

Tassi, Nina. *Urgency Addiction: How to Slow Down without Sacrificing Success*. Dallas: Taylor, 1991.

Theobald, Robert. *The Rapids of Change: Social Entrepreneurship in Turbulent Times*. Indianapolis, IN: Knowledge Systems, 1987.

Toffler, Alvin. *Future Shock*. New York: Random House, 1970.

Van Egeren, Lawrence F. "A 'Success Trap' Theory of Type A Behavior: Historical Background." In *Type A Behavior*, edited by Michael J. Strube, 45–58. Newbury Park, CA: Sage 1991.

Vries, Egbert de. *Man in Rapid Social Change*. Garden City, NY: Doubleday, 1961.

Whitrow, G. J., *Time in History: Views of Time from Prehistory to the Present Day*. New York: Oxford University Press, 1989.

Wright, Lawrence. *Clockwork Man*. New York: Barnes & Noble, 1992.

Young, Michael. *The Metronomic Society: Natural Rhythms and Human Timetables*. Cambridge, MA: Harvard University Press, 1988.

Zerubavel, Eviatar. *Hidden Rhythms: Schedules and Calendars in Social Life*. Chicago: University of Chicago Press, 1981.

THE MEANING OF PROGRESS

Bury, J. B. *The Idea of Progress: An Inquiry into Its Origin and Growth*. New York: Dover, 1955 (1932).

Durant, Will, and Durant, Ariel. *The Lessons of History*. New York: Simon & Schuster, 1968.

Edelstein, Ludwig. *The Idea of Progress in Classical Antiquity.* Baltimore: Johns Hopkins University Press, 1967.

Fukuyama, Francis. *The End of History and the Last Man.* New York: Macmillan, 1992.

Heilbroner, Robert. *Visions of the Future: The Distant Past, Yesterday, Today, Tomorrow.* New York: New York Public Library/Oxford University Press, 1995.

Jennings, Humphrey. *Pandaemonium: The Coming of the Machine as Seen by Contemporary Observers,* 1660–1886 New York: Free Press, 1985.

Kuhn, Thomas S. *The Structure of Scientific Revolutions. International Encyclopedia of Unified Science,* 2.2., 2d ed., enl. Chicago: University of Chicago Press, 1970.

Lasch, Christopher. *The True and Only Heaven: Progress and Its Critics.* New York: Norton, 1991.

Nisbet, Robert. *History of the Idea of Progress.* New Brunswick, NJ: Transaction Publishers, 1993.

Paepke, C. Owen. *The Evolution of Progress; The End of Economic Growth and the Beginning of Human Transformation.* New York: Random House, 1993.

Schumaker, E. F. *Small Is Beautiful: Economics as if People Mattered.* New York: Harper & Row, 1973.

Shattuck, Roger. *Forbidden Knowledge: From Prometheus to Pornography.* New York: Harvest Books, 1997.

Shils, Edward. *Tradition.* Chicago: University of Chicago Press, 1981.

Solzhenitsyn, Alexander. "The Relentless Cult of Novelty and How It Wrecked the Century." *New York Times,* National Edition, February 7, 1993, 7.3.

Van Doren, Charles. *The Idea of Progress.* New York: Praeger, 1967.

NATURE AND HUMAN NATURE

Arnheim, Rudolf. *Art and Visual Perception.* Berkeley: University of California Press, 1969.

Blakemore, Colin, and Cooper, G. F. "Development of the Brain Depends on the Visual Environment." *Nature* 228 (1970): 477.

Boden, Margaret. *Artificial Intelligence and Natural Man,* 2d. ed. New York: Basic Books, 1987.

Brady, John. *Biological Clocks* London: Edward Arnold, 1979.

———. *Biological Timekeeping.* Cambridge, England: Cambridge University Press, 1982.

Bronowski, Jacob. *The Ascent of Man.* New York: Little, Brown, 1976.

Brown, Lester R., et al. *State of the World: A Worldwatch Institute Report on Progress toward a Sustainable Society.* New York: Norton, 1994.

Buber, Martin. *I and Thou.* New York: Scribner's, 1958.

Chase, Alston. *In a Dark Wood: The Fight over Forests and the Rising Tyranny of Ecology.* Boston: Houghton Mifflin, 1995.

Commoner, Barry. *The Closing Circle: Nature, Man and Technology.* New York: Knopf, 1971.

Csikszentmihalyi, Mihalyi, and Selega Isabella. *Optimal Experience: Psychological Studies of Flow in Consciousness.* New York: Cambridge University Press, 1988.

Dichter, Ernest. *The Strategy of Desire*. Garden City, NY: Doubleday, 1960.

Donaldson, Margaret. *Human Minds: An Exploration*. New York: Allen Lane/Viking Penguin, 1992.

Dubos, René. *Man Adapting*. New Haven, CT: Yale University Press, 1965.

———. *So Human an Animal*. New York: Scribner's, 1968.

Edelman, Gerald. *Bright Air, Brilliant Fire: On the Matter of the Mind*. New York: Basic Books, 1992.

Egan, Timothy. "Havens Besieged: Civilization Closes in on National Parks.," *Detroit Free Press*, May 30, 1991, 17A.

Eldredge, Niles. *Dominion*. New York: Holt, 1995.

———. *The Miner's Canary: Unravelling the Mysteries of Extinction*. New York: Prentice Hall, 1991.

Elgin, Duane. *Voluntary Simplicity: Toward a Way of Life That Is Outwardly Simple, Inwardly Rich*. New York: Morrow, 1981, 1993.

Epstein, Lewis Carroll. *Relativity Visualized*. San Francisco: Insight Press, 1991.

Franck, Frederick. *Zen of Seeing*. New York: Random House, 1973.

Gallagher, Winifred. *The Power of Place: How Our Surroundings Shape Our Thoughts, Emotions, and Actions*. New York: Poseidon, 1993.

Gazzaniga, Michael S. *Nature's Mind: The Biological Roots of Thinking, Emotions, Sexuality, Language, and Intelligence*. New York: Basic Books, 1993.

Gibson, James Jerome. *The Perception of the Visible World*. Westport, CT: Greenwood, 1950.

Gombrich, E. H. *Art and Illusion*. London: Phaidon, 1959.

Gore, Al. *Earth in the Balance*. Boston: Houghton Mifflin, 1992.

Gore, Rick. "The March toward Extinction." *National Geographic*. 175.6 (June 1989): 662–98.

Gregory, R. L. *Eye and Brain: The Psychology of Seeing*. New York: McGraw-Hill, 1973.

Grudin, Robert. *The Grace of Great Things: Creativity and Innovation*. New York: Ticknor & Fields, 1990.

Hall, Edward T. *The Dance of Life: The Other Dimension of Time*. New York: Doubleday, 1983.

Harrison, Robert Pogue. *Forests: The Shadow of Civilization*. Chicago: University of Chicago Press, 1992.

Heilbroner, Robert. *An Inquiry into the Human Prospect*. New York: Norton, 1974.

Jantsch, Eric. *The Self-Organizing Universe*. Oxford, England: Pergamon, 1980.

Johnson, Mark. *The Body in the Mind: The Bodily Basis of Meaning, Imagination, and Reason*. Chicago: University of Chicago Press, 1990.

Kaufman, Lloyd. *Sight and Mind: An Introduction to Visual Perception*. New York: Oxford University Press, 1974.

Kohaz, Erazim. *The Embers and the Stars: A Philosophical Inquiry into the Moral Sense of Nature*. Chicago: University of Chicago Press, 1984.

Kramer, Peter D. *Listening to Prozac: A Psychiatrist Explores Antidepressant Drugs and the Remaking of the Self*. New York: Viking, 1993.

Krutch, Joseph Wood. *Human Nature and the Human Condition*. New York: Random House, 1959.

Lawlor, Robert. *Voices of the First Day: Awakening in the Aboriginal Dreamtime*. Rochester, VT: Inner Traditions, 1991.

Leakey, Richard, and Lewin, Roger. *Origins Reconsidered: In Search of What Makes Us Human*. New York: Doubleday, 1992.

Lederman, Leon, with Teresi, Dick. *The God Particle: If the Universe Is the Answer, What Is the Question?* Boston: Houghton Mifflin, 1993.

Leonard, George. *The Silent Pulse*. New York: Viking Penguin, 1992.

Levy, Steven. *Artificial Life: The Quest for a New Creation*. New York: Pantheon, 1993.

Lewin, Roger. *Complexity: Life at the Edge of Chaos*. New York: Macmillan, 1993.

Lifton, Robert Jay. *The Protean Self: Human Resilience in an Age of Fragmentation*. New York: Basic Books, 1993.

Lovelock, James E. *The Ages of Gaia: A Biography of Our Living Earth*. New York: Norton, 1988.

_____. *Gaia: A New Look at Life on Earth*. New York: Norton, 1988.

_____. *Healing Gaia: A New Prescription for the Living Planet*. New York: Crown, 1991.

Maybury-Lewis, David. *Millennium: Tribal Wisdom and the Modern World*. New York: Viking, 1992.

McHarg, Ian. *Design with Nature*. Garden City, NY: Doubleday, 1969.

_____. *A Quest for Life*. New York: John Wiley, 1996.

McKibben, Bill. *The Age of Missing Information*. New York: Random House, 1992.

_____. *The End of Nature*. New York: Random House, 1989.

_____. *Hope, Human and Wild: True Stories of Living Lightly on the Earth*. Boston: Little, Brown, 1995.

_____. "Not So Fast." *New York Times Magazine*, July 23, 1995, 24f.

McNeill, Daniel, and Freiberger, Paul. *Fuzzy Logic*. New York: Simon & Schuster, 1993.

Millar, Susanna. *Understanding and Representing Space: Theory and Evidence from Blind Children*. New York: Oxford University Press, 1995.

Mitchell, John Hanson. *Living at the End of Time*. New York: Houghton Mifflin, 1990.

Mitchell, William J. *The Reconfigured Eye: Visual Truth in the Post-Photographic Era*. Cambridge, MA: MIT Press, 1992.

Nearing, Helen, and Nearing, Scott, *Living the Good Life; How to Live Sanely and Simply in a Troubled World*. New York: Schocken, 1982.

Nietzsche, Friedrich. *Beyond Good and Evil*. In *Basic Writings of Nietzsche*, ed. and trans. by Walter Kaufmann. New York: Random House, 1977.

Ong, Walter. *Interfaces of the Word: Studies in the Evolution of Consciousness and Culture*. Ithaca, NY: Cornell University Press, 1977.

Penrose, Roger. *Shadows of the Mind: A Search for the Missing Science of Consciousness*. New York: Oxford University Press, 1994.

Prigogine, Ilya. "Thermodynamics of Evolution." *Physics Today* 25 (November 1972):23–28; (December 1972): 38–44.

_____. "Unity of Physical Laws and Levels of Description." In *Interpretations of Life and Mind: Essays around the Problem of Reduction*, edited by Marjorie Grene, 1–13. New York: Humanities Press, 1971.

Rifkin, Jeremy, with Howard, Ted, *Entropy: A New World View*. New York: Viking, 1980.

Roszak, Theodore. *The Voice of the Earth*. New York: Summit/Simon & Schuster, 1992.

Russell, Peter. *The Global Brain: Speculations on the Evolutionary Leap to Planetary Consciousness*. Los Angeles: Jeremy P. Tarcher, 1983.

———. *The White Hole in Time: Our Future Evolution and the Meaning of Now*. San Francisco: Harper, 1992.

Sagan, Carl. *The Dragons of Eden: Speculations on the Evolution of Human Intelligence*. New York: Random House, 1977.

———. *Pale Blue Dot*. New York: Random House, 1994.

———, and Druyan, Ann. *Shadows of Forgotten Ancestors: A Search for Who We Are*. New York: Random House, 1992.

Saint-Exupéry, Antoine de. *The Wisdom of the Sands*. Translated by Stuart Gilbert. New York: Harcourt, 1950.

Sarno, Louis, *Songs from the Forest: My Life among the Ba-Benelle Pygmies*. Boston: Houghton Mifflin, 1993.

Satchell, Michael. "The Rape of the Oceans." *U.S. News & World Report*, June 22, 1992, 64–75.

Schama, Simon. *Landscape and Memory*. New York: Knopf, 1995.

Scheler, Max. *Man's Place in Nature*. New York: Farrar, Straus, & Giroux, 1961.

Schick, Kathy, and Toth, Nicholas. *Making Silent Stones Speak: Human Evolution and the Dawn of Technology*. New York: Simon & Schuster, 1993.

Shabecoff, Philip. *A Fierce Green Fire: The American Environmental Movement*. New York: Hill & Wang, 1993.

Thomas, Lewis. *The Fragile Species*. New York: Scribner's, 1992.

Thoreau, Henry David. *Walden*. New York: Random House, 1991.

Tiger, Lionel. *The Pursuit of Pleasure*. New York: Little, Brown, 1992.

Waldrop, M. Mitchell. *Complexity: The Emerging Science at the Edge of Order and Chaos*. New York: Simon & Schuster, 1993.

Weinberg, Steven. *Dreams of a Final Theory*. New York: Pantheon, 1993.

Weiner, Jonathan. *The Next Hundred Years: Shaping the Fate of Our Living Earth*. New York: Bantam, 1990.

Weizsacker, Carl Friedrich von. *The Unity of Nature* New York: Farrar, Straus, & Giroux, 1980.

White, Lynn, Jr. "The Historical Roots of Our Ecological Crisis." *Science* 155 (March 10, 1967): 1203–7.

Wilson, Edward O. *The Diversity of Life*. Cambridge, MA: Harvard University Press, 1992.

———. *On Human Nature*. Cambridge, MA: Harvard University Press, 1978.

———, and Holldobler, Bert. *The Ants*. Cambridge, MA: Harvard University Press, 1991.

Wilson, James Q. *The Moral Sense*. New York: Free Press, 1993.

Wolport, Lewis. *The Unnatural Nature of Science*. Cambridge, MA: Harvard University Press, 1993.

Worster, Donald. *The Wealth of Nature: Environmental History and the Ecological Imagination*. New York: Oxford University Press, 1993.

Wright, Robert. *The Moral Animal: The New Science of Evolutionary Psychology*. New York: Pantheon, 1994.

Yamashita, Hiroaki. *Ancient Grace: Inside the Cedar Sanctuary of Yakushima Island*. San Francisco: Cadence, 1992.

Young, Arthur M. *The Reflexive Universe: Evolution of Consciousness.* New York: Delacorte, 1976.

THE IMPACT OF TECHNOLOGY

Aronowitz, Stanley, and DiFazio, William. *The Jobless Future: Sci-Tech and the Dogma of Work.* Minneapolis, University of Minnesota Press, 1994.

Barrett, William. *The Illusion of Technique.* New York: Doubleday, 1979.

Berger, Kevin Todd. *Zen Driving.* New York: Ballantine, 1988.

Boorstin, Daniel J. "Tomorrow: The Republic of Technology." *Time* 109 (January 17, 1977): 36–38.

Burke, James. *Connections.* New York: Little, Brown, 1980.

Cowan, Ruth Schwartz. *More Work for Mother: The Ironies of Household Technology from the Open Hearth to the Microwave.* New York: Basic Books, 1983.

Eisenstein, Elizabeth. *The Printing Press as an Agent of Change.* New York: Cambridge University Press, 1979.

_____ . *The Printing Revolution in Early Modern Europe.* New York: Cambridge University Press, 1983.

Ellul, Jacques. *The Technological Society.* New York: Knopf, 1964.

Ferkiss, Victor. *The Future of Technological Civilization.* New York: Braziller, 1974.

Fischer, Claude S. *America Calling: A Social History of the Telephone to 1940.* Berkeley: University of California Press, 1992.

Florman, Samuel C. *Blaming Technology: The Irrational Search for Scapegoats.* New York: St. Martin's Press, 1981.

Giedion, Sigfried. *Mechanization Takes Command: A Contribution to an Anonymous History.* New York: Oxford University Press, 1948.

_____ . *Space, Time, and Architecture: The Growth of a New Tradition.* Cambridge, MA: Harvard University Press, 1962.

Giscard d'Estaing, Valérie-Anne, and Young, Mark, eds. *Inventions and Discoveries 1993: What's Happened? What's Coming? What's That?* New York: Facts on File, 1993.

Grossman, Lawrence K. *The Electronic Republic: Reshaping Democracy in the Information Age.* New York: Viking, 1995.

Hay, Edward J. *The Just-in-Time Breakthrough: Implementing the New Manufacturing Basics.* New York: John Wiley, 1988.

Huxley, Aldous. *Brave New World.* New York: Penguin, 1968 (1932).

_____ . *Brave New World Revisited.* New York: Harper, 1958.

Kelly, Kevin. *Out of Control: The Rise of Neo-Biological Civilization.* Reading, MA: Addison-Wesley, 1994.

Klapp, Orrin E. *Overload and Boredom: Essays on the Quality of Life in the Information Society.* Westport, CT: Greenwood, 1986.

Lanham, Richard A. *The Electronic Word: Democracy, Technology, and the Arts.* Chicago: University of Chicago Press, 1993.

Lubar, Stephen. *InfoCulture: The Smithsonian Book of Information Age Inventions.* Boston: Houghton Mifflin, 1993.

Lyon, David. *The Electronic Eye: The Rise of Surveillance Society.* Minneapolis: University of Minnesota Press, 1994.

Mander, Jerry. *In the Absence of the Sacred: The Failure of Technology and the Survival of the Indian Nations.* San Francisco: Sierra Club, 1991.

McLuhan, Marshall. *Gutenberg Galaxy: The Making of Typographic Man.* Toronto: University of Toronto Press, 1962.

———. *Understanding Media: The Extensions of Man.* New York: New American Library/Dutton, 1966.

Muller, Herbert J. *The Children of Frankenstein.* Bloomington, IN: Indiana University Press, 1970.

Mumford, Lewis. *The Myth of the Machine.* New York: Harcourt, Brace, & World, 1966.

———. *Technics and Civilization.* New York: Harcourt Brace, 1934.

Norman, Donald. *Turn Signals Are the Facial Expressions of Automobiles.* Reading, MA: Addison-Wesley, 1993.

Orwell, George. *1984.* New York: Penguin, 1964 (1949).

Peters, Tom, *Liberation Management: Necessary Disorganization for the Nanosecond Nineties.* New York: Knopf, 1992.

———. *Thriving on Chaos: Handbook for a Management Revolution.* New York: Harper & Row, 1987.

"Please Turn Off the Dog." *Time,* February 19, 1988, 70.

Postman, Neil. *Technopoly: The Surrender of Culture to Technology.* New York: Random House, 1992.

Rifkin, Jeremy. *Declaration of a Heretic.* Boston: Routledge & Kegan Paul, 1985.

———. *Time Wars: The Primary Conflict in Human History.* New York: Holt, 1987.

———, with Howard, Ted. *Entropy: A New World View.* New York: Viking, 1980.

Rothe, J. Peter. *Beyond Traffic Safety.* New Brunswick, NJ: Transaction Press, 1993.

Rothenberg, David. *Hand's End: Technology and the Limits of Nature.* Berkeley, CA: University of California Press, 1993.

Sale, Kirkpatrick. *Rebels against the Future: The Luddites and Their War on the Industrial Revolution, Lessons for the Computer Age.* Reading, MA: Addison-Wesley, 1995.

Schement, Jorge Reina, and Curtis, Terry. *Tendencies and Tensions of the Information Age: The Production and Distribution of Information in the United States.* New Brunswick, NJ: Transaction Publishers, 1994.

Schiller, Herbert I. *Culture Inc.: The Corporate Takeover of Public Expression.* New York: Oxford University Press, 1989.

———. *Information and the Crisis Economy.* Norwood, NJ: Ablex Publishing Corp., 1984.

———. *Mass Communication and American Empire.* Boston: Beacon Press, 1969.

———. *The Mind Managers.* Boston: Beacon Press, 1973.

Schumaker, E. F. *Small Is Beautiful: Economics As If People Mattered.* New York: Harper & Row, 1973.

Searle, John. *Minds, Brains, and Science.* Cambridge, MA: Harvard University Press, 1985.

Seiden, Martin H. *Access to the American Mind: The Damaging Impact of the New Mass Media.* New York: Schapolsky, 1990.

Spretnak, Charlene. *The Resurgence of the Real: Body, Nature, and Place in a Hypermodern World.* Reading, MA: Addison-Wesley, 1996.

Springer, Claudia. *Electronic Eros: Bodies and Desire in the Postindustrial Age.* Austin: University of Texas Press, 1996.

Stock, Gregory. *Metaman: The Merging of Humans and Machines into a Global Superorganism.* New York: Simon & Schuster, 1993.

Teich, Albert. *Technology and Man's Future.* New York: St. Martin's Press, 1972.

Tenner, Edward. *Why Things Bite Back: Technology and the Revenge of Unintended Consequences.* New York: Knopf, 1996.

Toffler, Alvin. *Future Shock.* New York: Bantam, 1970.

_____. *Powershift: Knowledge, Wealth, and Violence at the Edge of the 21st Century.* New York: Bantam, 1990.

_____. *The Third Wave.* New York: Morrow, 1980.

Wallis, Allan D. *Wheel Estate: The Rise and Decline of Mobile Homes.* New York: Oxford University Press, 1991.

Winner, Langton. *Autonomous Technology.* Cambridge, MA: MIT Press, 1977.

Wurman, Richard Saul. *Information Anxiety.* New York: Doubleday, 1989.

THE POWER OF TELEVISION

Abramson, Jeffrey B.; Arterton, F. Christopher; and Orren, Gary R. *The Electronic Commonwealth: The Impact of New Media Technologies on Democratic Politics.* New York: Basic Books, 1988.

Addato, Kiku. "Sound Bite Democracy: Network Evening News Presidential Campaign Coverage, 1968 and 1988." Research Paper R-2. Cambridge, MA: Joan Shorenstein Barone Center, Harvard University, 1990.

Barsamian, David. *Stenographers to Power: Media and Propaganda.* Monroe, ME: Common Courage Press, 1992.

Berger, Arthur Asa. *Television in Society.* New Brunswick, NJ: Transaction Publishers, 1986.

Burns, Eric. *Broadcast Blues: Dispatches from the Twenty Year War between a Television Reporter and His Medium.* New York: HarperCollins, 1993.

Davis, Douglas. *The Five Myths of Television Power: Or, Why the Medium Is Not the Message.* New York: Simon & Schuster, 1993.

Frankl, Razelle. *Televangelism: The Marketing of Popular Culture.* Carbondale, IL: Southern Illinois University Press, 1986.

Gilder, George. *Life After Television: The Coming Transformation of Media and American Life.* Knoxville, TN: Whittle Communications, 1990.

Haddon, Jeffrey K. and Shupe, Anson. *Televangelism: Power and Politics on God's Frontier.* New York: Henry Holt, 1988.

Hoggart, Richard. *The Uses of Illiteracy.* New Brunswick, NJ: Transaction Publishers, 1991.

Jacobs, Norman, ed. *Mass Media in Modern Society.* New Brunswick, NJ: Transaction Publishers, 1992.

Keen, Peter G. W. *Competing in Time: Using Telecommunications for Competitive Advantage.* New York: Harper & Row, 1988.

Kneal, Dennis. "Zapping of TV Ads Appears Pervasive." *Wall Street Journal,* April 25, 1988, 27.

Kubey, Robert William, and Csikszentmihalyi, Mihaly. *Television and the Quality of Life: How Viewing Shapes Everyday Experience.* Hillsdale, NJ: Lawrence Erlbaum Associates, 1990.

Mander, Jerry. *Four Arguments for the Elimination of Television.* New York: Morrow, 1978.

Marc, David. *Bonfire of the Humanities: Essays on Television, Subliteracy, and Long-Term Memory Loss.* Syracuse, NY: Syracuse University Press, 1995.

McIlwraith, Robert; Jacobvitz, Robin Smith; Kubey, Robert; and Alexander, Alison. "Television Addiction: Theories and Data behind the Ubiquitous Metaphor." *American Behavioral Scientist* 35.2 (November–December 1991): 104–21.

McKibben, Bill. *The Age of Missing Information.* New York: Random House, 1992.

Merelman, Richard. *Making Something of Ourselves: On Culture and Politics in the United States.* Berkeley: University of California Press, 1984.

Meyrowitz, Joshua. *No Sense of Place: The Impact of Electronic Media on Social Behavior.* New York: Oxford University Press, 1985.

Minow, Newton N., and LaMay, Craig A. *Abandoned in the Wasteland: Children, Television, and the First Amendment.* New York: Hill & Wang, 1995.

Mitroff, Ian I., and Bennis, Warren. *The Unreality Industry: The Deliberate Manufacturing of Falsehood and What It Is Doing to Our Lives.* New York: Oxford University Press, 1989.

Neuman, W. Russell. *The Future of the Mass Audience.* New York: Cambridge University Press, 1992.

O'Neill, Michael J. *The Roar of the Crowd: How Television and People Power Are Changing the World.* New York: Random House, 1993.

Perkinson, Henry. *Getting Better: Television and Moral Progress.* New Brunswick, NJ: Transaction Publishers, 1991.

Price, Monroe E. *Television, the Public Sphere, and National Identity,* New York: Oxford University Press, 1996.

Provenzo, Eugene F., Jr. *Video Kids: Making Sense of Nintendo.* Cambridge, MA: Harvard University Press, 1991.

Rushkoff, Douglas. *Media Virus! Hidden Agendas in Popular Culture.* New York: Ballantine Books, 1994.

Schultze, Quentin J. *Televangelism and American Culture: The Business of Popular Religion.* Grand Rapids, MI: Baker, 1991.

Spigel, Lynn. *Make Room for TV: Television and the Family Ideal in Postwar America.* Chicago: University of Chicago Press, 1992.

Turkle, Sherry. *Life on the Screen: Identity in the Age of the Internet.* New York: Simon & Schuster, 1995.

Whisnant, Luke. *Watching TV with the Red Chinese.* Chapel Hill, NC: Algonquin Books, 1992.

Winn, Marie. *The Plug-In Drug.* New York: Viking, 1985.

———. *Unplugging the Plug-in Drug.* New York: Viking, 1987.

THE ROLE OF THE COMPUTER

Beniger, J. R. *The Control Revolution: Technological and Economic Origins of the Information Society.* Cambridge, MA: Harvard University Press, 1986.

Birkerts, Sven. *The Gutenberg Elegies: The Fate of Reading in an Electronic Age*. Boston: Faber & Faber, 1994.

Bolter, J. David. *Turing's Man: Western Culture in the Computer Age*. Chapel Hill: University of North Carolina Press, 1984.

———. *Writing Space: The Computer, Hypertext and the History of Writing*. Hillsdale, NJ: Lawrence Erlbaum Associates, 1991.

Brod, Craig. *Technostress: The Human Cost of the Computer Revolution*. Reading, MA: Addison-Wesley, 1984.

Dery, Mark. *Escape Velocity: Cyberculture at the End of the Century*. New York: Grove, 1996.

Dreyfus, Hubert. *What Computers Can't Do*. New York: Harper & Row, 1973.

Friedhoff, Richard Mark, and Benzon, William. *Visualization: The Second Computer Revolution*. New York: Abrams, 1989.

Gates, Bill. *The Road Ahead*. New York: Viking/Penguin, 1995.

Halacy, D. S. *Cyborg: Evolution of the Superman*. New York: Harper & Row, 1965.

Heim, Michael. *The Metaphysics of Virtual Reality*. New York: Oxford University Press, 1993.

Jacobs, A. J., *America Off-Line: The Complete Outernet Starter Kit*. Kansas City, MO: Andrews & McMeel, 1996.

Larson, Erik. *The Naked Consumer: How Our Private Lives Become Public Commodities*. New York: Henry Holt, 1992.

Negroponte, Nicholas. *Being Digital*. New York: Knopf, 1995.

Pimentel, Ken, and Teixeira, Kevin. *Virtual Reality: Through the New Looking Glass*. Blue Ridge Summit, PA: TAB Books/McGraw-Hill, 1992.

Rheingold, Howard. *The Virtual Community: Homesteading on the Electronic Frontier*. Reading, MA: Addison-Wesley, 1993.

———. *Virtual Reality: The Revolutionary Technology of Computer-Generated Artificial Worlds and How It Promises to Transform Society*. New York: Simon & Schuster, 1992.

Robinson, Phillip, and Tamosaitis, Nancy. *The Joy of Cybersex: An Underground Guide to Electronic Erotica*. New York: Brady Computer Books, 1993.

Rosenberg, Richard S. *The Social Impact of Computers*. Boston: Harcourt Brace Jovanovich, 1992.

Roszak, Theodore. *The Cult of Information: The Folklore of Computers and the True Art of Thinking*. New York: Pantheon, 1986, 1994.

Rothe, J. Peter. *Beyond Traffic Safety*. New Brunswick, NJ: Transaction Press, 1993.

Rothenberg, David. *Hand's End: Technology and the Limits of Nature*. Berkeley, CA: University of California Press, 1993.

Rothfeder, Jeffrey. *Privacy for Sale: How Computerization Has Made Everyone's Life an Open Secret*. New York: Simon & Schuster, 1992.

Seabrook, John. *Deeper: My Two-Year Odyssey in Cyberspace*. New York: Simon & Schuster, 1997.

Shenk, David. *Data Smog: Surviving the Information Glut*. New York: HarperCollins, 1997.

Simons, Geoff. *Silicon Shock: The Menace of the Computer Invasion*. New York: Blackwell, 1985.

Slouka, Mark. *War of the Worlds: Cyberspace and the High-Tech Assault on Reality*. New York: Basic Books, 1995.

Snider, James H., and Ziporyn, Terra. *Future Shop: How Future Technologies Will Change the Way We Shop and What We Buy*. New York: St. Martin's Press, 1992.

Staples, Brent. "Life in the Information Age: When Burma Shave Meets Cyberspace." *New York Times*, "Editorial Notebook," July 7, 1994, D18.

Stoll, Clifford, *Silicon Snake Oil: Second Thoughts on the Information Highway*. New York: Doubleday, 1995.

Turkle, Sherry, *The Second Self: Computers and the Human Spirit*. New York: Simon & Schuster, 1984.

Weizenbaum, Joseph. *Computer Power and Human Reason: From Judgment to Calculation*. New York: Penguin, 1984.

Wiener, Norbert. *The Human Use of Human Beings: Cybernetics and Society*. Boston: Houghton Mifflin, 1954.

———. "Some Moral and Technical Consequences of Automation." *Science* 131 (May 6, 1960): 1355–8.

AMERICA AND ITS VALUES

Albert, Susan. *Work of Her Own*. New York: Viking, 1987.

Alderman, Ellen, and Kennedy, Caroline. *The Right to Privacy*. New York: Knopf, 1996.

Assael, Henry. *Consumer Behavior and Marketing Action*. 4th ed. Belmont, CA: Wadsworth, 1992.

Bagdikian, Ben H. *The Media Monopoly*. 4th ed. Boston: Beacon Press, 1992.

Baker, Nancy C. *The Beauty Trap: Exploring Woman's Greatest Obsession*. New York: Franklin Watts, 1984.

Barlett, Donald L., and Steele, James B. *America: What Went Wrong*. Kansas City, MO: Andrews & McMeel, 1992.

Bellah, Robert N.; Madsen, Richard; Sullivan, William M.; Swidler, Ann; and Tipton, Steven M., *The Good Society*. New York: Knopf, 1991.

———. *Habits of the Heart: Individualism and Commitment in American Life*, Berkeley: University of California Press, 1985.

Bennett, William J. *The De-Valuing of America: The Fight for Our Culture and Our Children*. New York: Summit, 1992.

———. *The Index of Leading Cultural Indicators: Facts and Figures on the State of American Society*. New York: Simon & Schuster, 1994.

Berlowitz, Leslie; Donoghue, Dennis; and Menand, Louis. *America in Theory*. New York: Oxford University Press, 1989.

Bernstein, Richard. *Dictatorship of Virtue: Multiculturalism and the Battle for America's Future*. New York: Knopf, 1995.

Blankenhorn, David. *Fatherless America: Confronting Our Most Urgent Social Problem*. New York: Basic Books, 1995.

Block, Alan A. *Space, Time and Organized Crime*. 2d ed. New Brunswick, NJ: Transaction Press, 1993.

Bloom, Allan. *The Closing of the American Mind*. New York: Simon & Schuster, 1988.

Bok, Derek. *The Cost of Talent: How Executives and Professionals Are Paid and How It Affects America*. New York: Free Press, 1993.

Bok, Sissela. *Lying: Moral Choice in Public and Private Life.* New York: Random House, 1979.

Boorstin, Daniel J. *The Image: Or What Happened to the American Dream.* New York: Atheneum, 1962.

Bordo, Susan. *Unbearable Weight: Feminism, Western Culture, and the Body.* Berkeley: University of California Press, 1993.

Borgman, Albert. *Crossing the Postmodern Divide.* Chicago: University of Chicago Press, 1992.

Branscombe, Anne Wells. *Who Owns Information? From Privacy to Public Access.* New York: Basic Books, 1994.

Bronfenbrenner, Urie; McClelland, Peter; Wethington, Elain; Moen, Phyllis; and Ceci, Stephen J. *The State of Americans: This Generation and the Next.* New York: Free Press, 1996.

Campbell, Colin. *The Romantic Ethic and the Spirit of Modern Consumerism.* New York: Blackwell, 1989.

Captive Kids: A Report on Commercial Pressures on Kids at School. Yonkers, NY: Consumers Union Education Services, 1995.

Carter, Stephen L. *The Culture of Disbelief: How American Law and Politics Are Trivializing Religious Devotion.* New York: Basic Books, 1993.

Cheskin, Louis. *Color for Profit.* New York: Liveright, 1950.

_____. *How to Predict What People Will Buy.* New York: Liveright, 1957.

Clark, Eric. *The Want Makers: Inside the World of Advertising.* New York: Viking Penguin, 1990.

Cobb, Nathan. "The End of Privacy." *The Detroit Free Press Magazine,* August 23, 1992, 6–12.

Collier, James Lincoln. *The Rise of Selfishness in America.* New York: Oxford University Press, 1991.

Coontz, Stephanie. *The Way We Never Were: American Families and the Nostalgia Trap.* New York: Basic Books, 1992.

Critchfield, Richard. *Those Days: An American Album.* Garden City, NY: Doubleday, 1986.

_____. *Trees, Why Do You Wait?: America's Changing Rural Culture.* Washington, DC: Island Press, 1991.

_____. *Villages.* New York: Doubleday, 1981.

Cross, Gary. *Time and Money: The Making of Consumerist Modernity.* New York: Routledge, 1993.

Cushman, Philip. *Constructing the Self, Constructing America: A Cultural History of Psychotherapy.* Reading, MA: Addison-Wesley, 1995.

Daria, Irene. *The Fashion Cycle: A Behind-the-Scenes Look at a Year with Bill Blass, Liz Claiborne, Donna Karan, Arnold Scaasi, and Adrienne Vittadini.* New York: Simon & Schuster, 1990.

Dominguez, Joe, and Robin, Vicki. *Your Money or Your Life: Transforming Your Relationship with Money and Achieving Financial Independence.* New York: Viking Penguin, 1992.

Debord, Guy. *Society of the Spectacle.* Detroit: Black & Red, 1973.

Drucker, Peter F. *Post-Capitalist Society.* New York: Harper Business, 1993.

Dubin, Max. *Futurehype: The Tyranny of Prophecy.* New York: Penguin, 1991.

During, Alan. *How Much is Enough?: The Consumer Society and the Future of the Earth.* New York: Norton, 1992.

Ehrenhalt, Alan. *The Lost City: Discovering the Forgotten Virtues of Community in the Chicago of the 1950s.* New York: Basic Books, 1995.

Elgin, Duane. *Voluntary Simplicity: Toward a Way of Life That Is Outwardly Simple, Inwardly Rich.* New York: Morrow, 1982.

Ellul, Jacques. *Propaganda: The Formation of Men's Attitudes.* New York: Knopf, 1965.

Etzioni, Amitai. *The Spirit of Community: Rights, Responsibilities, and the Communitarian Agenda.* New York: Crown, 1993.

Ewen, Stuart. *All Consuming Images: The Politics of Style in Contemporary Culture.* New York: Basic Books, 1988.

———. *Captains of Consciousness: Advertising and the Social Roots of Consumer Culture,* New York: McGraw-Hill, 1976.

Fallows, James. *Breaking the News: How the Media Undermine American Democracy.* New York: Pantheon, 1997.

Frank, Robert H., and Cook, Philip J. *The Winner-Take-All Society: How More and More Americans Compete for Ever Fewer and Bigger Prizes, Encouraging Economic Waste, Income Inequality, and an Impoverished Cultural Life.* New York: Free Press, 1995.

Galbraith, John Kenneth. *The Affluent Society.* Boston: Houghton Mifflin, 1976.

Garment, Suzanne. *Scandal: The Crisis of Mistrust in American Politics.* New York: Times Books, 1991.

Gergen, Kenneth J. *The Saturated Self: Dilemmas of Identity in Contemporary Life.* New York: Basic Books, 1992.

Glassner, Barry. *Bodies: Why We Look the Way We Do (and How We Feel about It).* New York: Putnam, 1988.

Gleick, James. "Dead as a Dollar." *New York Times Magazine,* June 16, 1996, 26ff.

Grant, Anne, and Burrell, Web. *The Patriotic Consumer: How to Buy American.* Kansas City, KS: Andrews & McMeel, 1992.

Grant, James. *Money of the Mind: Borrowing and Lending in America from the Civil War to Michael Milken.* New York: Farrar, Straus, Giroux, 1992.

Greider, William, *Who Will Tell the People?* New York: Simon & Schuster, 1992.

Grinspoon, Lester, and Hedblom, Peter. *The Speed Culture: Amphetamine Use and Abuse in America.* Cambridge, MA: Harvard University Press, 1975.

Gross, Michael. "Fashion's Fickle Seasons." *New York,* August 21, 1989, 30–32.

Gusewelle, C.W. *Far from Any Coast: Pieces of America's Heartland.* Columbia, MO: University of Missouri Press, 1989.

———. *Quick as Shadows Passing.* Jefferson City, MO: Westphalia Press, 1988.

Hanson, F. Allan. *Testing: Social Consequences of the Examined Life.* Berkeley: University of California Press, 1993.

Harrell, Gilbert D. *Consumer Behavior.* New York: Harcourt Brace, 1986.

Harris, Louis. *Inside America.* New York: Random House, 1987.

Harrison, Lawrence E. *Who Prospers? Economic and Political Success.* New York: Basic Books, 1992.

Hawkins, Del I.; Best, Roger J.; and Kopey, Kenneth A. *Consumer Behavior: Implications for Marketing Strategy.* 3d ed. Plano, TX: Business Publications, 1986.

Hayden, Dolores. *The Power of Place: Urban Landscapes as Public History.* Cambridge, MA: MIT Press, 1995.

Himmelfarb, Gertrude. *The De-Moralization of Society*. New York: Knopf, 1995.

_____. *On Looking into the Abyss: Untimely Thoughts on Culture and Society*. New York: Knopf, 1994.

Hirsch, E. D., Jr. *Cultural Literacy: What Every American Needs to Know*. Boston: Houghton Mifflin, 1987.

Hochschild, Arlie Russell. *The Time Bind: When Work Becomes Home and Home Becomes Work*. New York: Henry Holt, 1997.

Hochswender, Woody. "How Fashion Spreads around the World at the Speed of Light." *New York Times*, National Edition, May 13, 1990, E5.

Hostetler, John A., *Amish Roots: A Treasury of History, Wisdom, and Lore*. Baltimore: Johns Hopkins University Press, 1989.

_____. *Amish Society*. 3d ed. Baltimore: Johns Hopkins University Press, 1980.

Howard, John A. "Ennobling Obligations: You Make a Life by What You Give." *Vital Speeches of the Day*, March 1, 1988, 314–17.

_____. "Lifting Education's Iron Curtain: To Rebuild the Civic and Moral Capital." *Vital Speeches of the Day*, October 1, 1991, 756–61.

Hughes, Robert. *Culture of Complaint: The Fraying of America*. New York: Oxford University Press, 1993.

Hunnicut, Benjamin K. *Work without End: Abandoning Shorter Hours for the Right to Work*. Philadelphia: Temple University Press, 1990.

Huxtable, Ada Louise. *The Unreal America: Architecture and Illusion*. New York: New Press, 1997.

Jacobs, Jane. *The Death and Life of Great American Cities*. New York: Random House, 1961.

_____. *Systems of Survival: A Dialogue on the Moral Foundations of Commerce and Politics*. New York: Random House, 1992.

Jacobs, Michael. *Short-Term America: The Causes and Cures of Our Business Myopia*. Boston: Harvard Business School Press, 1991.

Jamieson, Kathleen Hall. *Dirty Politics: Deception, Distraction, and Democracy*. New York: Oxford University Press, 1992.

_____. *Eloquence in an Electronic Age: The Transformation of Political Speechmaking*. New York: Oxford University Press, 1988.

Johnson, Warren. *The Future Is Not What It Used to Be: Returning to Traditional Values in an Age of Scarcity*. New York: Dodd, Mead, 1985.

Katz, Jack. *The Seductions of Crime*. New York: Basic Books, 1990.

Kennedy, Paul. *Preparing for the Twenty-First Century*. New York: Random House, 1993.

Kerr, Walter. *The Decline of Pleasure*. New York: Simon & Schuster, 1962.

Kerschner, Frederick, Jr., ed. *Tocqueville's America: The Great Quotations*. Athens, OH: Ohio University Press, 1983.

Keyes, Ralph. *We the Lonely People: Searching for Community*. New York: Harper & Row, 1973.

Kilpatrick, William. *Why Johnny Can't Tell Right from Wrong*. New York: Times Books, 1993.

Kirk, Russell *Enemies of the Permanent Things: Observations of Abnormality in Literature and Politics*. 3d ed. Peru, IL: Sherwood Sugden, 1988.

_____. *The Roots of American Order*. 3d ed. Washington, DC: Regnery Gateway, 1992.

Kraybill, Donald B. *The Riddle of Amish Culture*. Baltimore: Johns Hopkins University Press, 1989.

Kugelmann, Robert. *Stress: The Nature and History of Engineered Grief*. New York: Praeger, 1992.

Kurtz, Howard. *Media Circus: The Trouble with America's Newspapers*. New York: Times Books, 1993.

Lamm, Richard D. *American in Decline?* Denver: The Center for Public Policy and Contemporary Issues, University of Denver, 1990.

Lapham, Lewis W. *Money and Class in America: Notes and Observations on Our Civil Religion*. New York: Weidenfeld & Nicolson, 1988.

———. *The Wish for Kings: Democracy at Bay*. New York: Grove Press, 1993.

Larkin, Jack. *The Reshaping of Everyday Life, 1790–1840*. New York: HarperCollins, 1989.

Lasch, Christopher. *The Culture of Narcissism: American Life in an Age of Diminishing Expectations*. New York: Norton, 1979.

———. *The Minimal Self: Psychic Survival in Troubled Times*. New York: Norton, 1984.

Leach, William. *Land of Desire: Merchants, Power, and the Rise of a New American Culture*. New York: Pantheon, 1993.

Lebergott, Stanley. *Pursuing Happiness: American Consumers in the Twentieth Century*. Princeton, NJ: Princeton University Press, 1993.

Leonard, George. *Mastery: The Keys to Success and Long-Term Fulfillment*. New York: Penguin, 1991.

Linder, Staffan B. *The Harried Leisure Class*. New York: Columbia University Press, 1971.

Lutz, Tom. *American Nervousness, 1903: An Anecdotal History*. Ithaca, NY: Cornell University Press, 1991.

Mann, Charles C., and Plummer, Mark L. *Aspirin Wars: Money, Medicine, and 100 Years of Rampant Competition*. New York: Knopf, 1991.

Marc, David. *Bonfire of the Humanities: Essays on Television, Subliteracy, and Long-Term Memory Loss*. Syracuse, NY: Syracuse University Press, 1995.

Marchand, Roland. *Advertising the American Dream: Making Way for Modernity, 1920–1940*. Berkeley: University of California Press, 1985.

McCracken, Grant. *Culture and Consumption*. Bloomington, IN: Indiana University Press, 1988.

McNeal, James. *Kids as Customers: A Handbook of Marketing to Children*. Ithaca, NY: American Demographics, 1992.

Mitchell, Susan. *The Official Guide to American Attitudes*. Ithaca, NY: New Strategist, 1996.

Monninger, Joseph. "Fast Food." *American Heritage*, April 1988, 68–75.

Moon, William Least Heat. *Blue Highways: A Journey into America*. New York: Ballantine, 1982.

Moore, David W. *The Superpolluters: How They Measure and Manipulate Public Opinion in America*. New York: Four Walls, Eight Windows, 1992.

Moore, R. Laurence. *Selling God: American Religion in the Marketplace of Culture*. New York: Oxford University Press, 1994.

Moyers, Bill. *A World of Ideas: Conversations with Thoughtful Men and Women about American Life Today and the Ideas Shaping Our Future*. Edited by Betty Sue Flowers. New York: Doubleday, 1989.

Naisbitt, John. *Megatrends: Ten New Directions Transforming Our Lives*. New York: Warner, 1982.

_____ , and Aburdene, Patricia, *Megatrends 2000: Ten New Directions for the 1990's* New York: Morrow, 1990.

_____ . *Megatrends for Women: From Liberation to Leadership*. New York: Villard, 1993.

Neuhaus, Richard. *The Naked Public Square: Religion and Democracy in America*. Grand Rapids, MI: Eerdmans, 1984.

Newman, Katherine S. *Declining Fortunes: The Withering of the American Dream*. New York: Basic Books, 1993.

Nisbet, Robert. *The Present Age: Progress and Anarchy in Modern America*. New York: HarperCollins, 1989.

Osborne, David, and Gaebler, Ted. *Reinventing Government: How the Entrepreneurial Spirit Is Transforming the Private Sector*. Reading, MA: Addison-Wesley, 1992.

Packard, Vance. *The Hidden Persuaders*. New York: McKay, 1957.

_____ . *The Ultra Rich: How Much Is Too Much?* Boston: Little, Brown, 1989.

Postman, Neil. *Amusing Ourselves to Death: Public Discourse in the Age of Show Business*. New York: Viking Penguin, 1985.

Research Alert. *Future Vision: The 189 Most Important Trends of the 1990s*. Naperville, IL: Sourcebooks Trade, 1991.

Riesman, David. *The Lonely Crowd*. New Haven, CT: Yale University Press, 1961.

Roberts, Sam. *Who We Are: A Portrait of America Based on the Latest U.S. Census*. New York: Random House, 1993.

Roche, George. *The Legacy of Freedom*. New Rochelle, NY: Arlington House, 1969.

Samuelson, Robert J. *The Good Life and Its Discontents: The American Dream in the Age of Entitlement, 1945–1995*. New York: Times Books, 1995.

Schiller, Herbert I. *Culture Inc.: The Corporate Takeover of Public Expression*. New York: Oxford University Press, 1989.

Schlesinger Arthur M., Jr. *The Disuniting of America: Reflections on a Multicultural Society*. Knoxville, TN: Whittle Direct Books, 1991.

Schmookler, Andrew Bard. *Fool's Gold: The Fate of Values in a World of Goods*. San Francisco: Harper, 1993.

_____ . *The Illusion of Choice: How the Market Economy Shapes Our Destiny*. Albany: State University of New York Press, 1993.

_____ . "The Insatiable Society: Materialistic Values and Human Needs." *The Futurist*, July-August 1991, 17–19.

Schor, Juliet B. *The Overworked American: The Unexpected Decline of Leisure*. New York: Basic Books, 1991.

Sclove, Richard E. *Democracy and Technology*. New York: Guilford, 1996.

Sheehy, Gail. *Character: America's Search for Leadership*. New York: Morrow, 1988.

Shi, David, *In Search of the Simple Life: American Voices Past and Present*. Layton, UT: Gibbs Smith, 1986.

_____ . *The Simple Life: Plain Living and High Thinking in American Culture*. New York: Oxford University Press, 1986.

Shorris, Earl, *A Nation of Salesmen: The Tyranny of the Market and the Subversion of Culture*. New York: Norton, 1994.

Slater, Philip. *The Pursuit of Loneliness*. Boston: Beacon. 1976.

Straus, William, and Howe, Neil. *Generations: The History of America's Future, 1584–2069*. New York: Morrow, 1991.

Sykes, Charles J. *A Nation of Victims: The Decay of the American Character*. New York: St. Martin's Press, 1992.

———. *ProfScam: Professors and the Demise of Higher Education*. New York: St. Martin's Press, 1988.

Tarkington, Booth. *The Magnificent Ambersons*. Bloomington, IN: Indiana University Press, 1989.

Taylor, Charles. *The Malaise of Modernity*. Cambridge, MA: Harvard University Press, 1992.

———. *Source of the Self: The Making of the Modern Identity*. Cambridge, MA: Harvard University Press, 1992.

Testa, Randy-Michael. *After the Fire: The Destruction of the Lancaster County Amish*. Hanover, NH: University Press of New England, 1992.

Theobald, Robert. *Turning the Century: Personal and Organizational Strategies for Your Changed World*. Indianapolis, IN: Knowledge Systems, 1992.

Thomas, Andrew Peyton. *Crime and the Sacking of America: The Roots of Chaos*. McLean, VA: Brassey's, 1995.

Tocqueville, Alexis de. *Democracy in America*. translated by Henry Reeve, revised by Francis Bowen; edited by Phillips Bradley. 2 vols. New York: Knopf, 1948 (1835–1840).

Toffler, Alvin, and Toffler, Heidi. *Creating a New Civilization: The Politics of the Third Wave*. Foreword by Newt Gingrich. Atlanta: Turner Publishing, 1995.

Tolchin, Martin, and Tolchin, Susan. *Selling Our Security: The Erosion of America's Assets*. New York: Knopf, 1993.

Vidal, Gore. *United States: Essays, 1952–1992*. New York: Random House, 1993.

Wachtel, Paul L. *The Poverty of Affluence: A Psychological Portrait of the American Way of Life*. Philadelphia: New Society, 1989.

Withnow, Richard. *Poor Richard's Principle: Recovering the American Dream through the Moral Dimension of Work, Business, and Money*. Princeton, NJ: Princeton University Press, 1996.

Wolf, Naomi. *The Beauty Myth: How Images of Beauty Are Used against Women*. New York: Morrow, 1991.

LIVING, GROWING UP, AND DYING IN AMERICA

Arons, Stephen. *Compelling Belief: The Culture of American Schooling*. New York: McGraw-Hill, 1983.

Barnett, Rosalind C., and Rivers, Caryl. *She Works/He Works: How Two-Income Families are Happier, Healthier, and Better Off*. San Francisco: Harper, 1996.

Becker, Ernest. *The Denial of Death*. New York: The Free Press/Macmillan, 1973.

Becker, Gary. *The Economic Approach to Human Behavior: A Treatise on the Family*. Chicago: University of Chicago Press, 1978; enl. ed., Cambridge, MA: Harvard University Press, 1981.

Berger, Arthur A., et al., eds. *Perspectives on Death and Dying: Cross-Cultural and Multidisciplinary Views*. Philadelphia: Charles, 1989.

Bertman, Sandra. *Facing Death: Images, Insights, and Interventions*. New York: Hemisphere, 1991.

Callahan, Daniel, *Setting Limits: The Aging Society and the Goals of Medicine*. New York: Simon & Schuster, 1987.

_____ . *The Tyranny of Survival, and Other Pathologies of Civilized Life*. Lanham, MD: University Press of America, 1985.

Carper, Jean. *Stop Aging Now: The Ultimate Plan for Staying Young and Reversing the Aging Process*. New York: HarperCollins, 1995.

Carrick, Paul. *Medical Ethics in Antiquity: Philosophical Perspectives on Abortion and Euthanasia*. Norwell, MA: Kluwer Academic Publishers, 1985.

Cassel, John. "The Contribution of the Social Environment to Host Resistance." *American Journal of Epidemiology* 104.2 (1976): 107–23.

Chopra, Deepak. *Ageless Body, Timeless Mind*. New York: Harmony Books, 1993.

Ciardi, John. *I Marry You*. New Brunswick, NJ: Rutgers University Press, 1958.

Conner, Karen A. *Aging America: Issues Facing an Aging Society*. Englewood Cliffs, NJ: Prentice Hall, 1991.

Coontz, Stephanie. *The Way We Really Are: Coming to Terms with America's Changing Families*. New York: Basic Books, 1997.

_____ . *The Way We Were: Families and the Nostalgia Trap*. New York: Basic Books, 1992.

Dizard, Jan E., and Gaddin, Howard. *The Minimal Family*. Amherst, MA: University of Massachusetts Press, 1990.

Edelman, Marian Wright. *Families in Peril: An Agenda for Social Change*. Cambridge, MA: Harvard University Press, 1987.

_____ . *The Measure of Our Success: A Letter to My Children and Yours*. Boston: Beacon Press, 1992.

Elkind, David. *All Grown Up and No Place to Go: Teenagers in Crisis*. Reading, MA: Addison-Wesley, 1984.

_____ . *The Hurried Child: Growing Up Too Fast Too Soon*. Reading, MA: Addison-Wesley, 1981.

_____ . *Miseducation: Preschoolers at Risk*. New York: Knopf, 1987.

_____ . *Ties That Stress: The New Family Imbalance*, Cambridge, MA: Harvard University Press, 1994.

Epstein, Fred J., and Shimberg, Elaine Fantle. *Gifts of Time*. New York: Morrow, 1993.

Friedan, Betty. *The Fountain of Age*. New York: Simon & Schuster, 1994.

Fromm, Erich, *The Art of Loving*. New York: Harper & Row, 1956.

Greenfield, Lauren. *Fast Forward: Growing Up in the Shadow of Hollywood*. New York: Knopf/Melcher Media, 1997.

Grimes, Ronald L. *Marrying and Burying: Rites of Passage in a Man's Life*. Boulder, CO: Westview Press, 1995.

Hochschild, Arlie, with Machung, Anne. *The Second Shift: Working Parents and the Revolution at Home*. New York: Viking, 1989.

Hymowitz, Carol. "For Many Kids, Playtime Isn't Free Time." *Wall Street Journal*, September 20, 1988, 39.

Imber-Black, Evan, and Roberts, Janine. *Rituals for Our Times: Celebrating, Healing, and Changing Our Lives and Relationships*. New York: HarperCollins, 1992.

Kaminer, Wendy. *I'm Dysfunctional, You're Dysfunctional: The Recovery Movement and Other Self-Help Fashions*, Reading, MA: Addison-Wesley, 1992.

Kilpatrick, William. *Why Johnny Can't Tell Right from Wrong: Overcoming Moral Illiteracy*. New York: Simon & Schuster, 1992.

Lasch, Christopher. *Haven in a Heartless World: The Family Besieged*. New York: Basic Books, 1977.

Lickona, Thomas. *Educating for Character: How Our Schools Can Teach Respect and Responsibility*. New York: Bantam, 1991.

Longman, Phillip. *Born to Pay: The New Politics of Aging in America*. Boston: Houghton Mifflin, 1987.

Low, Richard. *Childhood's Future: Listening to the American Family: New Hope for the Next Generation*. Boston: Houghton Mifflin, 1990.

O'Neill, Nena, O'Neill, George, *Open Marriage: A New Life Style for Couples*. New York: Avon, 1973.

Oppenheimer, Todd. "The Computer Delusion." *Atlantic Monthly*, July 1997, 45–62.

Packard, Vance. *Our Endangered Children: Growing Up in a Changing World*. Boston: Little, Brown, 1983.

Pearsall, Paul. *The Ten Laws of Lasting Love*. New York: Simon & Schuster, 1993.

Pifer, Alan, and Bronte, Lydia, eds. *Our Aging Society: Paradox and Promise*. New York: Norton, 1986.

Postman, Neil. *Conscientious Objections: Stirring Up Trouble about Language, Technology, and Education*. New York: Knopf, 1988.

———. *The Disappearance of Childhood*. New York: Delacorte Press, 1982.

Rogers, Fred. *You Are Special*. New York: Viking Penguin, 1994.

Rosenberg, Charles E. *The Care of Strangers: The Rise of America's Hospital System*. New York: Basic Books, 1987.

Scarf, Maggie. *Intimate Worlds: Life inside the Family*. New York: Random House, 1995.

Selye, Hans. *The Stress of Life*. New York: McGraw-Hill, 1956.

———. *Stress without Distress*. New York: Lippincott, 1974.

Shapiro, Laura. "The Myth of Quality Time." *Newsweek*, May 12, 1997, 12ff.

Stacey, Judith. *Brave New Families: Stories of Domestic Upheaval in Late Twentieth Century America*. New York: Basic Books, 1993.

———. *In the Name of the Family: Rethinking Family Values in the Postmodern Age*. Boston: Beacon Press, 1996.

Whitehead, Barbara Dafoe, *The Divorce Culture: How Divorce Became an Entitlement and How It Is Blighting the Lives of Our Children*. New York: Knopf, 1997.

Witkin-Lanoil, Georgia. *The Female Stress Syndrome: How to Recognize It and Live with It*. New York: Newmarket Press, 1984.

NATIONALISM AND GLOBALISM

Anderson, Walter Truett. *Reality Isn't What It Used to Be: Theatrical Politics, Ready-to-Wear Religion, Global Myths, Primitive Chic, and Other Wonders of the Postmodern World*. New York: Harper & Row, 1990.

Ardrey, Robert *The Territorial Imperative*. New York: Atheneum, 1966.

Ash, Timothy Garton. "The Third Superpower." *World Press Review*, March 1990, 72.

Aslund, Anders. *How Russia Became a Market Economy*. Washington, DC: The Brookings Institution, 1995.

Barber, Benjamin R. *Jihad vs. McWorld: How the Planet Is Both Falling Apart and Coming Together*. Times Books/Random House, 1995.

Barnet, Richard J., and Cavanagh, John. *Global Dreams: Imperial Corporations and the New World Order*. New York: Simon & Schuster, 1994.

Center for Investigative Reporting and Bill Moyers. *Global Dumping Ground: The International Traffic in Hazardous Waste*. Cabin John, MD: Seven Locks Press, 1990.

Enzensberger, Hans Magnus. *Civil Wars: From L.A. to Bosnia*. New York: New Press, 1994.

Greenfield, Liah, *Nationalism: Five Roads to Modernity*, Cambridge, MA: Harvard University Press, 1992.

Greider, William. *One World, Ready or Not: The Manic Logic of Global Capitalism*. New York: Simon & Schuster, 1996.

Guéhenno, Jean-Marie. *The End of the Nation-State*. Minneapolis: University of Minnesota Press, 1995.

Hobsbawn, Eric. *The Age of Extremes: A History of the World, 1914–1991*. New York: Pantheon, 1995.

Kagan, Donald. *On the Origins of War and the Preservation of Peace*. New York: Doubleday, 1995.

Kaplan, Robert D. *The Ends of the Earth: A Journey at the Dawn of the 21st Century*. New York: Random House, 1996.

Kennedy, Paul. *Preparing for the Twenty-First Century*. New York: Random House, 1993.

Kohn, Hans. *The Idea of Nationalism: A Study in Its Origins and Background*. New York: Collier/Macmillan, 1944.

Kurtzman, Joel. *The Death of Money: How the Electronic Economy Has Destabilized the World's Markets and Created Financial Chaos*. New York: Simon & Schuster, 1993.

McLuhan, Marshall, and Powers, Bruce R. *The Global Village: Transformations in World Life and Media in the 21st Century*. New York: Oxford University Press, 1989.

Moynahan, Daniel Patrick. *Pandaemonium: Ethnicity in International Relations*. New York: Oxford University Press, 1993.

Nisbet, Robert. *The Twilight of Authority*. New York: Oxford University Press, 1975.

Orwell, George. *1984*. San Diego, CA: Harcourt Brace Jovanovich, 1977 (1949).

Pfaff, William. *The Wrath of Nations: Civilization and the Furies of Nationalism*. New York: Simon & Schuster, 1993.

Reich, Robert B. *The Work of Nations: Preparing Ourselves for 21st Century Capitalism*. New York: Knopf, 1991.

Rifkin, Jeremy. *The End of Work: The Decline of the Global Labor Force and the Dawn of the Post-Market Era*. New York: Putnam, 1995.

Ripp, Victor. *Pizza in Pushkin Square: What Russians Think about Americans and the American Way of Life*. New York: Simon and Schuster, 1990.

Spengler, Oswald. *The Decline of the West*. 2 vols. New York: Knopf, 1948 (1918–1922).

Toffler, Alvin. *The Third Wave*. New York: Morrow, 1980.

———, and Toffler, Heidi. *War and Anti-War: Survival at the Dawn of the 21st Century.* Boston: Little, Brown, 1993.

Toynbee, Arnold. *Surviving the Future.* New York: Oxford University Press, 1971.

Waters, Malcolm. *Globalization.* New York: Routledge, 1995.

Wolff, Michael, et al., *Where We Stand: Can America Make It in the Global Race for Wealth, Health, and Happiness?* New York: Bantam, 1992.

Wriston, Walter B. "Clintonomics: The Information Revolution and the New Global Market Economy." *Vital Speeches of the Day*, April 1, 1993, 375–80.

———. *The Twilight of Sovereignty: How the Information Revolution Is Transforming Our World.* New York: Scribner's, 1992.

Zha, Jianying. *China Pop: How Soap Operas, Tabloids and Best Sellers Are Transforming a Culture.* New York: New Press, 1995.

Index

About the Author

STEPHEN BERTMAN, Ph.D., is Professor of Classical and Modern Languages, Literatures, and Civilizations at Canada's University of Windsor. He is the author of *Art and the Romans* (1975), *The Conflict of Generations in Ancient Greece and Rome* (1976), *Doorways Through Time, The Romance of Archaeology* (1986), and the forthcoming *Cultural Amnesia* (Praeger). An educational consultant and nationally recognized speaker, he resides in West Bloomfield, Michigan.